## About the author

Antoni Kapcia is professor of Latin American history at the University of Nottingham, where he also directs the Centre for Research on Cuba. Since 1975, he has published extensively on aspects of modern and contemporary Cuban history, focusing especially on political and cultural history and on the questions of ideology and national identity. His books include *Cuba: Island of dreams* (2000), *Havana: The making of Cuban culture* (2005), *Cuba in Revolution* (2008) and (in conjunction with Par Kumaraswami) *Literary Culture in Cuba: Revolution, nation-building and the book* (2012).

# LEADERSHIP IN THE CUBAN REVOLUTION

## THE UNSEEN STORY

*Antoni Kapcia*

Zed Books
LONDON

Fernwood Publishing
HALIFAX | WINNIPEG

*Leadership in the Cuban Revolution: The unseen story* was first published in 2014 by Zed Books Ltd, 7 Cynthia Street, London N1 9JF, UK

www.zedbooks.co.uk

Published in Canada by Fernwood Publishing, 32 Oceanvista Lane, Black Point, Nova Scotia, B0J 1B0 and 748 Broadway Avenue, Winnipeg, Manitoba, R3G 0X3.

www.fernwoodpublishing.ca

Fernwood Publishing Company Limited gratefully acknowledges the financial support of the Government of Canada through the Canada Book Fund and the Canada Council for the Arts, the Nova Scotia Department of Communities, Culture and Heritage, the Manitoba Department of Culture, Heritage and Tourism under the Manitoba Book Publishers Marketing Assistance Program and the Province of Manitoba, through the Book Publishing Tax Credit, for our publishing program.

Set in Monotype Plantin and FFKievit by Ewan Smith, London
Index: ed.emery@thefreeuniversity.net
Cover designed by Dougal Burgess

A catalogue record for this book is available from the British Library
Library of Congress Cataloging in Publication Data available
Library and Archives Canada Cataloguing in Publication data available

ISBN 978-1-78032-527-9 hb (Zed Books)
ISBN 978-1-78032-525-5 pb (Zed Books)
ISBN 978-1-55266-692-0 (Fernwood Publishing)

# CONTENTS

Abbreviations and acronyms | vi
Spanish terms | ix  Stylistic notes | xi

INTRODUCTION: THE PROBLEM WITH 'FIDEL-CENTRISM' . . . 1

1 THE CORE LEADERSHIP: THE FAMILIAR TRIUMVIRATE . . . . 22

2 THE FORMATION OF 'THE VANGUARD': 1953–58 . . . . . . 41

3 TAKING STOCK AND FINDING DIRECTION: 1959–62 . . . . . 61

4 THE YEARS OF 'REVOLUTIONARY' FLUX: 1963–75 . . . . . 115

5 THE STABLE YEARS: SYSTEMS, INSTITUTIONS AND
BUREAUCRATS: 1975–86 . . . . . . . . . . . . . . . . . 132

6 THE RETURN OF FLUIDITY: 1986 TO THE PRESENT . . . . . 153

7 INCLUSION AND EXCLUSION: 'WITHIN' AND 'AGAINST'
THE REVOLUTION . . . . . . . . . . . . . . . . . . . . 182

8 INCLUSION AND COLLECTIVITY: A REVOLUTIONARY
CORPORATISM? . . . . . . . . . . . . . . . . . . . . . 198

Bibliography | 224
Index | 230

# ABBREVIATIONS AND ACRONYMS

Those listed appear more than once in the text or in a single usage but without an immediate translation.

**ACRC**     Asociación de Combatientes de la Revolución Cubana (Association of Veterans of the Cuban Revolution)

**AJR**     Asociación de Jóvenes Rebeldes (Association of Rebel Youth – the 26 July youth wing in 1959)

**ALBA**     Alianza Bolivariana para los Pueblos de Nuestra América (Bolivarian Alliance for the Americas)

**ANAP**     Asociación Nacional de Agricultores Pequeños (National Association of Small Farmers)

**CDR**     Comité para la Defensa de la Revolución (Committee for the Defence of the Revolution)

**CNC**     Consejo Nacional de Cultura (National Cultural Council)

**CNOC**     Confederación Nacional de Obreros de Cuba (National Confederation of Cuban Workers, 1925–39)

**COMECON**     Acronym for Council for Mutual Economic Assistance (CMEA), the Socialist Bloc's economic organisation, 1948–90

**CTC**     Confederación de Trabajadores de Cuba (1939–60)/Central de Trabajadores de Cuba (1960 onwards) (Confederation of Cuban Workers)

**CTC-R**     Confederación de Trabajadores de Cuba Revolucionaria (Revolutionary Confederation of Cuban Workers)

**DEU**     Directorio Estudiantil Universitario (University Students' Directorate – federation)

**DGI**     Dirección General de Inteligencia (General Intelligence Office)

**DR**     Directorio Revolucionario – 13 de Marzo) (1957–61) (Revolutionary Directorate – 13 March)

**DRE**     Directorio Revolucionario Estudiantil (1953–57) (Revolutionary Student Directorate)

**DSE**     Departamento de Seguridad del Estado (Department of State Security)

| | |
|---|---|
| EIR | Escuelas de Instrucción Revolucionaria (Schools of Revolutionary Education) |
| EJT | Ejército Juvenil de Trabajao (Youth Labour Army) |
| FAR | Fuerzas Armadas Revolucionarias (Revolutionary Armed Forces) |
| FEEM | Federación de Estudiantes de la Enseñanza Media (Federation of Secondary Education Students) |
| FEU | Federación Estudiantil Universitaria (until 1959), Federación de Estudiantes Universitarios (from 1959) (University Students' Federation) |
| FMC | Federación de Mujeres Cubanas (Federation of Cuban Women) |
| FONU | Frente Obrero Nacional de Unidad (National Workers' Unity Front) |
| ICAIC | Instituto Cubano de Arte e Industria Cinematográficas (Cuban Cinema Institute) |
| INDER | Instituto Nacional de Deportes, Educación Física y Recreación (National Institute for Sport, Physical Education and Recreation) |
| INRA | Instituto Nacional de Reforma Agraria (National Institute for Agrarian Reform) |
| INTUR | Instituto de Turismo  (Tourism Institute) |
| JS | Juventud Socialista (Socialist Youth – PSP's youth wing) |
| JUCEI | Junta de Coordinación, Ejecución e Inspección (Coordination, Execution and Inspection Board – local government structure in the 1960s) |
| JUCEPLAN | Junta Central de Planificación (Central Planning Board) |
| MINFAR | Ministerio de las FAR (see above) (Defence Ministry – literally Ministry for the Armed Forces) |
| MININT | Ministerio del Interior (Ministry of the Interior) |
| MNR | Movimiento Nacional Revolucionario (National Revolutionary Movement) |
| MSR | Movimiento Socialista Revolucionario (Revolutionary Socialist Movement) |
| OAS | Organisation of American States |
| ORI | Organizaciones Revolucionarias Integradas (Integrated Revolutionary Organisations) |
| OSPAAL | Organización de Solidaridad con los Pueblos de Asia, Africa y Latinoamérica (Organisation of Solidarity with the Peoples of Asia, Africa and Latin America) |

| | |
|---|---|
| PCC | Partido Comunista de Cuba (Cuban Communist Party) |
| PRC-A | Partido Revolucionario Cubano Auténtico (the Auténticos) (Authentic Cuban Revolutionary Party) |
| PSP | Partido Socialista Popular (People's Socialist Party) |
| PURSC | Partido Unido (occasionally Unificado) de la Revolución Socialista de Cuba (United Party of the Cuban Socialist Revolution) |
| SDPE | Sistema de Dirección y Planificación de la Economía (Economic Management and Planning System) |
| UIR | Unión Insurreccional Revolucionaria (Revolutionary Insurrectionary Union) |
| UJC | Unión de Jóvenes Comunistas (Union of Communist Youth) |
| UMAP | Unidad Militar para Ayuda a la Producción (Military Unit for Assisting Production) |
| UNEAC | Unión de Escritores y Artistas de Cuba (Union of Cuban Writers and Artists) |
| UN ECLA | United Nations Economic Commission for Latin America |

# SPANISH TERMS

Those listed are used more than once or not explained after the sole usage.

*ajíaco*  Cuban stew (mixing culturally different ingredients)

*autocrítica*  self-criticism/confession

*balsero*  literally 'rafter' (used of 'boat people' escaping in summer 1994)

*Batalla de Ideas*  Battle of Ideas

*batistiano*  following or supportive of Batista

*bonchismo*  student-based gangsterism of the 1930s to 1950s

*burocracia*  literally 'bureaucracy', but also referring to 'apparatchiks'

*caudillo*  leader or strongman (usually military)

*chibasismo*  following the ideas of Eduardo Chibás (Ortodoxo leader of 1947–51)

*choteo*  collectively self-deprecating Cuban humour

*Comandancia*  guerrilla Sierra headquarters in the last months of the 1956–58 struggle

*comandante*  major (in the army), but usually translated as 'commander'

*comunitario*  literally 'community' (adj.) but referring to collective self-help projects

*criollo*  native-born white (in late eighteenth and early nineteenth centuries), later it acquired a meaning of 'genuinely Cuban' (N.B. not 'creole')

*cuenta propia*  self-employment

*fidelista*  following or associated with Fidel Castro

*funcionario*  civil servant, official

*gusano*  literally 'worm', but used in public discourse inside Cuba for political émigrés between 1959 and the 1980s

*libreta*  ration book

*llano* (usually *Llano*)  literally 'plain', i.e. referring to those 26 July activists working outside the Sierra

*lucha*  struggle

*martiano*  following the ideas of José Martí

*mulato*  mixed race (black and white)

*municipio*  municipality (basic local government entity after 1976)

*negrista*  following the post-1930 artistic movement of *negrismo* (incorporation of Afro-Cuban elements into art)

*núcleo*  (party) branch

*parlamento obrero*  literally 'workers' parliament', i.e. a workplace forum

*patria*  homeland

*peninsular*  referring to someone born in Spain (opposite of *criollo*, above)

*quinquenio gris*  literally 'grey five years' (the period of artistic restriction and harassment from 1971 to 1976)

*tiranía*  literally 'tyranny', referring to 1952–58 dictatorship

*zafra*  annual sugar harvest

# STYLISTIC NOTES

**1** Since, throughout this book, both Fidel Castro and Raúl Castro are referred to frequently, for clarity only their first names (Fidel and Raúl) are usually used after the first mention.

**2** In common with all Spanish-speaking countries, Cubans have always had two surnames: a patronymic followed by a matronymic, hence the full version is usually the correct one. However, in practice, the tendency is often to use only one, namely the first surname or patronymic. Therefore, in this book, when dealing with key figures in the narrative, the first time that someone is introduced both names are given; thereafter, only one. The exceptions are those cases where both names are needed for clarity; however, in some cases (of the more frequent references to prominent activists, such as Faustino Pérez or Celia Sánchez), despite their first surname/patronymic being common, they are referred to in the text by their first name and first surname only. The same applies to the Cienfuegos brothers, to distinguish one from the other.

**3** Throughout the book, Cuban institutions are given in their Spanish form, immediately translated into English, with their Spanish-language initials; thereafter, they are referred to by those language initials, since that is mostly the form in which all Cuba scholars recognise them.

**4** The use of upper case and lower case for the word 'communist' follows the normal pattern: when referring to those who believed in communism (as an idea) but were unaffiliated to a party calling itself 'communist', lower case is used; when referring to a specific and named Communist Party, upper case is used for both initial letters.

**5** In the text, Sierra appears both as Sierra and *Sierra* (in italics): this is to distinguish between the former, the geographical location (the Sierra Maestra), and the name attached to the group of guerrillas who fought there (to distinguish them from the urban-based wing, the *Llano*).

# INTRODUCTION: THE PROBLEM WITH 'FIDEL-CENTRISM'

One fundamental problem that confronts anyone seeking to understand the complex processes and trajectory of the post-1959 Cuban Revolution is the conceptual fog created over the decades by what has been called 'Fidel-centrism' (Kapcia 1996), i.e. the overwhelming tendency of so much of the writing on the Revolution to focus exclusively on the person and personality of Fidel Castro.

This is, of course, easily explained: while undoubtedly rooted in familiar traditions of 'great men' approaches to popular history, for which we must blame partly Victorian historians and partly the media's sensationalising search for the human story or the 'potted' explanation, it also owes much to the effects of the February 1957 episode when the *New York Daily Times* reporter Herbert Matthews, having met the rebel leader, Fidel, in the Sierra, proceeded to report on, and talk up, both the guerrillas and their charismatic leader. Indeed, we should not ignore that supposed charisma, namely the impact that Fidel subsequently had on millions of Cubans of successive generations, and on many hundreds of thousands more non-Cubans, through his speeches and through the continuing reporting on, and films of, his dynamic and mesmerising leadership. Quite simply, he has dominated so much newsprint and so much air time in documentaries and news broadcasts that we cannot ignore him, and thus we easily fall into the assumption that he, and he alone, created, engineered, determined and (according to many, on one side of the 'for' and 'against' dichotomy in judgements of the Revolution) perhaps distorted and destroyed the Revolution. In this, of course, it does not help that we have fallen into similar traps before and since – about Hitler, Stalin, Saddam Hussein, Gaddafi, or any other supposedly despotic leader – therefore assuming that successful revolutions or long-lasting regimes are always attributable to the leader's strength and personality. Equally, it does not help that, since 1961 (when relations between the United States and Cuba were broken), US governments and policy-makers alike have repeatedly stressed that there could be no healing that break, or ending economic sanctions, while Fidel remained in power. Indeed, the 1996 Helms–Burton Act (which gave the embargo the force of a treaty, requiring a two-thirds majority of both Houses of Congress to reverse it) actually prohibits the ending of sanctions while a Castro is in power. So, if legal documents and formal US policies, as well as serious historical studies, continue to focus on Fidel, then we are unlikely to find ourselves straying away from that tendency.

Nor, of course, is that focus totally unhelpful for understanding modern and contemporary Cuba. For it would be a foolish historian who blindly argued that Fidel has not had a fundamental role in the whole process: in decision-making, determining policy, commanding loyalty from those around him and from generations of Cubans, in direct person-to-person relations with foreign leaders, and so on. The evidence for that is clear. Moreover, the longer that the post-1959 system has lasted and the more complex it has become, the greater the likelihood that more and more Cubans would continue to see it in terms of the person who dominated it all from the outset, either seeing him as the more easily comprehensible personification of a system that had become too complex, and even too contradictory, to understand completely, or, alternatively, trusting in his record of finding a way out of difficulties and emerging unscathed from crises. Indeed, many Cubans continued to assume that, whatever problems the country might be facing, Cubans would have a greater chance of solving them with him at the helm – even though that very complexity meant precisely the opposite, namely his inability to be the sole source of power or decision-making. One only has to think of the contradictory emotions and motives that constituted the popular support for Margaret Thatcher in Britain after 1983, despite a general unease at her persona or even a considerable distaste for many of her policies, to realise that, even in a long-established and highly aware political culture, a dominant individual politician can command loyalty and admiration despite, as much as because of, positive feelings or even rational beliefs.

So the point is not to deny Fidel's influence, power and popularity; it is to put these factors into perspective, going beyond stereotypical or superficial interpretations of the increasingly complex process as attributable mainly, or even solely, to one person – not least as the years since 2006 have demonstrated clearly that it did not depend on Fidel's constant presence at the helm. In fact, as Domínguez observed long ago, Fidel was always aware of the need for an organisation beyond the leadership: 'The politics of organization played a decisive role in the Cuban revolution from the very beginning' (Domínguez 1978: 206). This was something that even a firm adherent of 'Fidel-centrism' such as Theodore Draper realised in the 1960s, when referring to Fidel's belief in the need for a united and 'unbreakable body', based on 'ideology, discipline and leadership' (Draper 1969: 8) – although, predictably, Draper focused more on the last element of that trio than on the underlying belief in a vanguard (i.e. more collective) leadership.

Yet the problem remains that even relatively sophisticated and serious works – as opposed to either the hagiographic or demonising studies that have bedevilled the study of Cuba – have both created and perpetuated this mesmerising 'Fidel-centrism'. Several early commentators, for example, were enchanted by, or suspicious of, his evident 'charisma', usually seeing it as evidence of either megalomania or collective gullibility. This fascination with charisma continued well into the later decades, as the Revolution's survival continued to be attributed to such qualities. Generally, however, Fidel's 'charismatic authority' (to take Weber's phrase: Weber 1947) was seen as ephemeral or time-limited and limiting (González 1979), although Valdés (arguing that charisma also depended on the legitimacy bestowed by benefits that Cubans associated with Fidel) observed later that such interpretations of charisma owed more to Machiavelli than to a correct reading of Weber (Valdés 2008). Early on, others wrote glowingly of the 'direct democracy' that they beheld in the relationship between Fidel and Cuban crowds (Sartre 1961). Political scientists then attempted to fit '*fidelismo*' (or 'Castroism') into wider paradigms of either populist political culture or, more frequently, a new variant of what was seen as traditional Latin American *caudillismo*. While Draper argued that Fidel was 'a new type of *caudillo* with a need to justify his power ideologically' (Draper 1969: 49), he nonetheless, by using the term, saw a generic connection between Fidel and a Latin American stereotype. Thomas later took up this same stereotype

(Thomas 1971: 1292), and Horowitz saw Fidel's leadership as 'rooted in the Latin American tradition' of *caudillismo* (Horowitz 2008: 36), although he also elsewhere wrote that that same leadership was akin to Stalin's (ibid.: 3).

Indeed, what Draper actually argued in the end was that 'Castroism' (a term that he was happy to use at first but that he then steadily discarded in the same study, seeing it simply as 'the creation of Fidel Castro': Draper 1969: 16) should be seen as a variant of global 'Communism', seeing Fidel's apparent fixation on power and his ideological commitment to Communism as part of the same totalitarian phenomenon: 'Castroism gave Communism total power, and Communism gave Castroism an ideology of total power' (ibid.: 50). Indeed, this totalitarian reading of what was increasingly called 'Fidelism' became a commonplace throughout the following half century. There were also some who argued that we should read Fidel as being akin to Franco and fascism, often seeing his Spanish Jesuit education as inculcating corporatist or fascist ideas (Pardo Llada 1988: 30; Thomas 1971: 1490); even Draper thought his 'leadership principle' related to fascism or Peronism, suggesting that, although it had become associated with Communism, at a different time it might have gone in other (presumably fascist) directions (Draper 1969: 9).

The problem here was that, once this array of studies (mixing thoughtful political science analyses, serious historical works, passionately partisan accounts and sensationalist journalism) had established the pattern, the die was cast. By the time scholarly attention turned to examining the system or the political culture analytically (Domínguez 1978; Fagen 1969), the literature on Cuba was already dominated by 'Fidel-centrism', and it proved difficult to ignore it or not be influenced by it. Moreover, once the endless series of biographies began to be written, this tendency increased, and 'Castro's' became the standard epithet applied to Cuba, as in 'Castro's Cuba' or 'Fidel Castro's Personal Revolution' (Goodsell 1975), to the extent that Horowitz saw the 1965 creation of the Cuban Communist Party as a 'direct reflection of Castro's personal will and charismatic authority' (Horowitz 2008: 7) – although Jorge Domínguez came to precisely the opposite conclusion about that moment, seeing it as a 'shift to a slightly more collective style of public leadership' (Domínguez 1978: 197).

So what exactly is the problem with this? Most obviously, unless one believes in the power of regimes to indoctrinate whole societies for half a century (something which, given Cubans' evident contact with outside ideas, relatives and societies for sustained periods since 1959, seems unlikely in this case), it seems difficult to attribute the remarkable survival of the Cuban system – beyond its repeated crises (1963, 1968–70), the collapse of the Socialist Bloc, fifty years of sustained sanctions, and periods of active US hostility, and also beyond Fidel's retirement through ill health in 2006–08 – to the persuasive or coercive power of one man alone. Since most outside observers attest to Cuba's high educational levels, and while most historians see pre-1959 Cuba as a highly politicised society, it seems unlikely that millions of Cubans would easily give up their power of reason to allow themselves to be swamped by all that they are told by *el Jefe Máximo* (the Commander-in-Chief). For all that the Cuban media might be controlled by the party, and for all the restrictions on what can be published, such a perspective seems clumsy, belonging to the depths of the Cold War.

There is, however, something of an obligation to look beyond the obvious, not taking the easy option of echoing popular, partisan and journalistic interpretations of a complex subject, not least because to treat Cuba as a Caribbean version of what we assume North Korea to be – isolated, indoctrinated, dominated by a personality cult, coercive and monolithic – does not correspond to the reality of an island only 150 miles or so from the US mainland, open to over 2 million tourists a year, trading in the world economy (to the extent that US sanctions allow) and receiving inward investment since the late 1980s, with a vast diaspora that, since 1977, has increasingly been able to bring news of the outside world, and with greater access to external television, radio and the internet. So, apart from the period between 1962 and the mid-1970s (when the regional 'embargo' began to disintegrate) and the early 1990s (when economic isolation resulted from the collapse of COMECON and the Soviet Union), isolation has not been anywhere near total, and, in fact, has been decreasing since about 1994.

### Classic assumptions: personality cults, coercion and the military

As for the notion of a personality cult, one simply has to compare the visible Cuban signs with what was all too clear in Stalin's Soviet

Union, in North Korea since 1952 or in Mao's China. The Cuban authorities have studiously avoided any hint of a cult of any living person: no naming of places, airports, streets or squares, no statues and few portraits (apart from those in public offices and people's homes). Instead, the ubiquitous 'cult' is to the 1895 independence hero José Martí (in his multiple representations in busts, paintings, place names, and so on), with lesser homages paid to other historic leaders of the independence struggles (Antonio Maceo, Carlos Manuel de Céspedes, Máximo Gómez) or activists of twentieth-century political struggles (Julio Antonio Mella, Antonio Guiteras). In fact, since 1968, the only cult-like reverence to anyone associated with the Revolution has been reserved for Che Guevara, with the massive stylised portrait in Plaza de la Revolución (now accompanied by a similar one of Camilo Cienfuegos) and the huge mausoleum in Santa Clara, much larger than that of Martí in Santiago. There is certainly no shortage of books by Fidel in bookshops, and, while he was leader, the agenda of most party meetings would include the need to analyse one of his recent speeches. Even so, however 'Fidel-centric' it may seem to be, Cuba has clearly not had a cult to match those others referred to.

But what about coercion, a familiar accusation levelled at the Cuban system? There is little doubt that the Revolution took power with a ruthless determination to try, sentence and execute large numbers of active participants in Batista's repression before 1959; Guevara oversaw many such executions at the Cabaña fortress in the first few days, and Fidel himself admitted that about 550 people had been executed at that time (Szulc 1986: 386). Thereafter, at times of external pressure and hostility (notably 1962–68, when the 'siege' was at its height and Soviet support was tentative and unreliable, and in the early 1980s, when Reagan began to re-heat the Cold War, identifying Cuba as the source of the Central American conflicts and as his Secretary of State, Haig, commissioned the first of many Pentagon reports to assess the feasibility of military action against Cuba: Habel 1991: 138), tolerance of internal dissent or even non-conformity has been seriously restricted. The mid-1960s certainly saw the notorious UMAP (Military Unit for Assisting Production) 'work camps', designed, clumsily and vindictively, to 're-educate' those whose religious beliefs, sexuality or lifestyle were deemed unacceptable, until pressure from intellectuals led in 1968 to their closure as re-education camps for intellectuals (they remained in existence into the 1970s as bases for normal youth military service: Mesa-Lago 1974: 104). That same period also witnessed the height of the systematic demonisation of those leaving the island (by labelling them *gusanos* or 'worms') and the start of what would become a growing pressure on some 'aberrant' artists and writers. The early 1980s saw the now shameful episode of the exodus at Mariel of some 125,000 Cubans (Olson and Olson 1995: 81), who were allowed to leave in a boatlift but excoriated publicly for their 'lumpen' and anti-social tendencies; this included many prisoners released for the purpose and a handful of 'problem' intellectuals, notably those offending the system's assumed sexual mores. In addition, 1971–76 (and almost certainly beyond) saw the contentious *quinquenio gris* – the 'grey five years' – when certain writers and theatre people were marginalised and unable to find outlets for their work (Kumaraswami and Kapcia 2012: 101–7).

That said, however, it is perhaps significant that, firstly, the UMAP episode ended after three years, following pressure from UNEAC (the Union of Cuban Writers and Artists), showing that body's surprising level of autonomy (for what was assumed to be a Soviet-style state-run mechanism of control) and the leadership's surprising willingness to listen. Also, the few days of the Mariel exodus saw a change in official thinking, as excoriation gave way to a new awareness that many refugees were no longer the old 'political' émigrés but simply economic migrants. Finally, what ended the 'grey years', in 1976, was the creation of a comprehensive and nationally regulating Ministry of Culture, of the kind that, in the Soviet Union, would have led to expectations of rigid cultural control.

This issue is, of course, closely related to the notion that Cuba is a military-run system. This idea dates from the earliest days, as the ex-guerrillas continued to dominate political life, moving smoothly between 'military' and overtly civilian posts as what have been called 'civic soldiers' (Domínguez 1978: 341–78). Some later saw this attribute as fundamental to the Cuban system (Horowitz 2008: 104–41, 175–90), describing that system as a 'highly militarized revolution and regime' (Domínguez 1990: 47). However, the reality is inevitably more complex, as Klepak has shown eloquently (Klepak 2005): for all their professionalism, technical development and Soviet-linked modernisation in the 1970s, the Cuban armed forces – the FAR (Revolutionary Armed

Forces) – actually resemble more of a hybrid between the historic liberation army (the Rebel Army of 1956–58) and a popular militia, enjoying considerable public legitimacy and constituting not an elite group with separate corporate identity (which would describe most Latin American armed forces) but rather an institution that, born in a guerrilla war, remained committed to a guerrilla defence of Cuba. Moreover, with compulsory military service, a large military reserve and two periods of popular militias, most Cubans have had some close contact with, or service in, the military, which contributes to the greater fusion between the FAR and society than might otherwise be the case. Indeed, Domínguez argues that the FAR so accurately reflects Cuban society that its legendary efficiency is very much a myth (Domínguez 1990). Finally, we should remember that the FAR has its own party cells and structure, belonging firmly and loyally to the party-led system. Returning to the issue of coercion, it is worth noting that the very point when coercion might have been expected (1991–95) actually saw drastic cuts in troop numbers (by around 50 per cent), thereby weakening any capacity to coerce (Klepak 2005: 61).

A key element of the question of coercion is the vexed issue of political prisoners. Here we enter a minefield of partisanship, not least because the Cuban authorities and the US administration define that category differently: in Cuba it has long been an offence either to actively support the US embargo (since US sanctions were imposed under the Trading with the Enemy Act, the embargo became formally a declaration of war, as far as Havana was concerned), or, in common with many other countries, to receive political funding from a foreign government. Hence anyone sentenced for such offences is officially simply 'a prisoner', while the US administration and entities such as Human Rights Watch and Amnesty International all define such people as political prisoners. In fact, the peak of such imprisonments for crimes deemed political outside Cuba was probably reached in the first six years or so; Fidel admitted in 1965 that there were some 20,000 such prisoners, a category ranging from those taking up arms against the Revolution to those organising illegal protests. In 1969, the scarcely neutral Spanish ambassador Jaime Capdevilla gave a total of over 55,000 (Suchlicki 1988: 227). However, in 1987, the Cuban authorities themselves admitted that around 400 were serving sentences for 'crimes against the state', with

Amnesty International confirming 455, including sixty-eight who had taken up arms in the 1960s (Habel 1991: 97).

## The state and the monolith?

What, finally, of the notion of a monolithic Cuban state? At first sight, that notion seems accurate, given the tendency to centralisation from 1960, domination by one single ruling party since 1961, and our knowledge of post-1945 Communist systems. However, on examination, a somewhat different picture emerges, creating a quite different set of problems to analyse.

For, in the 1960s, a combination of processes worked against the creation of the powerful state which many Cubans felt that they needed after decades of neo-colonial rule and economic dependence. Firstly, within weeks, a process began to weed out unacceptable or *batistiano* (pro-Batista) office-holders in the civil service; by March 1959, some 50,000 out of 160,000 state employees had been expelled or replaced (Domínguez 1978: 234). This inevitably weakened an inherited structure, already weakened by nepotism and low morale.

Then the very process of revolution after 1 January 1959, transforming society totally within a few years, inevitably militated against such a state; whenever a state body seemed to be forming, the process of constant change proceeded to undermine that stability. Even if that had not been the case, the plethora of new institutions (including new ministries) that was set up in the wake of victory complicated the state structure at a time of profound change, each institution having its own, inevitably growing, bureaucracy.

However, the rebel leadership itself encouraged a tendency against 'institutionalism'; this was partly because of a growing and radicalised commitment, by January 1959, to making a real revolution rather than a revolution like the rhetorical ones of previous radical generations. However, it was mostly because, after 1961–62, when some in the pre-1959 Communist Party (the People's Socialist Party, or PSP) sought to take advantage of the post-victory chaos and inexperience to move the process in an orthodox communist direction (see later), many of the ex-guerrillas were determined to prevent a recurrence of that attempted takeover by encouraging a 'revolution in the revolution', adopting guerrilla-style tactics of constant movement in the face of what were seen as bureaucratic obstacles to that 'real' revolution. In 1966, Fidel argued that there was no rush to institutionalise, since eventual institutionalisation should reflect the changed social reality rather than precede it (Azicri 1988: 39). Thus, although the Revolution might have needed stability and structure in the mid-1960s (not least to distribute goods and services to all efficiently, and to allow for proper channels of communication on decision-making), the anti-bureaucracy campaign of that period (largely a political drive from 1964 to 1970 against the 'dangerous' elements who had threatened to take over) was also an anti-state campaign, weakening the morale of those loyal bureaucrats who were now often the target of committed activists and angry citizens (Domínguez 1978: 240).

A further factor preventing the growth of a strong state, however, was the effect of the mass exodus from 1960, largely draining Cuba of its middle class. While this had political benefits (making real opposition external rather than dangerously internal), it also drained a post-1959 state of its human resources; the middle class's education levels, experience and professional qualifications had made it the raw material for a national civil service to execute the government's constant flow of policies. Instead, therefore, new *funcionarios* (civil servants) and professionals had to be created expensively, either laboriously (despite the urgency) or too quickly to generate the necessary confidence and experience. Hence, for several years the 'new' Cuba lacked the human infrastructure necessary for a new and powerful state.

Meanwhile, the supposedly powerful single party refused to emerge. Plans were hatched early on, with the PSP's Aníbal Escalante given the task, as organisation secretary, of merging the three leading rebel groups of 1959 – the guerrillas' 26 July Movement, the communist PSP and the small student-based guerrilla group, the DR (Revolutionary Directorate – 13 March) – into one umbrella organisation, the ORI (Integrated Revolutionary Organisations). However, the 1962 'Escalante affair' so startled the rebels that its planned sequel, the United Party of the Cuban Socialist Revolution (PURSC), emerged without fanfare or inauguration, keeping a somewhat shadowy existence for three years. However, the PURSC was not, as is sometimes suggested (Anderson 1997: 759), a response to the ORI crisis, since it was always planned as the next stage after the ORI; in fact, in 1961, it was repeatedly mentioned as such in the press. The Escalante affair simply accelerated its appearance.

Then when, in 1965, the planned Cuban Communist Party (PCC) emerged, while it might have looked like its partner parties in Eastern Europe, it never had a founding congress and only really existed at the top (among the ex-guerrillas) and the bottom (among grass-roots activists). In between, there was no linking structure or national infrastructure of political involvement.

The effects of this weakness of the state were twofold. Firstly, the inchoate groupings that emerged, some organically and others haphazardly, often lacked control by an overarching state structure; instead, individuals or groups often exercised unrestricted local control, unless they offended openly or conflicted with other groups or individuals. For example, until 1965 there were two major national newspapers, the PSP's *Noticias de Hoy* (always abbreviated to *Hoy*) and the 26 July Movement's *Revolución*, which finally merged to become *Granma*. Equally, the lack of a single national cultural policy arose from a 'cultural state' that consisted of discrete organisations, often working separately from, or against, each other; thus, the National Cultural Council (CNC) from 1961, run by PSP members (often with orthodox Communist views about socialist art), had no control over the powerful cinema industry (ICAIC), which, under Alfredo Guevara, had free rein to create a 'Cuban' revolutionary cinema, or over the new Casa de las Américas cultural centre (under the ex-guerrilla Haydée Santamaría). Therefore, while arguments about culture and the state raged throughout the period from 1959 to 1968, that 'state' actually consisted of several 'islands', uncoordinated and rarely pursuing a single monolithic policy (Kumaraswami and Kapcia 2012: 77). Therefore, while the CNC could restrict literary production, for example (as in the notorious 'grey five years' of 1971–76), other cultural 'islands' were tolerant and imaginative. Indeed, as already observed, it was the new Ministry of Culture in 1976 that ended the CNC, and, by establishing an accountable single set of policies for people to pursue and execute, created a greater tolerance.

The second effect of state weakness was seminal: the absence of a state capable of effecting all the desired reforms meant that, to realise rapid change (guaranteeing immediate popular support), a series of 'mass organisations' (created in 1960–62) took over the state's tasks, not only enacting many of the reforms but also mobilising hundreds of thousands in 'the Revolution'. These bodies were foreshadowed by the volunteer National Revolutionary Militias, which, created on 26 October 1959 (to enrol ordinary Cubans in the defence of 'their' Revolution against external threat), numbered around 300,000 members by 1961 (Domínguez 1978: 208; Ruega Jomarrón 2009), showing the depth of active popular support and the possibilities of large-scale volunteering. Out of that came the mass organisations.

Hence, the CDRs (Committees for the Defence of the Revolution, 1960), the FMC (Federation of Cuban Women, 1960), the FEU (University Students' Federation), the CTC (Confederation of Cuban Workers) and ANAP (National Association of Small Farmers) all effectively substituted for the state, taking over the day-to-day running of the new Cuba and involving Cubans in the Revolution's processes, campaigns and emerging structures. However, most commentators argue that, of these, the CTC was the weakest (Azicri 1988: 44): given an inherent problem, familiar in the Socialist Bloc (of accommodating the idea of trade unions, designed to protect workers against employers, within a defined workers' state), the CTC went through a damaging period of internal conflict over control of the new CTC-R (i.e. the Revolutionary CTC), and then adopted the 'transmission belt' role that Lenin had described, executing decisions and focusing on production (Lenin 1920). That weakness was partly corrected in the 1970s, but, until then, the CTC played a less fundamental socialising role than the FMC or CDRs. Interestingly, however, it was in the 1980s, in the growing debates about corruption, that the CTC began to flex its muscles and depart from its previously problematic role in the Cuban system; it did so by putting constraints on managers' errors and malpractice (Habel 1991: 83).

Overall, the mass organisations became fundamental to the Cuban system; for many years there were seven – the CDR, CTC, ANAP, FMC and the three youth organisations for children: the Pioneers, established as a mass organisation in 1966, schoolchildren (FEEM) and students (FEU) – but a potential eighth was created in 1993, the ACRC (Association of Veterans of the Cuban Revolution). Crucially, these organisations almost all pre-dated, and then ran alongside, the state that eventually emerged, complicating later arguments about the 'state and civil society' (Gray and Kapcia 2008). At this point, incidentally, it should be said that neither the various formations of the single party (ORI, PURSC, PCC) nor their youth wing (the Union of Communist Youth, or UJC) were ever considered 'mass' organisations, since they have always remained selective, with membership achieved by invitation rather than application. The UJC was created in 1962, merging the 26 July Movement's AJR (Association of Rebel Youth), created in December 1959, and the PSP's pre-1959 Socialist Youth (JS) (Rodríguez Rodríguez 1989).

Later on, after the 1990–91 disappearance of the Soviet Union and the Socialist Bloc, the economy's 35 per cent collapse (by 1994) immediately weakened the state, which, with oil shortages handicapping transportation and energy, could not deliver goods, move people or guarantee the normal requisites of daily life. That 'Special Period' ('in Peacetime', declared as such in August 1990), therefore threatened the state's existence, which, in turn, threatened the Revolution's survival. While it did of course survive, the effects of the means used to guarantee that survival (notably the legalisation, and thus influx, of the US dollar, the opening up to tourism, and the legalisation of self-employment) were often serious. While outside media attention focused on the rise in petty criminality (although this was never on the scale of post-1991 Russia) and the return of prostitution, several studies observed the decline of collective solidarity and its replacement by a greater individualism (Eckstein 1994).

However, the issue is actually a little more complex, and there may even be an element of wishful thinking or exaggeration in some accounts of this problem. Certainly, the post-1993 economic reforms allowed much greater freedom than before for individuals to operate in the *cuenta propia* (self-employed) sector, and reforms since 2008 have extended this further; nevertheless, to a great extent what these reforms have done is legalise what was already happening illegally. In other words, the previous collectivism was more of a formal ethos, flouted considerably in the informal economy; hence, individualism already flourished under the radar, and was often tolerated by the authorities, and therefore rather than one 'ism' being replaced by another, such practices and patterns were now simply authorised.

In fact, most Cubans' material survival in the 1990s was, on examination, the result less of the perceived rampant individualism within a 'survivalist' culture than of the government's rapid restoration and protection of the ration book (*libreta*), which undoubtedly saved basic living standards, and also of the lower-level networks to which most Cubans had recourse. These included two especially: the family networks that had always operated (i.e. neither individualistic nor collectivist in the normal sense of the terms, but actually somewhere in between) and the government-led encouragement to local activists (in the mass organisations, People's Power local government, People's Councils, and local Communist Party branches) to mobilise locally and de facto stand in for the financially and organisationally hamstrung state structure. Hence, a 'localism' quickly emerged from the chaos, with local *comunitario* structures, workshops and campaigns to address localities' immediate problems until the national state might eventually be able to step in. Therefore, rather than being individualistic in ethos, this was actually a redefining of the state and therefore of the collective.

The basic point here is that the only period when the new Cuban state was strong, organised and potentially monolithic was 1975–89, i.e. only fourteen years out of the Revolution's fifty-five. This, of course, partly depends on one's definition of 'monolithic'. For a Hayekian Thatcherite, for example, any state intervention by definition tends towards the monolithic, and, according to this perspective, the term itself has always been associated with the notion of totalitarianism. From this point of view, Cuba's visible patterns of 'bureaucracy' are ample proof of a kind of monolith, with a structure seemingly inert, immovable and unresponsive.

But is all bureaucracy necessarily monolithic or bad, and is that what is meant by the term anyway? That question is valid, for it goes to the heart of the Cuban system and of our expectations, taking us back to Cold War terminology and, specifically, to standard interpretations of the Socialist Bloc. There, 'bureaucracy' could mean any one of a range of things, either negative or neutral. The former included the banal but annoying: the 'paper-pusher' whose job was due to nepotism or over-staffing (to prevent unemployment); the 'time-server' occupying a post for job security, determined to cling to it by making himself or herself indispensable, or creating a complex set of overlapping procedures; the 'jobsworth' exercising the power to deny access or permission; or simply the poorly educated or inexperienced clerk who, conscripted into a burgeoning civil service to replace those who had left but unable to cope, either acted inefficiently or declined to act at all. However, negative meanings also arose from a wider critique, as in the Trotskyist use of the term 'the bureaucracy' and 'bureaucratisation' to refer to the emerging class of apparatchiks, seen to be controlling the system for their own interests, a class of party members rather than of civil servants, using their power to subvert collective authority or workers' power (Harman 1974). As for the neutral use of the term, that was simply the reality that centralisation and a drive towards full employment created a vastly expanded civil service, at all levels. Hence, *funcionario* often meant any clerical worker, since most were employed by the state; this even included those in the cultural world who were freed of the need to sell in order to survive by occupying a notional post in a state-run cultural or educational institution.

This inevitably brings us to the complexity of the Cuban system, which, since 1959, has created more and more bodies and layers of operation, either to improve efficiency or to ensure delivery of material goods or opportunities. For example, the spread of the mass organisations meant a need for national and provincial coordination structures, and, as employment expanded, the party (always based on workplace branches) added more local branches and intervening levels of authority and operation; the People's Power electoral system from 1976 created fourteen new provinces out of the previous six (and 169 *municipios*), adding new layers of representation, accountability and authority, and each national body and ministry had its provincial and often municipal branches.

Given this complexity, the potential for bureaucratic and institutional confusion and inertia has always been immense. Inertia is especially likely given the extent of constant negotiation preceding and following any decision, nationally or locally: since the ruling party plays a constitutionally defined 'guiding role', any significant proposal is debated there first, but in several sub-stages. Any leadership proposal (from the Political Bureau, Central Committee or five-yearly Congress) is then filtered down for debate, each lower level (provincial and municipal) adding its own interpretation and guidance, before it is debated at the branch (*núcleo*) level; then the outcome is returned upwards, being again interpreted and filtered until it reaches its source. Meanwhile, all mass organisations are invariably involved in national consultations (before a Party Congress or National Assembly meeting, for example), so the party process is repeated within each organisation and also throughout the People's Power structures. Hence, every level and stage involves negotiation, give and take and amendment. This is also true of ministerial decisions; they are not simply handed down for local execution, but rather negotiated in every province, and even (although less likely) in every *municipio*, with the local party, People's Power delegates and mass organisations. Therefore, rather than decisions being handed down hierarchically within a rigidly centralised system, decision-making and debate are more of a constant, painstaking and inevitably dilatory process of negotiation. Of course, this reflects the daily reality for every Cuban, who must always negotiate their way along the individual–collective continuum within which the whole system operates (Kumaraswami and Kapcia 2012: 52–6).

Before leaving this issue, however, a major caveat has to be considered: while the case for the post-1959 Cuban state being much weaker institutionally than has often been alleged is convincing, that does not necessarily mean that it has not been effective. Not only has the state – mostly by enlisting one or more of the mass organisations – proved repeatedly able to cope with normally devastating hurricanes, it has also been spectacularly successful in the task of defending the Revolution. Most obviously this was seen in the April 1961 invasion, which was repulsed with considerable losses on the Cuban side but, nonetheless, with a revealing and (for the US government) embarrassing effectiveness. Then again, between 1961 and 1966, the suppression of counter-revolutionary rebels in the Sierra Escambray (substantially backed by the United States' Operation Mongoose programme) was prolonged but successful.

However, below the radar, at a less visible and spectacular level, the fifty-five years of the Revolution have seen the state maintain a highly effective continuous defensive operation of state security that has kept active dissent to a minimum and deterred or defeated active sabotage. Although, as one might expect from the known characteristics of the Cuban system, the whole operation has been achieved through a mixture of state and mass organisations, the latter most obviously consisting of the highly effective CDRs (both in April 1961 and since), it has always essentially been the state itself that has borne the brunt of the burden of defence.

That state defensive operation has consisted of the FAR (and its reserve force) and the intelligence and security services (most clearly the well-known G2 organisation, but also the different levels and corps of the police service and the militias). Although the militias were disbanded once the biggest threats of invasion had disappeared, a new version (the Militia of Territorial Troops) was created in 1981, in the face of the perceived threat from a rampant Reagan administration. The FAR, as already seen, was not only fundamental from the outset in cementing unity, enrolling Cubans (literally and metaphorically) in the tasks of defending the new Revolution and repelling invasion, but it also grew into one of Latin America's largest and most successful military forces, its achievement in Angola being its best known and most widely admired deployment. That said, however, it has mostly been the deterrent effect of such a formidable force, rather than its actual deployment, that has, since April 1961, been the cornerstone of the FAR's contribution to defence.

Alongside the FAR, the CDRs and the militia have stood the system's intelligence and security forces. Constructed from the earliest days (out of the most reliable elements of the Rebel Army) and then, from the early 1960s, trained or advised by both the KGB and the East German intelligence services, the two arms – the DGI (General Intelligence Office), dealing with overseas intelligence, and the DSE (Department of State Security), for domestic intelligence – soon became renowned for their efficiency and effectiveness. Abroad, probably the most notable achievements have been through constant and often highly successful infiltration of the Cuban-American community (and specifically of its most active and significant political groupings), thereby working to prevent externally based subversion. Indeed, it was in that role that the famous case of the 'Cuban Five' came to prominence. At home, however, the DSE's capacity to invigilate and infiltrate dissident groups (most spectacularly in the case of several of the groupings that were unmasked in the 2003 arrests of seventy-five dissident activists, many of whom were exposed by DSE agents and some of whom belonged to groups set up by the DSE itself) and to respond to active and open organised dissent has gained the organisation respect on the one hand, and opprobrium on the other. For supporters of the Revolution, the DSE's work has been vital to protecting a system whose very existence has, since 1961, been openly threatened by the United States and covertly undermined by externally funded opposition; for those opposing the Revolution, or even simply not supporting it, the DSE has been a much-feared source of repression and an arm of 'Big Brother', the sole reason why the Revolution has managed to survive. The latter especially see the DSE's hand in the so-called Rapid Response Brigades that have periodically harassed dissident activists.

The point of this is that, however weak the Cuban state may have been in its institutional structure and effectiveness in some respects, it has always demonstrated a remarkable degree of effectiveness in its various mechanisms of defence, however widely or narrowly defined that term may be.

## Debate

Finally, this discussion raises a further crucial aspect of the system: the idea of 'debate' itself, which might seem fanciful, given our expectations of a system with one single party, controlling the daily newspapers, radio and television, and with non-competitive elections. However, once again, Cuba is more complex than our expectations, and close examination reveals several instances where debate has been open, public and encouraged, and many more where, while not necessarily recognisable to those outside the parameters of the debate in question, real differences of opinion have been evident. The key issue is recognising such debates, for, as explained above, each process of party or National Assembly decision-making is ritually subjected to extensive consultation; consultation, of course, is not necessarily real discussion, and, since the parameters and guidelines are defined from above, and each discussion chaired by a suitably prepared party member, there are clear limits to its effectiveness.

Nonetheless, debates do clearly happen, sometimes formally but mostly in less structured ways, with the system depending on them. Indeed, one way of reading the Revolution's trajectory since 1959 is through a repeated series of cycles of crisis–debate–certainty (Kapcia 2008: 25–45). Although these debates are discussed in a later chapter, it is worth commenting that the Revolution's inherent tendency to crisis (often attributed to a whimsical leadership or the predominance of 'idealistic' political criteria over 'pragmatic' economic judgements: Mesa-Lago 1974) emanates from two causes: Cuba's dependency (as a sugar-exporting island) and the inevitable effects of a revolutionary process (after all, a revolution without crisis may not be revolutionising anything). Moreover, although the periods of 'certainty' are well documented by historians (such as the ambitious industrialisation drive of 1960–63, the late 1960s' 'moral economy', the campaign to liberate Latin America, and the institutionalisation of the 1970s), the intervening periods of debate often go unnoticed. However, there are usually tell-tale signs: when the required five-yearly cycle of Party Congresses is delayed (as in 1965–75, 1985–86, 1996–97, or 2002–11) – indicating a lack of consensus – when the press addresses controversial issues in letters' pages or in-depth examinations, or, as in the 1990s, when magazines are created precisely to address hitherto unquestionable issues.

The relationship between Party Congresses and debate is interesting: expectations (based on the Soviet experience) are that these events are ritually unanimous claques for leadership decisions, and so many ignore them as meaningful. However, if that were true, delay (in four of the Revolution's six Congresses) would make no sense; in fact, Congresses tend to meet in order to ratify not so much the leaders' decisions but rather the outcomes of the preceding debates, and, if there is no outcome as yet, there is nothing to legitimise. In 1986, that prior debate was clearly unsettled when the Congress met in February (its delegates failing to approve the 1986–90 plan and party programme: Habel 1991: 90), leading to the suspension of the Assembly until there was consensus; the reconvened December Congress thereupon confirmed 'Rectification' as a policy (this having been already announced between the two sittings: ibid.: 91). Therefore, the Congresses' behaviour and treatment demonstrate the opposite of our expectations, and, once debate is ratified, the Congress usually sets in train both the resulting period of certainty and the parameters for the next debate.

Debate has thus been central to the Revolution's trajectory, character and even survival over the decades; but to what other factors can the post-1991 survival be attributed? The most pragmatic was Cubans' fear of the alternatives that they saw facing them; many returned from the Socialist Bloc after 1989 with horror stories about the social effects of a 'transition' (to capitalism): mass unemployment (with privatisation), the collapse of social provision, a rampant criminality and high-powered corruption. As a neoliberal International Monetary Fund proceeded to apply the same conditions to the new post-Communist states (cuts in welfare and state subsidies, and rapid privatisation) that had been visited on Latin America in the 1980s – about which Cubans were well informed – many clung to the certainty of a state-backed provision of welfare and employment. Once the Cuban government protected expenditure on health and education, guaranteed the newly unemployed 60 per cent of their wages, and strengthened the *libreta*, the die was cast. No one wanted to risk a social implosion on the Eastern European or Latin American scale, a view shared even by a critical Catholic Church, which, like the Cuban leadership, was uneasy about the social effects of the post-1993 reform programme.

The second key factor was evident: the continuing (if damaged) effectiveness of the system's means of participation. These mechanisms (organisations, rallies, voluntary labour mobilisations and meetings) had long acted as either safety valves – at times of stress and discontent, creating a forum for complaints – or sounding boards, informing the authorities of grass-roots rumours, sentiments and complaints. But they also served another purpose: to provide a means of continuous involvement (which some saw as empowerment).

Historically, that had taken two forms, rarely running simultaneously. The first was the most characteristic: participation and involvement through mass mobilisation, often accompanied by 'politics of passion' (Fernández 2000). This has taken the form of repeated campaigns for labour, culture, defence, protest (against the United States), or whatever was deemed necessary at the time. It especially characterised the 1963–68 period (including the moral economy, volunteer labour, the Revolutionary Offensive of March 1968 and the campaign against bureaucracy), but it returned after 1986 (until interrupted by the 1989–91 crisis) and again after 2000 in the *Batalla de Ideas* (Battle of Ideas).

The second form of involvement has been more mundane and consolidated: the system of structures of accountability and communication, through the party, People's Power and mass organisations, usually involving a desire to satisfy materially. In other words, while 'passionate mobilisation' feeds 'the soul' but perhaps neglects the body, the latter feeds 'the body' but may well neglect 'the soul' (Kapcia 2009).

The final factor in the Revolution's survival has been equally evident: the enduring power of nationalism. Not only did the Revolution grow out of a powerful radical tradition of nationalist dissent, but it also built on that, emphasising 'nation', *patria*, and a history of struggle. Hence, by the 1990s, when Cubans referred to *la Revolución* they often meant *la patria* (Kapcia 2000); indeed, the campaign to rally support for the beleaguered system was increasingly defined as 'saving the nation', to which Cubans rallied willingly, especially when the United States responded clumsily to Cuba's plight by intensifying the embargo (in 1992 and 1997) and increasing hostility.

This, therefore, leads us naturally into a discussion of precisely why this happened and what it meant. What role did 'nation' really play in the process and what role should it play in our interpretation of the whole trajectory? Moreover, given the opening focus and underlying purpose of this book, how does it take us 'beyond Fidel'?

# 1 | THE CORE LEADERSHIP: THE FAMILIAR TRIUMVIRATE

Taking up this question and searching 'beyond Fidel', we find a familiar problem in the literature on modern Cuba: alongside (and perhaps as an extension of) the usual Fidel-centrism, there is a dogged focus on leadership with the same potential to distract and mesmerise. This refers to the idea that, at least during the early 1960s, Fidel partly shared power with, and was close to and even influenced by, Ernesto 'Che' Guevara, until Guevara's departure from Cuba in 1965 (according to some following a split with Fidel). Yet there is now also a third member of this leadership: Raúl Castro. Ignored for years – or, more typically, assumed to be either the 'red under the bed' that US policy-makers sought and always assumed was, and dismissed as, an 'ideologue' and pro-Soviet hardliner – he came back into most casual outside observers' reckoning in 2006 when given temporary responsibility for governing Cuba because of Fidel's ill health. In fact, the external reaction to this 're-emergence' was interesting: while his temporary accession was logical (he had been first vice-president since 1976 and was the last of the main guerrilla leaders to survive), it was initially either dismissed (by the Bush administration) as 'Fidel-lite' or (Raúl being Fidel's younger brother) assumed to reflect the Cuban system's dynastic nature. Since the reality was bound to be more complex than these simplistic approaches, what was the nature of the original 'triumvirate', and what roles did all three actually play from 1959 – a question that goes to the heart of a necessary understanding of the Revolution?

## Fidel Castro

Despite the case made against 'Fidel-centrism', understanding the triumvirate inevitably starts with Fidel, if only to set his significance within a proportional context. However, the question immediately arises as to where to limit this assessment, given the plethora of writing about the man and his role in the Revolution, making anything that can usefully be said in one-third of a chapter inevitably partial or narrowly focused. Thankfully, this book's subject (the activists and leaders beyond Fidel) allows us to ignore much of what has fascinated biographers: his childhood and youth, his character and personality, and his motivations. Instead, what matters here is an overview of his importance within the post-1959 process.

Of Fidel's leadership qualities, there can be little doubt. From his earliest political activism in the late 1940s he seems to have led those around him, using his decisiveness (occasionally becoming impetuousness), dynamism and charm to persuade people to accompany him on different ventures. These included the abortive 1947 plan to liberate the Trujillo-dominated Dominican Republic, which ultimately petered out into a frustrated wait on Cayo Confites by a group of mostly young would-be 'liberators'. These ventures did not, however, include the murky world of armed student politics in and around the University of Havana; here, although the so-called *bon-chismo* ('gangsterism') of the late 1930s and early 1940s had declined and had been channelled in different directions (Aguiar Rodríguez 2000), enough remained for Fidel to become attached to one of the supposedly political groups, the UIR (Revolutionary Insurrectionary Union). However, his involvement was never more than marginal. From 1952, though, there was no doubt about his tendency and capacity to lead: the Moncada episode (the attack on the Moncada barracks in Santiago de Cuba on 26 July 1953, which launched the rebellion against Batista, who had seized power on 10 March 1952) showed a remarkable degree of trust in his plans, since, even though almost all of the would-be attackers knew nothing about the plan until the last minute, only a handful left at that point, the rest following his lead into what many must have assumed was certain defeat if not death.

Likewise, his ability to command loyalty continued as others constructed the new 26 July Movement on his behalf, while he remained in prison or subsequently in Mexico. And so it went on: the *Granma* invasion, the bloody Alegría de Pío debacle immediately afterwards, the Sierra and so on. With each venture and defeat, Fidel's power to persuade seemed to grow, rather than dim. Indeed, with each defeat leading to yet another survival, this seemed to persuade more followers, and then, after 1959, more Cubans, of his ability to endure and recover, and of his evident determination to continue against all odds. Certainly, few could ever accuse him of an easy compromise; in the Cuba of the time, after a history of disillusion in successive leaders' compromise or corruption, this ability and determination undoubtedly helped to cement his popularity and people's trust.

If loyalty was one key to his leadership, another was his capacity to lead. Not only did he evidently exude charm, but his speeches could often be electrifying, if somewhat exhausting, always either pressing the right buttons or rallying support. That same capacity was also helped by his political acumen, whether balancing different viewpoints in Cuba or playing the international system. Indeed, Cuba's whole post-1960 relationship with the Soviet Union was influenced by his ability to gain leverage with Moscow, playing on their fears (about 'losing' Cuba to China), their embarrassment (for example over the missile crisis) and their needs, and even entrapping them into supporting Cuba, to ensure leeway to differ ideologically and politically. That same acumen produced perceptive judgements: during the insurrection (when negotiating with rival movements), in discussions with (and about) the PSP, in balancing Cubans' demands for change with the need to survive economically, and in judging the changing Latin American mood of the 1970s and then the 1990s.

Moreover, despite the frequently alleged impetuousness or whimsy, this astuteness led him into essentially pragmatic decisions, although the line between apparently 'ideological' decisions and policies and seemingly 'pragmatic' ones was often blurred: was the decision to opt for the supposedly utopian 'moral economy' of the late 1960s an ideological commitment with little practical benefit or a pragmatic recognition that, with the embargo in place and few manufactured goods available, paying Cubans to work harder was a recipe for inflation and economic weakness? Was the Cubans' commitment to insurrection in Latin America quixotic idealism or a realistic assessment that, since all but one Latin American government had isolated Cuba and the United States was committed not to invade, Cuba had nothing to lose and much to gain by fomenting revolution? Indeed, Cuba's external relations since 1959 have always been governed more by a practical need for allies and trading partners than by idealistic visions.

In this latter respect, Fidel's role has always been crucial in one particular way: his ability to cultivate close friendships with other countries' leaders, helping Cuba to cement formal diplomatic, commercial and political relations. Certainly, there was an evident special affinity with people such as Indira Gandhi, Omar Torrijos, Pierre Trudeau, Michael Manley, Daniel Ortega, Tomás Borge, Maurice Bishop, Hugo Chávez and Evo Morales.

Pragmatism has, however, been less evident in Fidel's occasional fixation on some scheme or other – the drive to produce a 'super-cow' in the first decade or his enthusiasm for the abortive 'energy revolution' in the early 2000s – but even these quirks have not lacked a logic. Therefore, overall, we are left with the conclusion that, for most of Fidel's five decades at the helm, decisions taken were more often than not the only ones possible in the circumstances or given the ideological, economic or political imperatives. Most obviously, for example, given the reality that US governments have lacked either the willingness or the freedom to engage in dialogue for most of the years after 1963, continuing a formal hostility on the Cuban part has often made more sense than chasing ephemera.

What is also clear is that, despite allegations and *Forbes* magazine's once annual inclusion of Fidel in its 'rich list', there is little evidence of either Fidel's accumulation of personal wealth or his overweening desire for total power, as opposed to an evident mistrust in people's ability to be as reliable or as effective as he is, and a preference for unnecessary and often inefficient micro-management.

That, however, leads on to a further dimension worth discussing: his politics. Since 1959, there have been various interpretations of his ideological development, his supposed pragmatic machinations in manipulating and dissembling (not helped by his own talk of deliberately remaining silent on the United States in his 1953 'History will absolve me' speech), or his whimsically reactive responses to ideological options or opportunities. However, what was always clear was a constant commitment to 'the Revolution' and a determination to achieve it by whatever means, develop it in whatever form, and protect it with whatever weapons (real or metaphorical). In that context, he was always prepared to meet would-be rebels from other organisations, including ex-President Carlos Prío, the FEU's Echeverría and even, in 1946, members of the PSP's youth wing, the JS (notably Raúl Valdés Vivó, Alfredo Guevara and Flavio Bravo: Castro Ruz 2010: XXXII).

However, although he may have come late to Marxism (compared with Raúl or Guevara), his ideological instinct was always radical. This led him from an unattached radicalism, through a commitment to the Ortodoxo Party (see Chapter 2), towards a more sympathetic view of Marxism, and finally to a more sui generis version. But that Marxism was never superficial; it grew out of the Marxisant elements in the Cuban political culture, enhanced by his reading and by those around him, and confirmed by the long but chequered relationship with Moscow and other socialist and nationalist states. Hence, by the 2000s, it was clear, deep and committed – but no less flexible and unique for all that.

So, apart from through his character and motivations, how did Fidel play a crucial role? One problem here, of course, is the dynamic nature of the whole Cuban system, changing Fidel's role continually to adapt to the increasingly complex structure, social changes and external pressures. What might have been true in the early 1960s was therefore less so ten years later, and very different thirty years later.

Overall, it is clear that he played a key role at moments of real or imminent crisis, such as in 1959 (when his authority was greatest but when the emerging system was most fluid), 1961 (when the Revolution reached several 'turning points') or 1970 (recognising the need for a reassessment). Equally, the 1991–95 crisis saw Fidel return to centre stage decisively, especially when quelling the August 1994 street disturbances, convincing fearful Cubans that all was not lost. Equally decisive were moments when his intervention changed things: the 1965 and 1980 decisions to hasten a mass exodus (Camarioca and Mariel), the latter being especially traumatic and politically damaging; the unrealistic scale of 1970's planned 10 million ton *zafra* (sugar harvest); and the post-2000 Battle of Ideas, which, while making some sense (since, after a decade of demoralisation and ideological doubt, there was a clear need to reinvigorate ideologically), almost certainly erred in its scale and impracticality. Beyond that, there is no doubt about his role in the creation of the 26 July Movement and the Sierra struggle, his early recognition of the importance of political unity, or his championing of the explosion of 'internationalism' in the 1970s and 1980s.

He also intervened decisively in many debates, either setting the parameters or summing up, or ending the debate by deciding on the outcome. Equally, however, we should not lose sight of the moments when he lost arguments: one such came in the early 1990s when he was successfully and publicly challenged by then UNEAC president Abel Prieto over his opposition to a controversial film that he had not yet seen, and, more crucially, in 1991–93 when the reform programme agreed and enacted was one with which he did not agree in principle.

Yet, overall, his legacy is likely to lie less in such decisions (many of which were unavoidable) than in the widespread loyalty that he commanded, a loyalty which, on the one hand, and as already observed, created a tendency for many Cubans to personify 'the Revolution' in him, and, on the other, generated an enduring faith in his ability to find solutions. Indeed, that faith will be precisely the crucial factor lacking over the coming years. The other side of this coin, however, is the contrary tendency for many, especially young, Cubans to blame him for everything, seeing him as the single obstacle to change, the father figure against whom to rebel, and an increasingly grey (and perhaps fragile, but still too influential) éminence grise.

This, of course, brings us to his most telling decision: to retire temporarily in 2006 and permanently in 2008. It was telling because US policy-making had long been based on the assumption that his thirst for power and mistrust of others would keep him in office until death (the so-called 'biological solution'). However, this overlooked another feature of Fidel's personality: his overwhelming sense of history. In 1953, his first public appeal was a rallying call to Cuba's historical destiny, and an awareness of the Revolution's historical importance was always central to his speeches, writings and beliefs. Hence, although he may initially have intended to retire temporarily in 2006, he was ultimately well aware that a power vacuum could seriously damage political stability and endanger the historical project to which he had dedicated his life. Therefore, by 2007, it became clear that this sense of history (and his astute reading of the political runes) was driving him to accept the inevitable and step down, rather than risk seeing that project unravel.

There was, however, a characteristically interesting final twist: not only did he not oppose his Santiago constituents' nomination of him for the National Assembly elections of February 2008, but only in the last days before the election did he confirm that he would not be standing, leaving the door open for his brother. Equally, in 2011, it remained unclear until very late what his intentions were about his post of general secretary of the party after the Sixth Congress, until he confirmed that his 2008 resignation had in fact included that post. Hence, on both occasions there remained some doubt about his intentions, suggesting the scenario of a reluctant Fidel being pressured to resign finally.

## Che Guevara

The problem with seriously assessing Guevara's role within the Revolution is separating fact from myth, for few political leaders have been subject to so much contrary mythification as 'Che', even before the moment and manner of his death in 1967. Moreover, apart from reasonably objective biographies (Anderson 1997) or analytical studies of his ideas (Sinclair 1979) and of his active role in government (Borrego 2001; Tablada Pérez 1987; Yaffe 2009), most interest in him has tended to focus on only a few aspects.

Firstly, there is the romanticising focus on his youth, and especially on the period of his 'iconic' journeys through Latin America in the early 1950s and their effect on his commitment. Secondly, there is Che the guerrilla: his participation in the Sierra rebellion until 1958 and then his activism outside Cuba after 1965, culminating in his death. Indeed, two recent successful feature films on Che focused, separately, on precisely those two periods. Thirdly, while there is some limited interest in his experience in government, that tends to be less significant than eye-catching moments: his United Nations (UN) speeches, his role in fomenting guerrilla warfare in Latin America, his famous signing of banknotes during his brief stint as president of the National Bank, and, of course, the whole decision to abandon his government work and leave Cuba, generating all manner of speculation about splits with Fidel. Finally, there has been serious interest among Marxists in his contribution to Marxist theory, assessing his theories on revolution, value, subjective conditions and consciousness (Lowy 1973). Yet, overall, the significance of what Guevara actually did in government in 1959–65 has largely been missed (Kapcia 1994).

Separating myth from fact is therefore not easy, especially as Guevara's whole trajectory, his probable culpability (for example in the executions of proven *batistianos* at his La Cabaña headquarters in January 1959: Castañeda 1998: 143) and his effectiveness have all become clouded in the familiar, highly partisan reporting. What we do know is that, while immediately striking up a rapport with Fidel in Mexico, he was initially simply the rebel expedition's doctor and thus an ordinary 'foot soldier' on the *Granma*; it was only as the guerrilla group survived into 1957 that his military skills and commitment became evident, winning respect and eventually (in July 1957) leadership of one of the three guerrilla columns (Fidel and Raúl leading the other two).

After 1959, Guevara was certainly at the centre of everything, even if his input was not always influential. In the Sierra, his clarity of political vision, his awareness of Marxism and his drive to educate made him crucial to the path to radicalisation of the 'core group' of guerrillas: it was 'universally recognized that Che played an important part in the political and intellectual maturation of the *guerrilleros*' (Karol 1970: 42). It also seems clear that not only did Guevara's commitment to socialism pre-date Fidel's, but that he helped push Fidel along that road after 1959 (Anderson 1997: 480).

He also seems to have been significant in driving active cooperation with the PSP, while his column was marching westwards towards Havana. Certainly, before 1959 he shared Fidel's view that the rebels should welcome the PSP's commitment and organisation, willingly incorporating PSP activists (such as Acosta and Núñez Jiménez) into his ranks, and even in prominent positions. After 1959, however, although continuing to stress cooperation, he became increasingly aware of Communist Parties' inability to make a revolution (Karol 1970: 59). Nonetheless, although his Marxism never persuaded him to join any Communist Party's ranks before 1959, he always had 'an almost visceral reaction' to manifestations of anti-Communism (ibid.: 45). Therefore, on those counts alone, he was influentially at the centre of things by 1959.

In that year, it was he who led the rebel troops into Havana on 2 January, and then imposed order from his base in the Cabaña fortress; this meant not only dispensing 'revolutionary justice' but also continuing to educate the rebel forces politically and culturally (including through a literacy programme that helped shape the leadership's determination to mount the 1961 literacy campaign). It was also he who established the new police force, ensuring the new Revolution's domestic stability, and he generally played a crucial role in creating the Revolution's new security apparatus (Castañeda 1998: 146).

That centrality and his charismatic image enhanced his popularity to such an extent that, on 7 February 1959, the Fundamental Law (which, by substantially amending the 1940 Constitution, became essentially the Revolution's charter) included a clause specifically allowing him, uniquely, to retrospectively acquire Cuban citizenship 'from birth'. This was achieved through the debate about allowing foreigners who had fought for the Revolution to become Cuban citizens, distinguishing between those who had fought for over two years (Guevara being the only one fitting that definition) and the rest, who were able to become only naturalised citizens (Anderson 1997: 397; Buch and Suárez 2009: 72).

The same year also saw him immediately playing leading roles in two areas: foreign policy and economics (Sinclair 2002: 55). For him, the two were increasingly related, since he was already developing his interpretation of Marxism into his very particular belief that Cuba, as an underdeveloped economy, could realise a socialist revolution that would develop rapidly into fully fledged communism.

In May 1959, he left Cuba on a three-month visit to fourteen developing and non-aligned countries; besides looking for markets for Cuba, he was also effectively laying the basis for Cuba's active participation in the Non-Aligned Movement. However, he also visited the Soviet Union and the Socialist Bloc early on, always arguing for close links. His 1960 two-month visit to the Socialist Bloc was certainly crucial in agreeing sugar purchases, preceding the United States' total cut in the sugar quota (Anderson 1997: 485–6). Then, in 1961, when Raúl returned from Moscow with a draft missile agreement, it was Guevara who was sent back to Moscow to finalise a much revised version (ibid.: 529), indicating that, for Fidel, he was perhaps then more 'senior' than his brother. Certainly, many observers believe that Guevara's input in this one area was 'instrumental', and that the Soviet Union considered him the 'architect' of the relationship (ibid.: 492).

However, Guevara soon became critical of the bourgeois lifestyles of the Soviet and Socialist Bloc elites (ibid.: 488), and, by 1964, some

Soviet politicians considered him a dangerous and unreliable Maoist (ibid.: 596). That may have engendered some tension between Raúl and Guevara, the former becoming closer to Moscow (ibid.: 596–7). However, it seems likely that, in the early years, Guevara pragmatically took the Soviet Union and Socialist Bloc at face value, recognising and welcoming the need for the Soviet link and the value of the Soviet model, especially for its 1920s and 1930s industrialisation experience. By 1964, however, he was more disappointed at Moscow's failure to support Cuba properly (Karol 1970: 42–53), a position that intensified into a wider disenchantment with the Soviet Union's lack of revolutionary commitment in the Third World.

This, therefore, takes us to the question of his contribution to a different dimension of foreign policy: Cuba's growing commitment to the theory and practice of guerrilla warfare. The former came through his two early books, *La guerra de guerrillas* (1960) and *Pasajes de la guerra revolucionaria cubana* (1963). While neither affected Cuban policies, they clearly laid down the theoretical basis for Cuba's enormous impact on the wider leftist movement in Latin America, specifically generating a widespread willingness of leftist elements (many separating themselves from less insurrectionary Communist Parties) to follow the Cuban lead and form guerrilla groups. That willingness was matched in principle by 1961, and by 1962 in practice, by a Cuban readiness to support this with training (in Cuba), funds, equipment and (occasionally) people, chiefly through a secret unit inside the Ministry of the Interior (MININT). Despite the ministerial location of that unit, it was clearly Guevara who oversaw it all. Here, however, he was pushing at an open door, for, while the form of the campaign owed much to his new theories (closely following Guevara's reading of the Cuban experience), the idea of 'spreading the Revolution' was already in several leaders' minds. Fidel himself, after all, had once tried to liberate the Dominican Republic and Camilo Cienfuegos oversaw a plan to repeat that in 1959 (Abreu Cardet and Coredero Michel 2009). The 1960 Declaration of Havana then threw down the challenge to the Latin American left to copy Cuba and overthrow other despots.

Therefore, while Guevara was influential in the policy's form and energy, it was not his policy alone; we can assume that something similar would have emerged anyway. Instead, as with other areas of Cuban political life, he articulated it better than anyone and theorised what others already wanted. Therefore, of course, he also partly contributed to the policy's failure, since his theory was based on a reading of the Cuban experience that seriously underplayed the contribution of the urban-based underground (partly arising from his growing frustration in 1957–58 with what he saw as an unreliable political force, compared with that of the guerrillas, whose determination and radicalism had been steeled in the heat of battle); it was that reading that led many Latin American guerrillas to neglect, occasionally fatally, the vital need for a close relationship with an urban movement (usually assumed to be the Communist Party) to supply them and to provide 'armed propaganda' in the cities, just as the 26 July Movement had done in Cuba.

Just as he articulated and theorised better than anyone, the same could be said in part of another area of his early contribution: economic policy. In 1959, he became president of the National Bank, taking over from the social democratic Felipe Pazos, who had become increasingly uneasy at the Revolution's radicalisation just when Guevara was becoming increasingly aware of the bank's crucial role in a more radical economic development strategy. He stayed there until 1961, using it as a base for his developing interpretation of Marxist economics. Then, on 23 February 1961, he moved to the newly created Ministry of Industries – born out of the old National Institute for Agrarian Reform's (INRA's) Department of Industries, which he had led – staying there until 1965. Once again, he used that position to develop and put into practice his readings of Marxist economics. In both positions, therefore, his contribution was crucial.

This brings us immediately to Guevara's most significant contribution to Marxist theory: his belief in the potential predominance of subjective over objective conditions and therefore also of the 'new man'. Normally, such theoretical notions might not be expected to contribute to strategies or policies; however, both ideas clearly accorded with, and articulated, notions developing among the rest of the leadership, and may even have influenced those notions.

Guevara challenged the conventional Marxist 'scientific' notion of the primacy of objective conditions (i.e. the appropriate stage of capitalist development and the resulting evolution and readiness of the industrial working class). He held that in certain circumstances and when objective conditions were insufficient, they could be super-seded by subjective conditions (i.e. the resolute actions of a politi-cally conscious vanguard), but also that political consciousness itself (conventionally seen as part of the 'superstructure' rather than the base) could substitute for objective conditions. As with his theories of guerrilla warfare, this was largely an empirical conclusion, based on the Cuban insurrectionary, and then revolutionary, experience, including episodes such as the literacy campaign and Playa Girón (the Cuban term for the Bay of Pigs), but he extended this observation to suggest specific policies and goals.

Firstly, the idea of the 'new man' (the ideal revolutionary – aware, committed and self-sacrificing) grew out of that basic premise, becoming a goal and an ethos about what to expect of true revolution-aries. Secondly, it justified the whole ethos of 'voluntarism' that took hold from the mid-1960s, emphasising the benefits and effectiveness of popular mobilisation, political commitment and volunteer labour as substitutes for Cuba's lack of material capacity. Thirdly, it both led to and reflected the idea that Cuba could turn conventional Marxist theory (and therefore both Moscow's and the PSP's conven-tional readings) on its head, by seeking to achieve the communist stage of development without passing through the requisite stages of advanced capitalism and a socialist 'people's democracy'.

It was the latter idea that generated the 1962–65 'Great Debate', which was far from abstruse, and informed the post-1965 'moral economy'; although Fidel essentially decreed a compromise between the two positions (adopting Guevara's notion of a rigidly centralised economic structure but also the opposing side's preference for a short-term sugar-based expansion), he was clearly influenced by Guevara's theoretical positions.

However, as with his ideas of guerrilla warfare, what Guevara theorised was not in a vacuum, since he largely articulated what others were already instinctively arguing. Voluntarism was already emerging as a modus operandi, and the urgency of social change and economic development was already pushing the leadership towards the idea of accelerating the model that they had enthusiastically borrowed from the Socialist Bloc.

The final issue on the role of Guevara, however, is the vexed question of his departure from power and Cuba in 1965, and the still extant idea of a supposed split with Fidel. In fact, there is no concrete proof of or witness to such a split; indeed, interviews in 1994–95 with several former colleagues of Guevara turned up no evidence of any major differences of opinion between the two (Kapcia 1994). The idea of the split therefore seems to have been rumour and speculation, given the suddenness of the decision; however, we immediately enter the familiar supposition and mythology of some branches of Cuban studies, where some expect a 'smoking gun' in the hands of Fidel, who was either unwilling to share the limelight in Cuba with another charismatic leader or determined to mend fences with the Soviet Union, despite Guevara's opposition, while others refuse to hear anything negative about either person. Ultimately, we are left with intelligent supposition, based on what we know about them both and about their relationship.

On that basis, it seems unlikely that any such argument happened. While we know that they disagreed occasionally, Guevara always either bowed to Fidel's leadership (which he never challenged or doubted) or persuaded Fidel of his own arguments. We also know that their relationship was close and mutually trusting, and that Guevara's departure and then death moved Fidel considerably. Moreover, the reasons usually suggested for the 'split' do not correspond to what we know of the two leaders' ideas, especially as the Cuban leadership began to adhere closely to many of Guevara's views after he had left Cuba (Balfour 2009: 80). There was also repeated evidence of the two seeing eye to eye as late as March 1965, on Cuba's Latin American policy and on the Soviet Union (Anderson 1997: 626–7).

Equally, we also know that, by 1964, Guevara was becoming restless in his determination to realise a promise made to Fidel in 1956, namely that, once the Revolution was firmly in place, he would pursue other battles (ibid.: 595); therefore, by 1965, it was clear to him that he could do more for Cuba by leading rebellions elsewhere than by remaining in government, especially as he was increasingly convinced that the Revolution's survival depended not on the Soviet Union (as he once believed) but on revolution in Latin America (ibid.: 595; Castañeda 1998: 271).

However, myth, speculation and romanticism aside, Guevara's six years at the crux of decision-making in revolutionary Cuba are what interest us here. We are helped enormously by Yaffe's 2009 study, but even that tells us only one part of his role and little of his influence. Indeed, the aforementioned interview-based research of 1994 may well be the truth (Kapcia 1994); this concluded that, although he articulated many of the rebels' ideas more clearly and more radically than anyone else, in reality much of his supposed influence turned out to be less substantial. However, while he may not have changed things or determined the Revolution's direction, he was clearly always at the centre of the decision-making circle in Cuba.

## Raúl Castro

This assessment finally brings us to consider the third member of the triumvirate, Raúl Castro, someone either largely ignored over the years or treated as a secondary adjunct to his older brother. Even after the interregnum of 2006–07, many in the Cuban-American community continued to allege that Fidel was still behind the scenes, pulling the strings.

However, there is little doubt about Raúl's centrality to decision-making, especially and increasingly after 1959. Yet his participation in the first act of rebellion, the Moncada assault, was a late decision (he was informed of the plan by Fidel the day before they left for Santiago) and he remained something of a foot soldier during the operation itself, as Lester Rodríguez's second-in-command in the seizure of the Palace of Justice. Until then, he was certainly not one of the five involved in the planning (Bourne 1986: 82).

Besides his early role, the other key question in his biography concerns his political commitment, about which much has been exaggerated. What Thomas wrote in 1971 still seems to be the most consistent version: that, in early July 1953, returning from the Moscow-sponsored World Youth Congress in Vienna and a subsequent visit to Prague and Bucharest, he was briefly arrested for possessing communist literature. On his release, he seems to have approached the PSP's youth wing, the JS (Thomas 1971: 826), although other accounts have him applying to join a month before the Moncada (Bourne 1986: 73; Szulc 1986: 54) or even in 1952 (Klepak 2010: 25). Certainly, he was politically aware and active; in January 1953, he was elected (with the PSP's Flavio Bravo) to the student committee to commemorate Martí's centenary by linking it to Cuban youth and thus generating student activism against Batista (Szulc 1986: 168).

Thereafter, however, he remained close to Fidel throughout the development of the rebellion; according to one account, he was the closest to Fidel personally and politically (ibid.: 310). Tried and sentenced with Fidel and the other Moncada attackers, he was also imprisoned on the Isle of Pines, and, after their release, accompanied Fidel to Mexico, where he joined in the military training (in preparation for the planned invasion of Cuba) and movement-building. In Mexico, he seems then to have had some unproductive contact with the PSP. However, he clearly rose to greater significance within the group, for, during the invasion, he was one of only three 'captains'. Becoming then one of the fifteen or so survivors of the *Granma* landing who gathered in the Sierra after 5 December 1956, he went on to demonstrate considerable military prowess, loyalty and organisation. Eventually, in March 1958, he was given command of a separate column (deliberately misleadingly called Column No. 6), opening up the 'Frank País Second Front' in the northern Oriente Sierra del Cristal.

From then on, he clearly had an autonomous importance in the rebel movement, building a micro-government in the Sierra, with 'ministerial' departments and a political education unit for the troops and local peasants (where he himself taught: Klepak 2010: 37–8). In addition to shifting military strategy in the east, he also developed links with the local PSP; indeed, when the PSP made overtures to the rebels, it did so through Raúl, Carlos Rafael Rodríguez making his way first to Raúl and only then onwards to Fidel.

After 1 January 1959, as Fidel began his eight-day 'Victory Caravan' to Havana, Raúl was left behind as military commander of Oriente, a significant post for the Revolution's security but not yet nationally influential. However, on 22 January, Fidel, speaking at the Presidential Palace, named Raúl as second-in-command of the 26 July Movement, thereby effectively designating him as his successor in the event of his death (Anderson 1997: 391; Thomas 1971: 1087). But it was Fidel's promotion to Prime Minister in February 1959 that created a real space for Raúl, when a government decree named him the new Commander-in-Chief of the armed forces. By 1961, his importance was even clearer, when he was confirmed as occupying the new post of Deputy Prime Minister (starting in 1962).

As well as running the new FAR, he succeeded his Sierra del Cristal lieutenant, Martínez Sánchez, as Minister of Defence on 15 October 1959 (the decision led to a major crisis within the movement by provoking Huber Matos's resignation: Thomas 1971: 1244). From those two positions, he proceeded to exercise a growing influence in many areas of Cuban political life, certainly becoming crucial to the vital task of defending the new Revolution.

He was also significant in building links with the Soviet Union, just as he had been in relations with the PSP. In September 1959, he dispatched a FAR delegation to the Soviet Union and China (Klepak 2010: 57), and then, in June 1960, he visited Moscow himself, seeking arms and establishing close links with the Soviet military. It was this relationship, and his leadership of the FAR, his previous association with the JS and his willingness to work with the PSP in 1958, that all conspired to create his standard image in Western circles as a 'hardliner', an 'ideologue' (as opposed to Fidel's supposedly more wayward approach to 'ideology'), and even something of a Stalinist, although there is no evidence of his taking any such position.

The political shifts of the 1970s enabled Raúl's influence to grow, using his long-cultivated Soviet contacts to develop his authority in the new environment; moreover, while he may not have directly influenced that shift, there can be little doubt that a return to a more consolidated system of structures, closer to the Soviet model, and the end of the highly inefficient 'moral economy' were closer to his preferences than the heady 1960s. It was then that the FAR became both militarily powerful and efficient and also economically strong. In fact, it was Raúl who took the emphasis on efficiency to its logical conclusion in the mid-1980s by bringing in Japanese management consultants to help streamline the economic decision-making and execution of plans within the FAR (Domínguez 1990).

Finally, of course, the debate after 1991 about saving the Revolution saw him at the heart of discussions and decisions; with a characteristic desire for finding the best, rather than the most ideologically satisfactory, solution, he backed the emerging programme of economic reforms that was put to consultation in 1990–91 and approved by the 1991 Party Congress. It was that programme which, ultimately, ensured the Revolution's survival and, with it, his own reputation as an economic reformer and pragmatist, rather than the supposed 'Stalinist' of the 1960s.

That new reputation emerged fully after 2007. After a hiatus of authority following Fidel's retirement (with most Cubans, party members and bureaucrats unsure whether to expect a resumed *fidelista* system or to adapt to a new leadership), Raúl began to display a determination to take a firmer hold of authority, to ensure that the year of drift and inertia was not prolonged damagingly. On 26 July, he used the annual Moncada speech to voice a series of trenchant criticisms of different aspects of the Revolution, past and present. Then, in September, he used those criticisms as the basis for a nationwide consultation exercise that he launched; the outcome, exactly as expected, provided him with ammunition for his embryonic reform programme. In the meantime, he had quietly downgraded the Battle of Ideas, a strategy whose inefficiency and cost were anathema to his practical sensitivities, and, simultaneously, he had begun to change both the party's middle ranks and government personnel.

Once elected president, in February 2008, he began reshaping the government and launching the process of economic reform. The former showed a characteristic determination and a degree of ruthlessness: not only did he steadily replace the cabinet that he had inherited, bringing in younger, more efficient and dedicated specialists and similarly reliable FAR people, but he also shocked many in March 2009 by sacking the two most obvious heirs apparent, Carlos Lage and Felipe Pérez Roque. He also went on to sack several ministers deemed to be failing in their duty to prevent corruption.

On the reform process, he proved both determined and flexible. The programme itself was launched with a series of criticisms of aspects of Cuban life and work practices (including its 'dependency culture' and shallow egalitarianism) and, specifically, with the shocking plan to shed a million public sector jobs, half within six months, to be soaked up by an enlarged self-employed sector. The general reaction proved his flexibility, as the resulting negotiations with the CTC slowed and watered down the proposals and the timescale, although without changing the plan's purpose.

His determination, however, was more ably demonstrated by his approach to institutional resistance to reform, evidently still powerful and reflecting a growing unease among older Cubans. Indeed, the lack of a Congress since 2002 had probably allowed recalcitrant elements to use the party as a base for resistance. One of Raúl's first acts after his election was thus to call the long-overdue Sixth Party Congress, and, when it failed to materialise, he issued a public threat to call a special National Conference and to make what he called necessary generational changes to party personnel, pre-empting a conservative-dominated Congress. The deadlock broken, the Congress duly took place in April 2011, discussing and approving the revised reform programme. By 2013, therefore, Raúl was clearly in the saddle, with a programme of modernisation under way. The 2013 elections also confirmed something else: that this would be his last presidential term, having declared twice his intention to change the Constitution to prohibit more than two terms of office – thereby heralding the end of a 'Castro-led' Revolution in 2018.

However, a caveat should be expressed here: the frequent observation made outside Cuba that Raúl is determined to press ahead with a long-overdue transition to capitalism, based on the 'Chinese model', seems wide of the mark. Not only has he always shared Fidel's commitment to 'the Revolution', differing only on the precise means of defending and furthering that process, but his proposals evidently do not amount to 'liberalisation' or privatisation. Instead, what he has largely done is, firstly, to formalise and legalise what many Cubans were already doing informally (thereby decreasing the extent to which the morality of the system is undermined) and, secondly, to seek to loosen the state's hold in areas where small-scale private initiative can deliver goods or services more efficiently and cheaply, thereby increasing both income and supply. Indeed, the parallel commitment to a high level of cooperative enterprise as part of the new Cuba suggests that he has never sought a capitalist Cuba.

As for China, Raúl's characteristic distaste for corruption and his awareness of the sensitivity of the question of inequality (especially following the effects of the dual currency since 1993) make him unlikely to follow the Chinese path, aware that Cuba, as a small, close-knit and still relatively equal society, cannot afford to allow Chinese levels of either corruption or inequality to flourish.

## Conclusion

What the above discussion has therefore demonstrated is that the substantial and influential role of the two other leaders besides Fidel warrants attention, but also that, at least for the 1959–65 period, decision-making in revolutionary Cuba was not simply a case of one man's whim or megalomaniac control; rather, Cuba was at the very least governed by a triumvirate. Moreover, the pattern that this brief analysis has highlighted is revealing: one of the three (Raúl) was given a free hand in areas such as defence, the FAR, links with the Soviet Union and, eventually, in spearheading much-needed reform, and he was allowed at least to differ substantially from Fidel and, more likely, to persuade him, while the other (Guevara) was given similarly free rein in economic policy-making, foreign policy and the ideological definition of the early Revolution, and so there was evidently a wider leadership than one-man rule. Therefore, if these two were trusted enough for their influence and expertise to be acknowledged, then the possibility also exists that, looking beyond the triumvirate to the larger cast of potentially significant activists and role-holders, we may find other areas of influence.

The following three chapters therefore take up that thread, over the course of three defined periods. A focus on these three leaders highlights the reality that, in Cuba since 1959, there was always a core group leading the insurrection and then the Revolution, at the heart of which stood the two or three leaders (obviously, after Guevara's death, only Raúl remained alongside Fidel), but beyond whom there always existed an 'inner circle', with its origins clearly in the insurrectionary experience of 1953–58 and with contours changing relatively little over the following five decades or more. The following chapters will trace that circle and those contours and explain their components.

## 2 | THE FORMATION OF 'THE VANGUARD': 1953–58

When assessing the evolution and nature of the 'inner circle' in Cuba after 1959, we necessarily start by understanding the way in which the group was formed, which essentially means understanding the people who formed the rebel movement before 1959. For, like the three 'historic' leaders, all of those around them also owed their legitimacy and influence to their role in the successful rebellion; indeed, as the following chapters make clear, membership of the original and evolving guerrilla group and participation in the rebellion's key moments constituted both a badge of honour (lasting well over half a century) and membership of one of the several concentric circles of power and influence. This chapter therefore focuses on details of the insurrectionary years, less for their biographical value (although this can have some relevance) than to explain the process by which the 'inner' and other 'circles' emerged.

The starting point is therefore Fulgencio Batista's coup on 10 March 1952, which sparked the rebellion and the wider opposition, but, more importantly, showed a general lack of opposition that allowed the guerrilla rebels to fill the void. The coup was a shock to the Cuban political system: however corrupt the preceding twelve years of constitutional rule might have been (following thirty-eight years of a somewhat embarrassing sequence of questionable independence, unstable and corrupt politicking, violent unrest, brutal authoritarianism and then finally reforming populism – the latter two experiences effected by Batista), Batista's return was a rude awakening, seen by many as yet another milestone in a recent history of shame (Ameringer 2000; López Civeira 1990; Thomas 1971: 737–86; Whitney 2001). Hence, formal opposition, especially from the two major parties dominating politics, was expressed immediately.

The main political force was the Authentic Cuban Revolutionary Party (PRC-A, better known as the Auténticos), consciously borrowing the name of José Martí's party of 1892–99 (he had founded the

PRC, but the Auténticos added the epithet 'authentic'), which had led the last rebellion against Spain. The Auténticos were formed in Mexico in 1934 by ex-students then in exile, all of them veterans of the 1927–33 movement against Gerardo Machado's dictatorship and, more pertinently, of the brief '100 days' government' and 'revolution' of September 1933 to January 1934. The latter had been ended by Batista, who seized power, having previously led a mutiny of non-commissioned officers (NCOs) in alliance with the rebellious students (of the University Students' Directorate or DEU). Under that revolution's president, Ramón Grau San Martín, the party remained in exile while Batista ruled Cuba with a firm and often repressive hand (always through 'puppet' presidents); when he eased up his indirect control in 1938 (eventually even winning elections in 1940), it allowed the PRC-A back. The Auténticos eventually won both the 1944 and 1948 elections, as a supposedly nationalist, revolutionary and anti-corruption party, in the *martiano* tradition; however, in power, they proved to be largely pro-United States, conservatively anti-Communist, and as corrupt as any pre-1933 government.

As a result, a second major party arose in 1947 from within the Auténtico ranks (especially among its younger members and the branches in the far east, Cuba's Oriente province), the Cuban People's Party, known as the Ortodoxos and led by the charismatic leader Eduardo ('Eddy') Chibás, opposing corruption and soon gaining votes. Indeed, although Chibás committed suicide in 1951, the Ortodoxos seemed likely to win the 1952 elections, almost certainly contributing to Batista's and the military's decision to stage a coup. However, the key issue here is that the Ortodoxos were really the crucible for the eventual opposition to Batista, since several of the early conspirators around, and including, Fidel, were members; Fidel, in fact, was both a founding member and congressional candidate in 1952, and, until 1958, often described the rebellion as 'armed *chibasismo*'. As confirmation, the first edition of the movement's newspaper was called *Aldabonazo* (literally 'the knock at the door'), copying Chibás's well-known 'call to arms'.

Most other parties of the time were relatively insignificant; the exception was the (Communist) PSP. The PSP was not large – it had only 199 members in 1927 (Rojas Blaquier 2005: 64), although numbers increased to over a thousand by 1932 (ibid.: 139) and then

2,480 by 1935 (ibid.: 256), and grew to somewhere around 15,000 to 16,000 in 1958 (Goldenberg 1966: 163; Habel 1991: 93); however, it was well established, having been founded in 1925 as the Cuban Communist Party, and was solidly based in the trade union movement (eventually becoming significant in the hitherto militant and even anarcho-syndicalist CNOC confederation). In fact, it was the communist spectre in the unrest of 1930–33 that largely drove the military, urged by the United States, to remove Machado in August 1933 in order to seek to head off discontent; later, in 1933, it was the party's union activities outside Havana that persuaded the United States to seek Batista's intervention in 1934. In both cases, the United States was frightened more by the spectre than by the reality of the new party's size – in August 1933, there were no fewer than 367 strikes (Rojas Blaquier 2005: 205) and the US assumed that the party was behind them all, although, in fact, it was not. In 1935, Batista's clampdown on leftist dissent, following a general strike, targeted the Communists, who went underground; their leader, Blas Roca, called for a 'popular front' against the 'fascist' Batista (Karol 1970: 81–2).

In fact, in 1937, a coincidence of the Soviet Union's international strategy – expressed through the Communist International (or Comintern) – which then became one of forming 'popular fronts' against fascism, with Batista's own plans for constitutional rule led to a strange, but pragmatic, alliance between Batista and the Communists, announced by Roca to the party's Central Committee in July 1938 (ibid.: 85). Hence, for the 1939 Constitutional Convention elections, the party was legalised (and allowed to hold its Third Congress), officially merging with a specially created 'front' party to form the Communist Revolutionary Union Party (Batlle Reyes 2008: 94) under Juan Marinello Vidaurreta as president and Blas Roca as general secretary. Although the party won only six seats (out of eighty-one), it was clearly back in the fold, and, in 1939, it organised a welcome demonstration for Batista's return from the United States (Karol 1970: 85). This alliance (formalised as the Democratic Socialist Coalition) then went on to win the 1940 general election.

Meanwhile, the party was free to establish its daily newspaper (*Hoy*) and also to create and run a new national trade union confederation, the CTC. In 1942, after the Soviet Union entered the war on the Allies' side, Batista appointed two Communists to his cabinet,

Carlos Rafael Rodríguez and Marinello, although neither was in a significant or powerful position. Finally, in 1944, continuing this collaboration, the party changed its name again to the PSP.

The PSP, therefore, had a long but somewhat chequered history, but it was certainly a significant player and often well respected. It was chequered because, on a few occasions, partly following the Comintern's tortuous changes in 'line' and partly making pragmatic judgements on the ground, it had refused to support seemingly popular and even revolutionary protest movements, which the Comintern had dismissed as 'national-reformist' (Rojas Blaquier 2005: 119). In 1933, the PSP had even tacitly agreed with Machado to suspend strikes, until overtaken by the groundswell of popular activism; in the 'revolutionary' autumn of 1933, it consistently refused to support the Grau government; and the 1935 general strike was not organised by the PSP, although it was involved through its role in the CNOC and certainly suffered in the aftermath. Moreover, by the 1940s, the party tended to be Stalinist, having shed its maverick, 'Cuban' tendencies in the late 1920s. These had been largely associated with one of the founders, Julio Antonio Mella, who had been briefly expelled for 'indiscipline' (ibid.: 53–5). The PSP's declining membership reflected this, falling from 87,000 (1942) to 20,000 (1952); in addition, in the first meeting of the 1959 CTC, only 170 out of 3,240 delegates were PSP members (Karol 1970: 97), although another source has a figure of 260 (Thomas 1971: 1250). Despite this, however, the party always retained a justifiable reputation for effective trade union organisation and activism, being the only major party to recruit actively and extensively among Cuba's black workers (Rojas Blaquier 2005: 167–78).

However, despite their respective strengths and formal declarations, none of these three major parties seriously entertained the idea in 1952 of active or forceful opposition to the coup. At one level, this was pragmatic self-preservation, but it possibly also reflected either uncertainty about Batista's political longevity or even a distant hope that a deal might be struck with him. Both the PSP and the Auténticos had already cooperated with him after 1938, although, in the new Cold War context (although, unusually in Latin America, the PSP remained legal), there was little chance of a fresh Batista–PSP alliance.

This general quiescence (or acquiescence) was crucial, as the established parties' lack of opposition did not sit well with many Cubans, especially the students. The University of Havana, indeed, had historically been a site of activism, from a notable radicalisation in 1923 to the DEU of 1930–33; by the 1950s, however, that activism had degenerated into *bonchismo*, where supposedly political groups with 'revolutionary' names, such as the Revolutionary Insurrectionary Union (UIR) or the Revolutionary Socialist Movement (MSR), competed for control of the campus, fought in the streets or even hired themselves out to the Auténticos (the MSR had strong-armed the PSP out of CTC influence in 1948). Nonetheless, some dormant radicalism remained, and, within three hours of the coup, the FEU directorate met at the campus and then approached the ousted President Prío for arms to resist Batista (Nuiry 2007: 17). Later, after 1955, under José Antonio Echeverría's subsequent presidency, the FEU developed a sustained campaign of protests and conspiracy, the latter through a new armed wing, the Revolutionary Student Directorate (DRE) (García Oliveras 1988).

Another movement also grew up in May 1952, the National Revolutionary Movement (MNR), under a highly respected academic, Rafael García Bárcena, and based largely among Catholic activists, students and ex-students, many following new notions of 'Catholic Action' (Llerena 1978: 47). The MNR was small, however, with little public support or awareness of its existence until its ambitious plan to attack Cuba's main military base, Havana's Campamento Columbia, on 5 April 1953, was pre-empted by the security forces, who arrested most of the plotters. Several MNR activists and sympathisers, including Armando Hart, Faustino Pérez Hernández, Vilma Espín, Frank País (Szulc 1986: 163–4) and Enrique Oltuski (Oltuski 2000), then gravitated towards a new movement that was being constructed by Fidel.

This was the context for that new movement, initially simply called 'the Movement' but soon christened the 'Generation of the Centenary', since its creation coincided with (and was partly stimulated by) the fiftieth anniversary in 1953 of Martí's birth (Rojas 1973). With a plethora of publications about, and by, him, Martí now began to represent a collective self-image of Cuban nationalism, even more than he had previously done – betrayed, self-sacrificing, deeply patriotic and highly moral (Hennessy 1963). Fidel himself was already relatively well known as a student activist in the late 1940s (in the always 'political' law faculty), close to (and perhaps even in) the UIR, and then as an Ortodoxo.

In the face of others' inactivity and of the MNR's failure, Fidel and a handful of others then conceived the idea of an MNR-style dramatic action to galvanise opposition and, by capturing weapons, to begin a guerrilla struggle to overthrow Batista. That action was the twin attacks, on 26 July 1953, on two Oriente garrisons, the Moncada in Santiago (by 132 people) and the much smaller outpost in nearby Bayamo. While the attacks failed spectacularly and resulted in dozens of often brutal deaths (the attackers being surprised early on and then being outnumbered and outgunned, with many killed after arrest), it brought Fidel to the attention of all Cubans. After the mass trial, Fidel's defence speech became the rebellion's first real manifesto (Mencía 1986).

Given its importance in the trajectory traced in this book, this episode immediately raises the need to examine the precise details of many of those who actually participated. Such details are often complicated by the tendency in much of the literature (and even in some Cuban accounts) to conflate the two simultaneous attacks (Santiago and Bayamo), often ignoring Bayamo, and to neglect those who ultimately failed to take part in either attack: several either abandoned the venture beforehand (when, at the rebels' base at the nearby Siboney farm, Fidel outlined the plan and allowed any conspirators to leave) or never joined the actual attacks, having got lost on the way to the barracks or their vehicle having suffered a puncture. Therefore, the usual figure of approximately 165 mentioned actually referred to those in the original plans; in fact, only 110 attacked the Moncada and twenty-two attacked Bayamo. Of those, seventy-one survived the attack and the subsequent executions. One of those who got lost, thereby missing the attack, Angel Díaz, was not excluded from subsequent activism, as he became personal aide to President Urrutia in 1959; however, this did leave a legacy of suspicion, or resentment, among those who had fought (Buch and Suárez 2009: 118–19).

One further significance of the Moncada is that it gives us an early sense of who might have constituted an 'inner circle', for it was planned by very few people: Fidel himself (without Raúl), Jesús Montané (who part-funded it), Antonio (Ñico) López and the ex-

Ortodoxo Abel Santamaría (Karol 1970: 133), but also Abel's sister, Haydée, who hosted most of the meetings, and Melba Hernández. As we will see, apart from López and Abel Santamaría, who died soon afterwards, those who survived after 1959 enjoyed a special importance and considerable leeway.

The next stage in the rebellion's evolution was the imprisonment of many Moncada rebels in the Model Prison (Presidio Modelo) on the Isle of Pines; from there the movement was given a name – the 26 July Movement – and direction. It was formally founded on 12 June 1955 (Bell Lara 2007: 17), taking shape quickly under those not imprisoned, mostly in Havana and Santiago (the latter under Frank País). Ideologically, it still saw itself as a dissident Ortodoxo force, loyal to the memory of Chibás, a character that it retained until 1958, by which time most activists had shifted to more radical positions.

Once Fidel and the others were released on 15 May 1955, then going into a strategic exile in Mexico on 7 July, the Movement acquired another clear function: to prepare for a rebellion that would coincide with the landing of an armed force, all promised before the end of 1956. This plan was agreed at the last meeting of the National Directorate, on 12 June 1955 in Havana, a meeting that again serves to identify an emerging 'inner circle'; this included people such as Hart, Pérez, Pedro Miret Prieto, Montané, Hernández, Haydée Santamaría (Szulc 1986: 247), López and some lesser provincial coordinators. In fact, in all, that meeting included eight Moncada veterans and two former MNR members (Graña Eiriz 2008: 39).

The landing eventually materialised on 2 December 1956, with eighty-two rebels aboard the small yacht *Granma*; like the Moncada, this was a notable failure, due to the combination of bad weather, marine incompetence and a lack of fuel. Not only did it arrive late (failing to coincide with the soon-supressed 30 November rebellion in Santiago), but the yacht ran aground at a location somewhat distant from the planned beach (where disembarkation would have been easy and where transport and supplies were waiting), with an impenetrable mangrove swamp separating the rebels from dry land and safety and taking several hours to cross. The only advantage of this was that they were not attacked as they landed; however, within three days, their progress inland was interrupted at Alegría de Pío by an air force bombardment and an encounter with the army, resulting in many deaths and the dispersal of the rebel force, after which only a handful made it into the nearby Sierra Maestra as planned, to regroup and to form the basis of the guerrilla force.

At that point, even more than with the Moncada, the exact details become shrouded in imprecision, and even myth. The numbers landing are uncontested and the identity of those on the *Granma* likewise: it is enough at this stage simply to identify those who remained central or influential thereafter, notably (besides Fidel, Raúl and Guevara) Faustino Pérez (who had run the Mexico 'training farm' and went on to become 26 July national coordinator), Juan Almeida, Camilo Cienfuegos Gorriarán, Universo Sánchez, Efigenio Ameijeiras, Ciro Redondo, and two Moncada veterans, Montané (like Almeida, formally a 'captain' in the force) and Ramiro Valdés Menéndez.

The mythical aspect refers to the notions that soon sprang up around the 'mystical' figure of 'the twelve' who supposedly survived the Alegría encounter. One of the prime causes of this confusion was Carlos Franqui's 1967 book *El libro de los Doce* (*The Book of the Twelve*), which did not in fact refer to the 'original group' at all (as many have since imagined), but rather it dealt with autobiographical accounts of the experiences and views of eleven activists whose contribution to the urban and rural struggle had, in Franqui's view, been crucial, and also an account of Frank País's death in 1957. These activists included Almeida, Juan Ponce (a Moncada and *Granma* veteran, who never fought in the Sierra, being arrested in 1956 and remaining in prison until 1959), Ameijeiras, Universo Sánchez, Celia Sánchez, Haydée Santamaría, Guillermo García, Manuel Fajardo, Faure Chomón, Camilo Cienfuegos, Guevara and Espín. However, Franqui deliberately exploited the mythical force of the figure 'twelve', as he explained in his prologue:

> El libro se llama *De los Doce*, porque DOCE fueron los hombres que después del desastre incial, batidos cercados y acorralados por miles de soldados, prosiguieron la lucha hasta terminarla con la victoria dos años después. [The book is called *The Twelve* because TWELVE was the number of those who, after the initial disaster, shot at, surrounded and harassed by thousands of soldiers, pursued the struggle until it ended in victory two years later.]

In other words, Franqui either believed or manipulated the myth of the twelve survivors; indeed, later in the book, he himself counted sixteen or seventeen (Franqui 1967: 234).

However, together with early accounts (including Guevara's *Reminiscences*) that mentioned twelve survivors at some early stage, and helped by many Cubans' knowledge of Cuban history (referring to the episode in the 1868–78 independence struggle when the rebel leader, Céspedes, declared that 'with twelve we have enough'), the idea soon grew up that that was the number gathered round Fidel as the core of the Sierra group. The reality was more mundane and fluid: after Alegría, where twenty-four were killed during or after the fighting (Thomas 1971: 899), twenty-one were arrested and put on trial, and nineteen escaped from the encirclement and the area (making their way to the cities). That left twenty-one, divided into at least four small groups, who then regrouped over several days. Eight of these were with Fidel by 18 December (Alvarez Mola and Ravelo López 2007: 14) and other straggler groups arrived in the following days, gradually totalling fifteen (Bourne 1986: 137) and then eighteen, fourteen of whom began the march to the Sierra. In other words, at some point between 5 December and 18 December there were indeed something like twelve survivors gathered together, but that was a fleeting moment, before the eventual fifteen emerged, these consisting of the Castros, Guevara, Universo Sánchez, Faustino Pérez, Valdés, Ameijeiras, Camilo Cienfuegos, Redondo, Armando Rodríguez, René Rodríguez, Reinaldo Benítez, Calixto García, Calixto Morales and Chao Morán (Thomas 1971: 901).

Thereafter, precision about numbers and names becomes much more difficult, given the fluidity of the guerrilla formations, the deaths, arrests and departures of activists, the movement between the Sierra and the cities, and the numbers of new recruits flowing into the Sierra from mid-1957. Moreover, once two columns were formed (then followed by more), and once Camilo Cienfugos and Guevara started their march westward, members flooded to the rebels' ranks, swelling numbers from an original figure of a commonly estimated 300 or so in early 1958 to around 3,000 by the end of the year (Habel 1991: 93). Hence, after mid-1957, we have to identify individuals, rather than simply a category of 'service', when it comes to assessing the possible 'inner core'. Before that, however, one historian identifies an 'inner council' consisting of the two

Castros, Guevara, Camilo Cienfuegos, Jorge Sotús, Almeida, Ciro Frías, Guillermo García and Fajardo (Thomas 1971: 934–5), but that was limited to those in the Sierra, ignoring the urban movement. Fajardo was killed by counter-revolutionary rebels in the Escambray in November 1961, so his membership of any such 'inner council' was short-lived.

The urban wing had also changed significantly since 1955; as the rebellion developed and opposition to Batista grew, the Movement created several adjacent organisations, to draw different groups into the struggle under their leadership and give the Movement a broader image. By 1958, the wider rebellion therefore consisted of several component parts: the 26 July Movement itself, with its armed wing in the Sierra (by 1958 known as the Ejército Rebelde or Rebel Army), the Frente Estudiantil Nacional (National Student Front) and the Frente Obrero Nacional (National Workers' Front), founded in 1957 to organise a trade union base for the Movement but replaced, in late 1958, by the broader United National Workers' Front, designed to encompass grass-roots PSP activists (Bell Lara 2007: 18). There was also the Movimiento de Resistencia Cívica (MRC or Civic Resistance Movement), created as a parallel 'front' organisation to organise urban bourgeois and professional class opposition to Batista (Oltuski 2000: 111) under Mario Llerena. All were increasingly identified as the *Llano* ('the plains', i.e. as opposed to the Sierra). After 1959, of course, one problem in dealing with the details of the *Llano* was its previous clandestine nature, creating a permanent uncertainty about its size and membership. We therefore still lack a clear idea how many belonged to the Movement, but we can be sure that, in 1955, it consisted of dozens rather than hundreds, perhaps growing to hundreds by 1959.

Within the Movement, it was clear by 1958 that the guerrillas (known now as the *Sierra*) were the core and vanguard, with the greatest popular respect and political legitimacy. They, after all, were the ones who had survived the *Granma* (some having previously survived the Moncada) and had fought under arduous conditions in the Sierra for just over two years, and then in open warfare across the Cuban countryside. In fact, this prestige and the guerrillas' sense of their importance were a source of tension between the *Llano* and the *Sierra*, the latter often complaining about inadequate supplies and about the fiasco of a general strike organised in April 1958. That fiasco, indeed, resulted in a special meeting of the Movement's National Directorate in Mompié, in the Sierra, on 3 May 1958, which confirmed the *Sierra*'s primacy and removed some leading *Llano* people from positions of command, notably Faustino Pérez, René Ramos Latour (who had succeeded País as Santiago coordinator) and David Salvador; all three were then given posts in the *Sierra* and Marcelo Fernández Font became national coordinator (Szulc 1986: 351).

By late 1958, two further groups had joined the rebels. The first was the small DR, founded as the DRE in December 1955 by Echeverría; it was a cellular organisation whose most dramatic, but ultimately disastrous, act was the 13 March 1957 full-frontal attack by fifty members on the presidential palace and a Havana radio station. In, and after, that attack, Echeverría and several others were killed, leaving the remaining leaders, notably Fructuoso Rodríguez and Chomón, to pick up the pieces and regroup (Chomón 1969). Chomón soon became the DRE's main leader, therefore taking part in the Miami meeting of opposition groups in late 1957. However, being small, damaged and relatively new, the DRE lacked the strength and spread of the 26 July Movement, although it still had the prestige of association with Echeverría's memory. After March 1957, the DRE dropped the 'E' and added '13 de Marzo' to its name, but, in practice, became known simply as the DR.

In February 1958, Chomón landed with fourteen others at Nuevitas, on the north coast. They made their way southwards to the Sierra del Escambray, where they established a planned guerrilla base, with Eloy Gutiérrez Menoyo, Rolando Cubela and William Morgan. Hence, when Guevara's southern-route column arrived in late 1958 and sought the DR's fusion with the Rebel Army, Chomón eventually (if somewhat reluctantly) agreed, in the so-called 'pacto de Pedrero' on 1 December 1958 (Bell Lara 2007: 38), his followers then taking part in the crucial battle of Santa Clara. However, Gutiérrez Menoyo and Morgan refused and kept their force apart from the wider rebellion; then, as Chomón's wing joined the rebel alliance after 1959, the two recalcitrant leaders took their faction into armed opposition to the new order.

The second group to join the rebellion in 1958 – the PSP – was more significant and preceded the DR's attachment. The party's reaction to the 1950s rebellion was interesting: in 1953, it condemned the Moncada attack as brave but senseless, as 'adventurism' and 'putschism' (Karol 1970: 139) – the latter accusation being then a standard Communist definition of political plotting (Rojas Blaquier 2010: 43). In 1956, it also distanced itself from the *Granma* landing and attempted rising, again seeing it as 'adventurism'. The party was also, of course, concerned about its visibility, aware that, in any clampdown (as in 1935), its members would suffer. However, the leadership soon came under pressure from the JS youth wing and members in Oriente, who argued for a closer relationship with, and even support for and involvement in, the rebellion. Indeed, as early as 1955, PSP members in Havana had made contacts with the new Movement (Thomas 1971: 944), this being repeated in Mexico before the *Granma* expedition. In October 1957, PSP member Ursinio Rojas went to the Sierra to inform Fidel that the PSP had now allowed its members to join the rebels (Szulc 1986: 338); finally, in February 1958, two PSP leaders went to the Sierra and added their organisation to the revolutionary alliance, the party thereafter encouraging its members to support and even join the rebels (Thomas 1971: 981). As we have seen, once Raúl Castro set up a new front in the Sierra del Cristal, he willingly collaborated with local PSP members, some of whom joined his column, and, when Guevara and Camilo Cienfuegos began their westward march, Guevara was content to work with local PSP groups and alongside PSP guerrillas.

Thus, by late 1958, there were actually three distinct 'parties' to the final rebel alliance. However, while these were the core of the alliance (although never in an easy relationship), on the eve of the victory, on 31 December 1958, the wider if inchoate anti-Batista 'coalition' was much broader and looser. Moreover, it had changed considerably since 1952, the leading politicians having moved from empty protest to a growing awareness of the need to be seen to act; for example, ex-President Prío tried to head off the 26 July Movement's growing popularity and leadership by setting up small (but failed) invasion forces and supplying limited funds to the Movement. Throughout the period from 1955 to 1958, attempts were made to unite disparate opposition groups into a unified front; leading members of the exiled or Havana-based Movement sometimes joined these discussions, and even tentatively agreed on declarations. However, Fidel remained consistently aloof from such attempts, unless those groups acknowledged the Movement's primacy. This all meant that, while, on 1 January 1959, there was a ready welcome for the rebellion's military victory, there was little consensus on the next steps or the character of 'the Revolution'.

By then, of course, the guerrillas' prestige had grown and, with it, the prestige of those leaders or activists associated with the *Sierra*. Hence, Fidel, Guevara and Raúl were unquestionably the leading protagonists of the Rebel Army and three of the nationally best known rebels, with a special and unchallenged legitimacy and popularity.

They shared that, however, with a fourth person, Camilo Cienfuegos. While holding no 'officer' rank during the *Granma* invasion (he had not been at the Moncada and joined the group only in August 1956), Cienfuegos rapidly rose to a prominence that he retained. This protagonism, and his evident charisma, made him one of the most photogenic and popular of the guerrillas. Finally, on 21 August 1958, he was, with Guevara, chosen to lead one of the two columns (thereupon becoming a *comandante*) that, after the defeat of Batista's last Sierra offensive, began a rapid march westwards, along the length of the island, to take the Revolution towards Havana. While Guevara went along the southerly route, Cienfuegos led his 143 men (the 'Antonio Maceo' Invading Column Number 2) along the north route, reaching the central province of Las Villas by 8 October (Batista Moreno 2008). However, although by then the rebels were attracting hundreds of new recruits, by December Cienfuegos's column still had only 160 men (Aladro Cardoso et al. 2007: 207).

There were, however, already a number of ex-guerrillas becoming well known, and certainly already significant. Foremost among these was Ramiro Valdés. More radical than most other Moncada participants, being identified as 'vaguely familiar with Communist textbooks' before 1959 (Thomas 1971: 826), he was clearly a key player from the start. He trained for revolution in Mexico (being one of the twenty-four arrested there), sailed on the *Granma* and was part of the earliest *Sierra* group. He was therefore unquestionably part of the 'inner circle'. In March 1957, he was a lieutenant in Raúl's 'company' (ibid.: 934); then, in June 1957, with Redondo and Lalo Sardiñas, he led one of three platoons for the new column (Aladro Cardoso et al. 2007: 78).

In this short list of other prominent *Sierra* veterans, Guillermo García also stands out, not least because of his historic role. As a politically aware peasant from Plátano (in the Niquero region of south-western Oriente), he was already enlisted, by Celia Sánchez, in the 26 July Movement before the *Granma* beached (Alvarez Tabío 2004: 167). Subsequently, he famously became the first peasant to help the rebels after Alegría de Pío, thereafter remaining part of the guerrilla group. Hence, he held a special place in the pantheon.

Pedro Miret was also visible from early on; indeed, one account refers to him being generally 'considered second only to Castro at the beginning of the movement' (Llerena 1978: 25). A former Ortodoxo (and long a *chibasista*: Thomas 1971: 869), he became a versatile and always loyal activist. Sharing lodgings with Raúl before 1953 (Guanche 2013: 4), he helped to train the Moncada plotters militarily at the university (Bourne 1986: 69) and was part of the Moncada attack force, being one of only five who knew the plans beforehand (ibid.: 77). In 1955, he naturally joined the 26 July Movement National Committee in Mexico (Thomas 1971: 868). Crucially, he also moved easily between Mexico and Cuba, and, originally designated in 1955 as regional Oriente coordinator, he played a key role in reconnaissance in the Manzanillo area (with Celia Sánchez and País) in preparation for the planned invasion (Szulc 1986: 251). He also brought the necessary funds to Mexico for training and for the acquisition of the yacht *Granma*. However, he was arrested in Mexico in November 1956 – for possessing arms (Thomas 1971: 891) – and therefore was unable to participate in the actual invasion (Almeida Bosque 2008: 386). Nonetheless, he joined the rebels in the Sierra in April 1958 (flying from Mexico to the Sierra, complete with a cargo of arms), eventually becoming a *comandante*, and so his 'credentials' were solid, if not complete.

Within this cast of historically prominent activists before 1959 (who were therefore destined to become eventual 'heroes'), three 'heroines' are always selected as enjoying a special prestige: Vilma Espín, Celia Sánchez and Haydée Santamaría. Espín, daughter of a Bacardí lawyer in Santiago, studied engineering in the United States (graduating from MIT); after 1955, she went to Mexico to meet the rebels, becoming a key member of the Movement and its infrastructure. She was a member of the 26 July National Committee in 1955

(Thomas 1971: 868), and finally joined the guerrillas (in the Sierra del Cristal) in March 1958 (ibid.: 1001), where she met – and eventually married – Raúl.

Celia Sánchez was even more crucial to the rebels' success and is usually seen (after 1959) as enjoying a special position. Daughter of the doctor of the Julio Lobo 'Isabel' sugar estate in Pilón, south of Niquero in Oriente (in one version he was the estate's dentist: ibid.: 936), she was born in Media Luna, near Niquero, in a district (Pueblo Nuevo) where most of the estate's workers lived. She remained there till 1940, when the family moved further south to nearby Pilón, on the coast. More significantly, her father was an active Auténtico (Alvarez Tabío 2004: 106), then joining the Ortodoxos in 1947 and becoming a local party leader (ibid.: 124) – significant in a town whose sugar workers were actively political. Celia too became politically active, also as an Ortodoxo, and she eventually met Chibás in Havana (ibid.: 109) and hosted him when he campaigned politically in Pilón. After the Moncada, she gravitated towards the more radical groups, eventually setting up the Movimiento Revolucionario Masó (Masó Revolutionary Movement) in the Manzanillo area in 1954 (ibid.: 147–8), and finally joining the 26 July Movement itself in July 1955 (ibid.: 152), after which she soon became its local leader. In that capacity, she was instrumental in the preparations for the *Granma*, arranging for transport and supplies to be waiting at the scheduled landing place – although she was arrested in nearby Campechuela on the morning of 2 December (Bourne 1986: 135) – and then in helping the post-Alegría fugitives to leave the area. She had apparently asked to participate in the invasion, but had been told that her Manzanillo role was more important (Szulc 1986: 318).

She remained a crucial figure, as Manzanillo's geographical location (on the routes between Havana and the Sierra) made it the main conduit for communications, arms supplies and recruits. From her first meeting with Fidel (16 or 17 February 1956) in the Sierra foothills, she became a stalwart of the whole operation, until, after joining the guerrillas herself, she became both Fidel's close confidante (and effectively his secretary) and a participant in the fighting (at El Uvero). Later, in September 1958, she led the women's 'Mariana Grajales' platoon (Alvarez Tabío 2004: 269–70). Evidently, her local experience and leadership, and her proximity to, and respect from, the guerrilla leaders, made her an integral part of that leadership by 1958, as close to Fidel as Guevara was (ibid.: 249). Indeed, all reports talk about that closeness, Bourne (1986: 145) confirming that she remained by Fidel's side throughout the Sierra campaign after she joined the rebel group.

Santamaría was perhaps less crucial than either of the other two, but, because of her role in the Moncada attack, she retained a special place in the inner circle. Initially, she simply hosted the many meetings at her Vedado flat in Havana (shared with Abel) where the Moncada plan was hatched; however, at her own insistence, she became part of the attack force itself, in the hospital contingent. Therefore, she too was sentenced in October 1953, and was imprisoned with Melba Hernández at the Guanajay women's prison (ibid.: 94). After their release in February 1954, she remained a part of the key female group of 26 July members, who, using their gender to evade surveillance, linked the *Sierra* and *Llano*. She was part of the Movement's National Committee from 1955 (Thomas 1971: 868) and also played a vital role in fundraising in the United States; in fact, she was there when the rebellion triumphed, on 1 January 1959, but flew the next day to the Sierra, with José Llanusa, to consult Fidel.

In many respects, these three female protagonists acted as a valuable bridge between the *Llano* and the *Sierra*, falling into both 'camps' but never really being 'tainted' by association with the *Llano* in the minds of the *Sierra*, mostly because of their participation in either the Moncada attack or the guerrilla campaign. That was less true, however, of those whose 1955–58 activism was wholly focused on the cities, with the prominent exception of País; in the latter case, however, his inclusion in the pantheon was almost certainly enhanced by his 'martyrdom' in 1957, his participation in armed action and the fact that Santiago, his base of operations, had always been seen in Cuban nationalist mythology as more naturally rebellious, genuinely Cuban and less effete and cosmopolitan than Havana.

The leaders of the Havana underground therefore did not share Santiago's prestige. First among these was Armando Hart. Despite often being dismissed by observers as a political lightweight, an opportunist or an unprincipled loyalist, Hart was actually a significant player at most stages of the rebellion and then in the post-1959 Revolution. He was certainly crucial in the urban underground before

1959, having been told to remain in Cuba after June 1955 specifically to coordinate the Movement in Matanzas (Graña Eiriz 2008: 42). However, his arrest in late 1956 prevented him from full involvement throughout – which may, indeed, have meant that, to some extent, he remained free of the 'taint' of failure and inadequacy attached to others of the *Llano*. Certainly, he was always part of the inner circle of the emerging movement, despite his previous association with the MNR; this association may have led to the story that, during leadership discussions before 1959, he opposed the post-victory legalisation of the PSP (Thomas 1971: 944). As a lawyer, he defended the MNR leader, García Bárcena, after the would-be conspiracy (Szulc 1986: 173), and he was still in the MNR in 1954 (Pérez Llody 2007: 144). However, he seems to have been vital to persuading the MNR remnants (after that conspiracy) to merge with the 26 July Movement (Bourne 1986: 110). Of all the *Llano* people, Hart was undoubtedly the most significant and trusted after 1959 (Hart Dávalos 2004).

Others especially prominent in that underground included three who went on to remain in positions of some influence after 1959. The first was Marcelo Fernández Font, the former student leader in Havana's law faculty (like Fidel), who became the national coordinator of the 26 July Movement in Havana, from April 1958 and well into 1959 (Thomas 1971: 1221). The second was Enrique Oltuski (often misspelled Oltusky) Ozacki, who, an engineer by training and a former MNR member (1953–55), joined the 26 July Movement in Las Villas in 1955; he became head of the Civic Resistance in 1956 (Oltuski 2000: 111) and remained in that role until Manuel Ray Rivero took over in 1958 (Thomas 1971: 918). After that, he ran the Movement in Las Villas (ibid.: 1012), although Buch writes that this happened in September 1957 (Buch and Suárez 2009: 231).

Finally, Faustino Pérez was prominent throughout; indeed, he was clearly fundamental to the urban insurrection and the creation and maintenance of the pro-*Sierra* infrastructure in Cuba. This perhaps contributed to his continuing presence in the decisive circles – although some argue that he was never 'invited to join the inner circle' (Szulc 1986: 22). Having also been a member of both the Ortodoxos and the MNR, he and others were persuaded on their release from prison (having been there from October 1954 until March 1955) to merge the MNR remnants with the 26 July Movement (Bourne 1986:

110). In fact, in the MNR, he had led a faction seeking to shift that organisation towards a more mass-based strategy (Oltuski Ozacki et al. 2007: 125–30).

Despite being instructed to remain in Cuba in July 1955, specifically to coordinate the Movement in Las Villas (Graña Eiriz 2008: 42), he joined the rebels in Mexico in October 1955, becoming one of only two chiefs of staff on the *Granma* (Szulc 1986: 10). He was then one of the small group of survivors of the Alegría attack, being among the handful hiding with Fidel for some time. In January 1957 (as Fidel realised the importance of a propaganda coup), it was he who organised the visit to the Sierra of Herbert Matthews of the *New York Times*; Pérez himself went to Havana and brought Matthews to the Sierra. After that, he became a link between the Sierra and the cities, coordinating the Movement's urban infrastructure to supply the Sierra struggle. However, in 1958, he returned there (following the Mompié meeting) and ran the 'Civil Administration of Liberated Territory' (Bell Lara 2007: 39).

Beyond these, there was a handful of figures who, exclusively associated with the *Llano*, were crucial before 1959 and briefly prominent afterwards; two with a major role in the underground were David Salvador (organiser of the Movement's trade union body) and Manuel Ray (a leading activist of the *Llano*). However, by moving into opposition after 1959, their protagonist positions decisively changed, thereby probably also contributing to the perceived 'contamination' of the *Llano*.

Given the overwhelming hegemony of the *Sierra*, which was already affecting adversely the *Llano*'s authority (and eventual influence), it was clear that no one outside the 26 July Movement could challenge its authority. This included, of course, the PSP, which, despite (or perhaps because of) joining the rebel alliance late on, still – in the eyes of most rebels and some among the wider population – had to earn its spurs. In fact, only a handful of PSP activists were accommodated within the rebel ranks before 1959, and only two PSP leaders enjoyed any real acceptance by all of the rebels.

The most obvious of these was Carlos Rafael Rodríguez, partly because, in the PSP, he was always seen as the rebels' greatest supporter and the most adaptable leader, but also because of his own respected political past. Briefly mayor of Cienfuegos (in 1933, after Machado's overthrow), he joined the Communist Party in 1936 (Suchlicki 1988: 244), rising to join the Central Committee by 1939 (ibid.: 245). He then became a long-standing leader, enjoying the distinction of being highly respected outside the party (as an intellectual) and powerful within it; from 1933 to 1944, he edited party magazines and taught at the University of Havana, and then, in 1944, he was named Batista's minister without portfolio.

In August 1957, it was he who contacted Haydée Santamaría (after País's death), to broach the question of possible PSP support (Thomas 1971: 980), and, in July 1958, he was one of the two PSP leaders who went to the Sierra del Cristal (to make contact with Raúl) and thence to the Sierra Maestra, where he remained until the end (ibid.: 1002).

The other 'acceptable' PSP leader was Blas Roca Calderío, respected more for his political past and party authority than for his amenable attitude to the Movement; indeed, he often differed from Rodríguez on the latter issue. There was little doubt about his historical importance within the PSP, and therefore within the post-1959 Revolution (Batlle Reyes 2008); that past already made him one of Cuba's most powerful and influential communists, leading the party for long periods. Under his real name (Francisco Calderío López), he started his political trajectory in 1929, aged twenty-one, when he was elected general secretary of the Manzanillo Shoemakers' Union (ibid.: 12); he then became general secretary of the Regional Workers' Federation in Manzanillo, eventually becoming secretary of the Manzanillo Communist Party (still aged only twenty-one) under the pseudonym of Julio Martínez. He was imprisoned in 1930 and 1932. By 1931, he was a member of the party's Central Committee; from 1933, he lived in Havana, changing his assumed name to Blas Roca after his arrival, although still also using 'Marcos Díaz' as a pseudonym for his writings (ibid.: XII). In Havana he was immediately invited to lead the still small Communist Party there (ibid.: 12), and by 1934 he was general secretary of the party's Central Committee (ibid.), a post he retained until 1961 (Suchlicki 1988: 36). In March that year, he took over the editorship of *Hoy* from Rodríguez (until it merged with *Revolución* in 1965). Meanwhile, from 1940 until 1952, he sat in parliament as an elected deputy.

Therefore, by 31 December 1958, the contours (if not always the membership) of an emerging 'inner circle' could be detected, consisting essentially of the leading guerrillas, the leading 'link' people (between the *Sierra* and the *Llano*) and, albeit somewhat at arm's length, the leading activists in the *Llano* underground. Within that circle, there was already an implicit hierarchy, separating those who had fought in the Sierra (the December 1956 veterans being the most valued) from those who had not, with intermediate stages according to each individual's actions in 1953–58, the Moncada and *Granma* counting the most. Outside this 'inner circle' stood people such as Chomón (whose position was unclear in late 1958, but whose decision to work with Guevara gave him kudos among the rebels), and, at a slightly greater distance, the few trusted PSP leaders.

The composition of that circle, and of other circles beyond, would change in many ways over the coming years of power and revolution, with some activists moving into the inner circle as the process radicalised. Nonetheless, it was of some considerable significance for the Revolution's survival over the following decades that the nucleus of the core 'inner circle' remained largely unchanged, affected only by death and retirement; what did change, however, in response to the post-1959 developments, were the character and identity of those beyond the 'core'.

# 3 | TAKING STOCK AND FINDING DIRECTION: 1959–62

Almost all historians of modern and contemporary Cuba inevitably tend to divide the Revolution's trajectory into periods or phases. At one level, this is sensibly didactic: those fifty-four years, and especially the first decade or so, were so eventful and so full of contradictions and confusing policy changes that a careful 'parcelling' of processes into potentially clumsy, but nonetheless digestible, 'chunks' makes sense. On another level, however, it can simply be a mechanism for demonstrating that the whole process has been run by Fidel, with shifts from one phase or policy to another seen as proof of the whimsical nature of the single leader or the inherent instability and unpredictability of any personalist system.

More seriously, this periodisation can mislead, because the usual patterns followed rarely work across all aspects of Cuban life. Those patterns tend to be as follows: 1959–60, early confusion and euphoria; 1960–63, proximity to, and influence of, Soviet and Communist models; 1963–70, the 'Guevarist' phase of unorthodox communism; 1970–85, Soviet-style institutionalisation and limited economic restructuring, decentralisation and consumerism; 1986–90, 'Rectification'; 1990 onwards, the post-Soviet crisis, the Special Period and urgent reform, with maybe 2000–05 seen as a discrete 'Battle of Ideas'. However, taking but one example, while the Special Period began formally in 1990, so too did the crisis, continuing until at least 1995, by which time the process of substantial unprecedented reform had begun. Moreover, the question of when, or whether, the Special Period ended is a vexed one, the leadership always being aware of the risks of either declaring it over (leading to dangerously unrealistic expectations of material improvement) or insisting that it was still extant (thereby risking increased frustration, especially among the young). Equally, if 'Sovietisation' began in 1970 (with Cuba accepted into the Socialist Bloc trading system, COMECON, in 1972), why did the notorious 'Padilla affair' in culture begin in

1968, or even 1966, and continue into 1971, signalling the start of the seemingly Stalinist period of selective censorship, marginalisation and silencing, known in Cuba as the 'grey five years' (*quinquenio gris*), a policy that seemed especially to target some older writers (in particular those who had lived abroad before or after 1959) and some theatre people, and which included the harassment of known homosexuals among the artistic community?

Hence, periodisation, for all its merit, carries a health warning. However, it does highlight one reality of Cuba from 1959 onwards: that the Cuban leadership rarely enjoyed an unfettered freedom to act, always being limited by several parallel, and occasionally countervailing, pressures.

## External and internal pressures on Cuba

The reasons are clear. Firstly, the Revolution coincided with, and was facilitated by, a particular stage of the Cold War, which created an enforced choice between compromising any promises made during the insurrection (in order to remain within the US orbit) or realising those promises and risking retaliation (as seen in Guatemala in 1954) from a United States still with its 'backyard' mentality and its special blind spot for Cuba, and still driven by a powerful and somewhat paranoid anti-Communism. For example, if the leadership pursued nationalisation that included US interests, this risked US retaliation.

The Cold War therefore most obviously constrained options. However, that same Cold War also offered Cuba an economic outlet that had not been available to earlier Latin American challenges to dependency on the United States: this was the Soviet Union, a market now desperate for extensive sugar imports. This coincided with Cuba, still the world's largest sugar exporter, being desperate for an alternative to the traditional US preferential market; for, by the 1930s, the world sugar economy had changed from the traditional pattern (of limited supply resulting in growers' domination) to one of oversupply, forcing underdeveloped cane-sugar producers to seek preferential deals with a single market. By the 1950s, the Soviet Union was the only such unexploited market. This, of course, also coincided with the Soviet Union gaining status as a superpower looking to outflank Washington geopolitically, at a moment when the Soviet leadership judged the US presidency to be weak and inexperienced.

However, on balance, the Cold War limited rather than enhanced Cuba's options.

The fundamental reason for this was that Cuba in 1959 – for all its relative (i.e. statistical) 'development' – was still a small, primary-dependent economy, with an unproductive and problematic crop; pressures such as fluctuating prices or the nature of the market were therefore bound to restrict the government's capacity to act on its promises. Indeed, it was this awareness that generated the 'Great Debate' of 1962–65 (see later).

However, we should also add to the catalogue of pressures such factors as the US trade embargo from 1960 (formalised and intensified from October 1963), which placed even more limits on Cuba's trading, credit and currency opportunities. Equally, the exodus of the middle class played a role, removing half a million actual or potential skilled workers and professionals, all having to be replaced expensively or slowly (or with a resulting temporary dependence on the Soviet Union); one estimate has 60,000, half of Cuba's 'professional group', leaving by early 1961 (Thomas 1971: 1301). Finally, of course, the very process of revolution destabilised everything, implying constant challenges to be confronted; here, the process often happened despite, as much as because of, what the leaders intended, generating its own momentum as demands increased, empowerment took hold, and US opposition created gaps and provoked greater nationalism. Thus, sometimes the leadership was ahead of developments, but often it was catching up with, and adapting to, them. In this sense, the Revolution has always been in crisis or 'at the crossroads'.

The Revolution's passage through different periods often simply reflected Cuba's place in the world, regardless of leadership or ideology. However, there is another dimension that affects the argument of this study: if we examine the leaders' and activists' roles and influence within an emerging structure, logically the crucial factor may sometimes have been the nature, stability or context of the state itself rather than external pressure. Simply, if the state was weak, fluid or fragmented, individuals or groups were more able to influence decisions, while greater stability would have had the opposite effect.

For that reason, this chapter and the following three, which analyse in detail the patterns of influence or power, focus on only four periods (instead of the usual six), these being measured by the extent or absence of fluidity of the state and governing structures. Therefore, while the first period was necessarily short (1959–62), it showed a remarkable but unsurprising level of continual activity and change, including ideological change (Díaz Castañón 2001). The second period (1963–75) was somewhat longer, but, despite its degree of ideological certainty, it was no less contested, once the early challenges were defeated. Nonetheless, although these two periods shared similarities (on the road to stable nation-building), the first few years clearly had a distinct character, with rapid, exciting and always bewildering change, with certainties constantly being destroyed, with new patterns being created, and with a fluidity that often seemed directionless but that responded to, and was shaped by, an underlying momentum.

## Understanding divisions

The result was a continual process of constant change of gaps and spaces, with processes other than state-building tending to act as a substitute; these included personal friendships and loyalties (based largely on specific collective experiences, region of origin, and so on), new and old group identities (regional, generational or ideological), individual 'power bases' (usually in institutions that, in the still inchoate state, were often quasi-autonomous) and factions. When discussing the latter, however, caution is advisable: while all post-revolutionary processes inevitably produce factions (as the easy unity of opposition to 'tyranny' becomes the reality of hard decision-making, creating differences over definitions of the future and the means to get there) and while studies of the Soviet Union and the Socialist Bloc were often phrased in terms of factional conspiracies or pressures, the Revolution's trajectory, after the early splits (discussed below), was actually remarkably faction-free. While a group might form over a given issue, that same group would rarely be identical with respect to other issues, since factions proved as fluid and unpredictable as other aspects of the process.

Splits and divisions, however, were fundamental to the 1959–62 period. While such divisions were inevitable, given the apparent but probably fragile unanimity before, during and immediately after the widely popular victory against the unpopular *tiranía*, they also arose from the radicalisation within the rebel ranks since 1953. After 1959, given the reality of governing a country in the face of popular euphoria and growing demands on the one hand, and growing external and internal pressure on the other, that radicalisation changed the definitions guiding the Revolution's progress and decisions. Although this meant radicalisation at the top, among the ex-guerrillas, it was also a grass-roots radicalisation, with many Cubans, although unable to keep up with the pace of change that they experienced daily, tending to find their own perspectives and demands steadily radicalised.

One example was the sudden, if somewhat passing, reference to the Revolution's 'socialism' (on 16 April 1961, at the funeral of those killed in the pre-Playa Girón aerial bombing). While it was hardly the 'declaration of the Revolution's socialist character' that most Cuban and non-Cuban histories record (a form of words that, through constant repetition, has become an 'official' version), it was ultimately significant. Yet most Cubans hearing those words – precisely, 'What the imperialists cannot forgive us is that we are making a socialist revolution under their very noses' (*Revolución* 1961) – or reading them the next day found them unremarkable, since by 1961 most assumed that that was precisely where Cuba was headed anyway, especially as 'socialism' (either the PSP's version, or that of people such as Guiteras and other radicals in the recent past) had long been a component of Cuban dissent.

However, that general radicalisation both reflected the growing divisions and helped to widen them. There were three divisions: that between 'moderates' and 'radicals', especially within, and over the character of, the first governments and the broader rebel movement of 1958–59; that between the revolutionary process, leaders and supporters and the United States; but also that between the three component parts of the emerging revolutionary coalition.

The first division was, perhaps, inevitable, as already observed. However, in Cuba, that likelihood was increased by the clear difference of objectives between those who saw themselves, essentially, as the 'clean' face of the old system (broadly a centrist and centre-left perspective) and those arguing for a total break with that system, without knowing exactly with what to replace it. The former were the many Ortodoxos, Auténticos and 26 July Movement activists who did not share the ex-guerrillas' new radicalism or who feared the PSP; they were all anti-Batista, but reluctant to go beyond a corruption-free and socially progressive version of the Cuba of 1940–52. The latter 'radicals' were mostly either gathered within the ranks of the Rebel Army, especially those fighting since 1956–57, or in the PSP.

The wider division was also partly replicated within the ranks of the 26 July Movement, although (with some prominent exceptions, which soon became *causes célèbres*) 'division' overstates what were often little more than doubts (usually among the *Llano*) about the wisdom or desirability of close relations with the PSP. These views often arose from old suspicions about the party, or, conversely, doubts (among the radicals) about the reliability of the former *Llano*. Guevara was one of the instigators of those latter suspicions; in 1958, he had clashed angrily with Oltuski (the Movement's Las Villas coordinator) over his plans to rob banks to finance the rebellion and over his radical ideas of agrarian reform (Oltuski 2000: 193). He also argued with Faustino Pérez over strategy, seeing him (along with Franqui) as leading opposition in the Sierra to the presence of the PSP's Rodríguez (Anderson 1997: 335). Both confirmed to him that the *Llano* people were inherently untrustworthy and un-revolutionary (ibid.: 347). He confirmed this later in an article in *Verde Olivo*, recounting the Mompié National Directorate meeting of 1 May 1958, where arguments over strategy included Guevara's accusation that the *Llano* leaders' reluctance to develop PSP links had seriously weakened the failed general strike (ibid.: 318–19). Indeed, the subsequent decision to move some of the *Llano* leaders to the Sierra was probably intended to remove obstacles to closer collaboration (ibid.: 319).

The second division (between the Cuban revolutionaries and various US interests, commercial and political) was equally inevitable, given the historical baggage that was bound to make each other's positions mutually incomprehensible. The Cubans had inherited feelings from decades of pent-up (if not always obvious) resentment at the post-1898 military occupation and subsequent occupations, the Platt Amendment, economic dependence and, latterly, US support for Batista until late 1958. Meanwhile, US interests were influenced by the blind spot that Cuba always represented in US views of the region and the world, allowing politicians to make proprietorial assumptions about Cuba's importance to the United States, unaware of Cuban sensitivities, in addition to the new Cold War and post-McCarthy inability to distinguish between radical nationalism and Communism.

The final division took longer to emerge, but was equally pre-dictable, if somewhat multi-layered: the tensions within the rebel alliance of January 1959, specifically between the two guerrilla-based movements (the 26 July Movement and the much smaller DR) and then between the 26 July Movement and the PSP.

## Early unity

Initially, in January 1959, unity was obvious, expressed in the popularity of the victory and in the character of the first government. Largely a centre-left coalition, it represented the cream of Cuba's 'clean' politicians, with some prominent respected independents, di-verse 'radicals', and a small contingent of 26 July Movement members or sympathisers, mostly from the *Llano*. Under the indeterminately liberal ex-judge Manuel Urrutia Lleó as president, José Miró Cardona became Prime Minister, with the Ortodoxos' Roberto Agramonte Pichardo (presidential candidate in 1952) as Foreign Minister, and Luis Orlando Rodríguez Rodríguez (heading the Ministry of Government – which, after June 1961, became the Ministry of the Interior, known as MININT), Rufo López Fresquet (Finance), Raúl Cepero Bonilla (Commerce), Angel Fernández Rodríguez (Justice), the ex-MNR act-ivist Manuel Fernández García (Labour), Regino Boti (Economy), Elena Mederos (Social Welfare) and Felipe Pazos (the National Bank). Alongside these centre-left representatives were the 26 July Move-ment's Faustino Pérez (Ministry of Confiscated Property), Humberto Sorí Marín (Agriculture), Manuel Ray (Public Works), Armando Hart Dávalos (Education), Augusto Martínez Sánchez (Defence), Enrique Oltuski (Communications) and Julio Martínez Páez (Health), with Luis M. Buch Rodríguez as secretary to the Cabinet (Bell Lara et al. 2006: 16–19; Thomas 1971: 1065–7). On 13 February 1959, after a crisis, Fidel replaced Miró Cardona as Prime Minister (confirmed on 16 February).

However, in early 1959, there was a difference between the formal power (in that first government) and real power, then in the hands of the Rebel Army, allied with the other two rebel groups. Hence, although Fidel was not a member of that government (but attached, as Commander-in-Chief of the Rebel Army), there was no doubt either that it was he who most influenced decisions or that the government was in office rather than power. Moreover, it was clear that some rebels tolerated the government's moderate character as being an interim measure, to assuage bourgeois sensitivities; they had no faith in its capacity to effect the change that, they argued, was needed. Even before that, in December 1958, a meeting at the guerrilla Sierra headquarters at La Rinconada, to discuss the proposed post-victory government nominations, saw Raúl observing that, whatever its formation, the new government would be incapable of advancing at the necessary pace (Buch and Suárez 2009: 30–1).

The Rebel Army was, of course, the real power, because of its special role in the insurrection and the popularity and authority of its leaders. In the post-Batista vacuum, it was therefore the Rebel Army that held the fort (literally in the case of Guevara), defending the new Revolution, ensuring normal life as soon as possible, and, two years later, defeating 'the United States' at Playa Girón.

This mismatch, between a nominal government's weakness and the rebels' real power, really created all of the divisions. For, if real power lay outside the government, the politics of the Rebel Army and Fidel were of fundamental significance. However, that army was much broader than before and now essential to the new order, representing the most coherent and visible manifestation of the popular 26 July Movement. In fact, interviews carried out in 1994 confirmed that local army units soon began to act as the Movement's local branches, ex-guerrillas always having more political clout than others. Hence, when the fusion of the three allied forces began in 1961, it was those local units or branches that constituted the Movement's grass-roots elements.

### The rebel alliance of 1959

While those tensions were evident, however, the issue that was ostensibly at the heart of the divisions was the presence and status of the PSP within the rebel alliance; this soon became the question on which all definitions and positions depended, at least formally. Ultimately, this was often a somewhat superficial issue, since the underlying division arose from the growing differences within the broad rebellion since 1953 over the definitions and direction of 'revolution' and 'socialism'. The division also arose from PSP-focused fears on one side and, on the other, a growing doubt about the commitment of some in the leadership or government (notably Urrutia) to the emerging radical plans. This, indeed, led to a further government reshuffle in June 1959 (see below), although, interestingly, not all of the replacements were as revolutionary as Miret (Agriculture) and Raúl Roa, the latter replacing Agramonte while he was dining with the US ambassador, Philip Bonsal (Buch and Suárez 2009: 119).

The fusion of the three groups within the rebel alliance proved not to be as easy or as organic as many had hoped (or as subsequent Cuban accounts suggest); the idea of that fusion was often hotly contested, not least because the DR's origins (evident, to some extent, in its residual ideological position) were firmly rooted in Catholicism, at a time when the Vatican was still threatening excommunication of any Italian voting for the Communist Party. Hence, the deep-rooted anti-Communism in some DR activists never quite disappeared.

Relations between the DR and the 26 July Movement were also occasionally tense, differences emerging early on over what the former saw as a degree of marginalisation. In early January 1959, for example, a few days after arriving in Havana with Guevara's column, and then occupying the presidential palace, the Capitolio, the university and the airbase at San Antonio de los Baños (ibid.: 49), the DR was instructed by the new leadership to vacate the palace; this was a sore point, given that the building held a special place in the Directorate's history, after the March 1957 attack (remembered, indeed, in the DR's full name). The DR also complained bitterly about the lack of posts in the first governments (Thomas 1971: 1033).

### The 26 July Movement and the PSP

However, it was the uncomfortable relationship between the PSP and the 26 July Movement that was more significant, as these were the two major groups of the alliance. The relationship was complex, often depending on individuals and circumstances. As we have seen, some of the Rebel Army leaders had, by 1959, warmed towards the PSP (or at least towards collaboration); most notable among these were Raúl and Guevara, both ideologically clearer than Fidel before 1959 and closer instinctively to the Communist position, but both also having accommodated PSP members comfortably within their respective columns in the Sierra del Cristal and the westward march. From January 1959, in fact, Guevara continued to rely on a number of PSP members whose political judgement he trusted, most notably

Armando Acosta, Francisco ('Pancho') García Vals (Anderson 1997: 384, 405), and Ramón Nicolau (Rojas Blaquier 2005: 145).

However, many grass-roots 26 July Movement members still held doubts, resentment or hostility towards the PSP; this even seems to have included Aleida March, soon to be Guevara's new wife (Anderson 1997: 359). Doubts and resentment both focused on the wisdom or desirability of full collaboration with a force that had twice publicly dismissed the rebels' actions, seemingly 'jumping on the bandwagon' very late in the day, and with a history of prior collaboration with Batista. There were also generational differences between the two groups (the rebels being generally much younger than the stalwarts at the top of the PSP) and also differences of attitude, with the rebels' loose ideological mix and guerrilla-trained determination to always be flexible contrasting with the PSP's overall quasi-Stalinist, or at least very orthodox and occasionally doctrinaire, postures.

One such posture, indeed, focused on the feasibility of socialist revolution in an underdeveloped country such as Cuba: as already seen, according to orthodox Communist theory and Soviet policy, this could not happen before the 'semi-feudal' structures of that underdevelopment had disappeared and capitalism had begun to develop. The hostility, however, more clearly arose from the context of the times, i.e. the previous anti-Communist feeling of several within the 26 July Movement, especially those previously associated with the MNR. Hence, even when the PSP declared its unconditional support for the Revolution – at a time when, with Batista either about to be overthrown (1958) or already defeated (1959), all other pre-1959 groups and parties were busily laying out their demands and conditions for involvement in the revolutionary alliance – some continued to see this as Machiavellian – no doubt recalling the reputed machinations of the Communist Parties of Eastern Europe in 1945–48, when participation in 'popular fronts' after liberation led to a steady takeover by those parties. Indeed, while Fidel and others were arguing for unity of the rebel forces, the PSP's leadership echoed this enthusiastically, the term 'unity' seeming to become the party's 'watchword' (ibid.: 399); this was partly logical, because it guaranteed the PSP's inclusion in the new order, but it was also seen by some as a sinister echo of those previous takeovers.

As a result, caution characterised the grass roots and suspicion was expressed even among some more prominent local leaders. One incident in June 1959 almost led to Urrutia's resignation: an ex-guerrilla, Calixto Morales, had been appointed by Guevara as military governor of Las Villas province in late 1958, a post in which, after January 1959, he proceeded to rely heavily on local radicals, including some from the PSP, just as Guevara had. He did so, in part, because his angry opposition to the racism that he encountered in Santa Clara aroused local opposition, until the local PSP, under Félix Torres, came to his rescue and gave him support (ibid.: 399–400). This led in June to Urrutia calling a meeting in Havana specifically to accuse Morales, the meeting consisting of Buch, Camilo Cienfuegos (as army chief), Valdés (already nationally responsible for internal security), Oltuski, Quintín Pino Machado, and Morales himself; ultimately, after Urrutia had presented an ultimatum ('him or Morales'), Cienfuegos defused the crisis by reassigning Morales to another post (Buch and Suárez 2009: 125).

However, a more serious case followed immediately. Huber (some-times spelled Hubert) Matos had joined the guerrillas in 1957, being then detailed to go to Costa Rica to acquire arms; this he duly did, bringing them back by plane in March 1958. As a result, he rose through the rebel ranks to become *comandante* in August, and, in January 1959, was designated military commander of Camagüey province. However, having already proposed banning the PSP after the victory (Karol 1970: 183), in October he was arrested for plotting with other liberals to prevent the PSP having any influence in the army. Later rumours about his disobedience as a guerrilla com-mander (Buch and Suárez 2009: 278) or alleging corruption (ibid.: 130) and even an ambition to be named the first Minister of Education (ibid.: 276) remain unproven; what clearly sparked his arrest was his letter of resignation to Fidel, on 20 October 1959, in response to the formal designation as Commander-in-Chief of the armed forces of Raúl, whom Matos had long considered a dangerous pro-Communist plotter. Quite apart from the act itself (and the accusations against one of the Revolution's leaders), the resignation coincided with a leafleting flight over Havana by the renegade air force commander Pedro Luis Díaz Lanz, who had recently fled Cuba and even testi-fied before the US Senate about the supposed Communist threat in Cuba. The leadership's resulting anger meant that Matos simply pressed the wrong button at the wrong time, thereupon feeling the full force of that anger.

Unlike others falling out over the developing radicalism, however, Matos was no liberal but simply an anti-Communist radical, outraged by the growing evidence of some rebel leaders' collaboration with local and national PSP activists; that outrage had already led him to communicate with other like-minded rebels, and also with Urrutia, and to write to Fidel asking for a meeting of the 26 July Movement's National Directorate to discuss what he saw as Communist infiltration in both the army and INRA (Anderson 1997: 449). Therefore, the ferocity with which the leadership dealt with his rebellion spoke volumes about the seriousness of his challenge. Firstly, Camilo Cienfuegos (as army chief) was sent to Camagüey to arrest him and also twenty others in his branch of the army, followed there by Fidel himself – although some authors refer to Camilo and Fidel flying together to arrest Matos (Scheer and Zeitlin 1964: 108) – then a high-profile trial produced a twenty-year sentence. Interestingly, since his release and emigration, Matos consistently kept his distance from the main body of the United States-based émigrés, dismissing their right-wing politics and adopting a 'Revolution-betrayed' perspective. One interesting account sees the arrest as largely coming at Raúl's instigation, Raúl seeing Matos's mutiny as a threat to his own authority and to military unity. According to this uncorroborated version, Fidel's approach to the PSP was less to collaborate than to bring the PSP-linked radicals under his 'umbrella', but he sided with Raúl out of loyalty and also to prevent a 'far left' faction forming, in a classic example of co-optation (Bourne 1986: 191).

Yet Matos was not alone (indeed, fourteen of his fellow Rebel Army officers resigned with him); much of the rapid deterioration of relations between the 'liberals' and the 'radicals' arose from a fear of the PSP's role and intentions, and even of the 26 July Movement leadership's own intentions. This was compounded by another reality: that the deliberately loose nature of the pre-1959 26 July Movement (in order to guarantee its flexibility as an active opposition movement) was never corrected after 1959. Instead, while the PSP's organisation remained tight and disciplined, the Movement remained loosely structured, lacking systematic channels of internal communication. In fact, by about mid-1960, it was steadily losing force as an organised political entity (compared with either the Rebel Army or the PSP) and, under Emilio Aragonés, the new national coordinator, it lacked real power (Domínguez 1978: 206).

This was not least due to the fact that not only was real power (as well as public legitimacy) held by the Rebel Army for the first few months, but also because a parallel power was in existence very soon after the takeover. This power was essentially held by the 'inner circle', whose composition changed according to the time, the circumstances and the purpose of each meeting, but which could be identified in several instances.

### Hidden government?

Thus, for example, there was the so-called 'Tarará group', named after its main location, east of Havana, in Guevara's house where he was convalescing from March 1959 after a bad asthma attack. It was created to plan the promised agrarian reform, as 'an agrarian reform task force' (Anderson 1997: 406); as early as 10 February 1959, the Agriculture Minister, Sorí Marín, had been instructed by the government to set up a commission to do just that, but it never really worked as a commission (Buch and Suárez 2009: 104). Whether this was because of the Tarará group's existence (making such a commission redundant) or the cause of that group's creation is not clear.

It is worth clarifying some confusion about this group, and others, which has given rise to some misreadings. One problem with our knowledge of the group is that at least two later chroniclers seem to have confused three separate, but related, sets of meetings, all taking place in close proximity to each other. The first was a series of meetings in early 1959, in a villa owned by a former Ortodoxo senator (Agustín Cruz) and lent to Fidel for the duration, in the small port of Cojímar, east of Havana. This gathering seems to have included Guevara, Raúl, Valdés, Camilo Cienfuegos and (for the PSP) Carlos Rafael Rodríguez, Aníbal Escalante and Roca, the purpose being, according to one account, to 'meld' the 26 July Movement and the PSP (Anderson 1997: 384). The second was a series of meetings of PSP leaders alone, held (also in Cojímar) in the house of Francisco García Vals, by then a lieutenant under Guevara and also his personal assistant (ibid.: 405). Finally, the third was the Tarará group, based several miles to the east of Cojímar.

What is clear is that the Tarará group's real original purpose was indeed the land reform, as is shown by its composition: Fidel, Guevara, the geographer Antonio Núñez Jiménez, Vilma Espín and Alfredo Guevara Valdés. Two others were also there – Segundo Ceballos Parejas and Oscar Pino Santos – whom Anderson describes as 'two senior PSP advisors' (ibid.: 406), although neither was at all senior and both were agrarian specialists to some extent (Buch and Suárez 2009: 104; Szulc 1986: 380). According to one account, Miret was also involved (Anderson 1997: 406). The specialist presence of people such as Ceballos, Pino Santos and Núñez Jiménez indicated that the group's prime purpose was indeed to focus on a reform that all agreed went to the heart of Cuba's ills and the Revolution's future.

What is noticeable is that only four PSP members were directly involved, but three of them were far from orthodox. Pino Santos – according to one account, simply 'associated with the Communists or the extreme left' (Thomas 1971: 1215), but by his own account (in an interview) actually in the PSP – was already the economics editor of the 26 July Movement's newspaper, *Revolución*. Núñez Jiménez, an academic, had become part of the Guevara column in the last months of 1958. Alfredo Guevara was an old student colleague of Fidel's, with a long commitment to Communism, but whose approach was always more maverick than the PSP liked; his main activity before 1959 had been to support the Nuestro Tiempo group of radical Marxist artists and film-makers (Kapcia 2005: 98).

However, the presence of people such as Espín and Alfredo Guevara (neither of them expert in things agrarian) suggests that, apart from the two specialists, they were all involved for the nature of their likely contribution to a wider project – although, if so, the absence of Raúl is curious. In that capacity, in fact, the group went on to plan a merchant marine law and even a national bank (Szulc 1986: 381), although it is not clear if the group's composition remained unchanged once the agrarian reform was drafted, given that at least three of the original participants had been incorporated for their specific expertise. Indeed, the absence from the group of clearly 'inner circle' members such as Celia Sánchez and Raúl Castro suggests that it was not the 'hidden government' imagined but, rather, a specific task force.

In fact, given the confusion between these three groups, it is not clear which of them was actually the reputed 'hidden government', namely the Office of Revolutionary Plans (Balfour 2009: 60) or of Plans and Coordination (Szulc 1986: 380), described as meeting regularly over several weeks to map out the new government's plans and guide the steady radicalisation of the whole process. Since the Tarará group's focus was so specific, it seems likely that this refers to the group meeting in Fidel's house, with selected PSP leaders. Nonetheless, the fact that 'secret' meetings were being held, seemingly to hatch unseen plans with known radicals, was enough to scare those ready to see the rise of 'communism'.

This applied especially to US government circles, as the issue of 'communism' preoccupied, if not obsessed, US policy-makers before 1959 (Paterson 1994), who were concerned about the unknown politics of people such as Guevara and about the possible talks with the PSP. After 1959, a number of issues and disputes then soured already tense relations: the public trials of known *batistianos* (which the US government condemned, to the anger of many Cubans who recalled the United States' failure to condemn Batista's repression), the failure to call promised elections, and, above all, the May 1959 agrarian reform.

Indeed, even without the role of PSP members in formulating that reform, the fact – rather than the detail – of the reform was enough to set alarm bells ringing in Washington, despite the reality that the reform (with its protection of productive large landholdings, its focus on cooperatives, and the preservation of the principle of smallholdings) was less radical than either the Mexican or Bolivian reforms of 1910–40 and 1952–53. In fact, the long-term implications of the reform process turned out to be more radical than the reform itself seemed at the time, threatening a momentum of change, especially given the power allocated to the new National Institute of Agrarian Reform (INRA) under the presidency of Fidel Castro but with Núñez Jiménez as director and Pino Santos as assistant director (Thomas 1971: 1218). Indeed, INRA rapidly became one of the Revolution's key structures, with a vast remit, effectively becoming the ad hoc instrument for wide-ranging reform: besides addressing land reform, it also housed two powerful departments – Industrialisation (later becoming a ministry) and Commercialisation (taking over the former Commerce Ministry) – ran its own militia of 100,000 and constructed roads and houses (Szulc 1986: 396).

What was clear to many inside Cuba, however, was that what Washington and many liberals saw – or feared – as 'communism' was still a confusing, and often confused, fusion of a rapidly radicalising leftist nationalism, a cautious but probably ambitious neo-Stalinism, and a political determination by many ex-guerrillas not to compromise on their intention to transform Cuba into an independent and more equal society. What Washington did not realise was that relations between the PSP and the 26 July Movement continued to be tense and mutually suspicious, although that did not fully surface till 1962. Indeed, within the PSP there were also divisions, notably between Rodríguez and Roca, over how to approach, and how far to work with, the 26 July Movement: the former was enthusiastic about collaboration and the latter decidedly lukewarm (Anderson 1997: 399), although, in August 1960, Roca instituted a process of collective self-criticism about the party's failure to appreciate the post-1953 rebellion's significance (Karol 1970: 149). Indeed, Roca's shift towards Rodríguez's more amenable position probably tipped the balance within the PSP leadership, where (perhaps significantly) Escalante continued to lead those doubting the rebels' ability or willingness to progress towards socialism (Draper 1969: 31, 84; Karol 1970: 147). Escalante, in fact, still read the Revolution as 'bourgeois democratic' change, which probably explains his determination to take over the structures of power in the Revolution in 1961–62.

In the meantime, the Revolution's leadership gave plenty of ammunition to those seeing a drift towards communism. For example, in late 1960 new political Schools of Revolutionary Education (EIR) were created, for Rebel Army and 26 July members, but directed by the PSP's Lionel Soto and using Marxist textbooks (Fagen 1969: 104–37), not least Roca's explanation of socialism (Roca 1961). One writer sees these as growing directly out of Raúl's Second Front political education schools under the PSP's Jorge Risquet (Szulc 1986: 379), although there is no direct evidence of this; another sees them as coming from Che Guevara's *Sierra* organisation (Castañeda 1998: 152). Furthermore, leading PSP activists were often given prominent positions, such as Marinello's nomination in 1962 as rector of Havana University; above all, Escalante, one of the PSP's most renowned and longest-serving leaders, was given authority to set up the planned umbrella organisation for the three rebel groups, the Integrated

Revolutionary Organisations (ORI). Not only did this seem to put enormous power in the hands of a long-time Communist, but it also suggested the creation of the single party feared by those vigilant of a repetition of 1945–48 European experiences.

## The battles within the CTC

With all these tensions, conflicts and suspicions within the rebel alliance in 1959–62, it is worth reflecting here on one particular battleground that is revealing for its complexity: the trade union confederation, the CTC (more precisely the CTC-R as it became almost immediately after January 1959). The background to this internal conflict was the previous history of conflict within the CTC, the PSP's role, prestige and base within it, and tensions and antagonisms between 26 July Movement activists and PSP members over the PSP's history (including its alleged role in weakening the April 1959 general strike) and suspicions over the history of 26 July people.

The CTC, since its creation in 1939, had always been such a battleground. Established as part of the electoral deal between Batista and the Communist Party, with the understanding that the party would be allowed to exercise hegemony within the organisation, it remained a Communist-led body until the late 1940s; then, with the rise of the Cold War (and US anti-Communist pressure) from 1947 coinciding with Auténtico hegemony in Cuban politics, the PSP's prominence in the CTC was challenged by Auténtico-backed strong-arm tactics, marginalising PSP activists. Finally, from 1952, the previously pro-Auténtico leader, Eusebio Mujal, sided with Batista, and swung the organisation into neutrality and covert support for Batista. Hence, by 1956, few rebels held any respect for the organisation, and they created their own trade union movement, the Frente Obrero Nacional de Unidad (FONU or National Workers' Unity Front), led by David Salvador.

Salvador himself, however, had a somewhat questionable political pedigree, with previous membership of the Communist Party or PSP (1939–46), the Auténticos (1946–48), the Ortodoxos (from 1948) and (from 1952 to 1955) the would-be rebel organisation led by Aureliano Sánchez Arango, the Triple-A (Thomas 1971: 872). Hence, while recognising his protagonism in the *Llano*, there were some among the rebels who entertained doubts about his political reliability and his effectiveness (notably in the April 1959 strike), while PSP members saw his former communism as leading to a worrying anti-communism.

These suspicions and tensions soon came into the open. In May 1959, the PSP criticised the *Llano* (including Salvador) for being insufficiently trusting of Fidel's political judgements, to which *Revolución* responded by criticising the PSP's past collaboration with Batista. This generated a series of accusations and counter-accusations, with even Fidel publicly criticising the PSP's role in fomenting labour unrest in Oriente, prompting *Hoy* to criticise Fidel for his divisive stance (Guerra 2012: 65). Indeed, the sugar workers' union (FNTA), Salvador's former base, voted by 885 votes to thirteen to denounce the PSP's divisive allegations (ibid.: 65).

Both sides, however, stepped back from this political confrontation: the PSP mounted a campaign within the CTC for a 'unity' platform and slate (for elections), while Fidel began to praise the PSP's record for working for social equality before 1959. Then, at the CTC's first post-victory Congress, in November, despite the paucity of PSP delegates, Salvador was persuaded (by the Minister of Labour, Augusto Martínez Sánchez, presumably under pressure from the rebel leadership: Suárez 1967: 77) to nominate a slate of thirteen for the CTC executive elections; these included three PSP activists (Thomas 1971: 1250). When this slate was overwhelmingly defeated by the Congress, the FONU gaining the upper hand in twenty-eight out of the CTC's thirty-three federations (Guerra 2012: 65), the PSP remained on the margins of the renewed organisation, and seemed to be frozen out of labour politics.

However, with the ministry steadily taking over some of the CTC unions' former roles, and with a steady rapprochement and even closer affinity between some of the rebel leadership, on the one hand, and the PSP, on the other – each gradually persuaded that an alliance was mutually beneficial – the PSP slowly found its way back into influence in the CTC. This was partly achieved as the arguments over the PSP's role resulted in a growing tendency among 26 July leaders to see overt anti-communism as dangerous and weakening the front, at a time of growing tensions with the United States, leading to the marginalisation and demotion of some of the more prominent union leaders (who had indeed made their mark before 1959 through a decidedly anti-communist stance). It was also achieved as the PSP activists at the grass roots used their experience, discipline and previous reputation as reliable and effective trade unionists to gain positions of local and then regional authority. Hence, gradually, the CTC began to show a greater role for PSP leaders and activists, as the old pro-26 July activists (many of them sharing Salvador's chequered political history) were sidelined or even removed and arrested (including Salvador in 1960), as their anti-PSP campaigning turned into plotting.

In other words, what had happened within the CTC was that an organisation that had once been famous for its effectiveness and political protagonism, then questionable for its corruption and political subservience, fell foul of both the radicalised rebels' distaste and distrust for those bodies associated with the *ancien régime* and the growing alliance between many rebels and the PSP. In this evolution, the non-PSP activists' pasts, as well as the CTC's own past, counted against them.

### The 'Escalante affair'

The outcome of the unification process, however, confirmed the tensions rather than the affinity between the ex-guerrillas and the PSP. For Escalante seized the opportunity (as many in the 26 July Movement later saw it, while others had their attention focused on the tasks of defending Cuba and pursuing the revolutionary process) to create a national structure and a network of local bases that clearly favoured the PSP. At the bottom, for example, many local ORI branches were soon dominated by the better organised PSP activists. But it was, above all, the announcement (on 9 March 1962) of the ORI National Directorate that really caused those tensions to emerge in anger and recrimination; for that Directorate (of twenty-five members) allocated fourteen places to the 26 July Movement (specifically Fidel, Raúl, Guevara, Valdés, Osmani Cienfuegos, Augusto Martínez Sánchez, Almeida, Santamaría, García, Sergio del Valle, Hart, Osvaldo Dorticós, Emilio Aragonés and Raúl Curbelo), but as many as ten to the PSP (Roca, Rodríguez, Aníbal and César Escalante, Lázaro Peña, Severo Aguirre, Joaquín Ordoqui, Manuel Luzardo, Flavio Bravo and Ramón Calcines) (Thomas 1971: 1377), and only one seat for the DR (Faure Chomón).

The furore that this caused within the rebel ranks remained

unseen for a few weeks, but bubbled away under the surface; not only had the PSP (which, after condemning the rebellion twice in 1953–56, had joined the rebels only in 1958) taken a substantial share of the seats, but Escalante had also marginalised the DR completely. Both 'sins' angered the rebels, seeing their Revolution seemingly hijacked by a force that several had never fully trusted or respected, giving themselves 40 per cent of the collective leadership and demeaning the forces that had acted so bravely in 1957 and remained loyal to the 26 July leadership. Indeed, the underlying 'sin' may have been not so much to aggrandise the PSP (by giving it more seats – and power – than its historical contribution merited) as to diminish and marginalise one of the three component rebel groups. Unity had been compromised.

That furore confirmed that the DR's treatment was a major part of the problem. On 13 March, a leading PSP activist gave a speech on the anniversary of Echeverría's death but neglected to mention the latter's Catholicism; that gave Fidel the pretext he needed, and, a few weeks later (27 March), he seized the opportunity to criticise that omission but then extended the criticism to Escalante, for what he had done more generally. By then, Escalante had already been dispatched to the USSR, being eventually given a diplomatic post in Prague. Most significantly, the eventual ORI Secretariat that was announced on 22 March contained only one PSP member (Roca).

The significance of the whole affair was that it made clear which group was dominant within the supposedly equal rebel alliance: the 26 July Movement. It also made clear (not least to those in the Movement who had entertained doubts about the PSP) that the PSP was not, and would not be, in control of the Revolution, and that its role would thereafter be secondary to the Movement. Not only did the new ORI Secretariat have five 26 July people and only one from the PSP, but the resulting purge of ORI saw 82.1 per cent of the Oriente membership and 50 per cent of Havana members expelled (Domínguez 1978: 212–14).

From that point onwards, the PSP leadership remained quiet about any differences with the 26 July Movement's direction of the Revolution; whatever doubts they (or Moscow) had, they realised the value of silence and cooperation. Indeed, one possible interpretation of the whole affair might be that it was a leadership device to remove the PSP activists most opposed to unity between the three main rebel forces.

All of this, however, makes things clear for this book's purposes: while, in 1959–61, influence, power and leadership might have been confused, the 'affair' clarified everything. What it confirmed was a hierarchy of respect, power and influence, dependent largely on the individuals' 'historic' pedigree, within a structure that resembled an onion rather than a pyramid, with real power at the centre (an 'inner circle'), outside which were layers of lesser influence, weakening the further from the 'core' one went. What constituted that 'core' was still clear (with some exceptions, most notably Guevara): participation in the Moncada, the *Granma* landing and the Sierra.

### The early 'inner circle' and its historic 'core'

Therefore, what really mattered for authority was combat experience, especially as a guerrilla; indeed, the unity of the ex-guerrillas remained one evident feature of the Revolution until the 2000s. However, that unity had subtle variations: thus, while those who had participated in the Sierra struggle were considered part of, or close to, the inner group, those who were there from the early days of December 1956 were especially anointed. Moreover, those among them who were also veterans of either the Moncada or Bayamo attacks of 1953 (twenty-one of the eighty-two who landed on the *Granma*: Aladro Cardoso et al. 2007: 22–3) were clearly among the innermost inner group.

However, while guerrilla combat was mostly the sine qua non for trust within those circles, that was not always the case, as with Hart. Nevertheless, even those who had participated at the Moncada or in the *Granma* landing but had not then become guerrillas for the most part tended to be valued later on the basis of their earlier 'heroic' participation, especially if enhanced by some short-term involvement in the *Sierra*. Most obviously, that included Melba Hernández Rodríguez del Rey, a lawyer and part of the Ortodoxo group of 1953 that met in the Santamarías' Vedado flat (Bourne 1986: 68), who became one of the four people on the Moncada 'general staff' – with Fidel, Abel and Haydée Santamaría – planning the attack (Szulc 1986: 161).

Hernández was certainly involved in that attack (occupying the hospital) and was subsequently sentenced in October 1953. However, together with Haydée Santamaría, she was then imprisoned in the Guanajay women's prison in Pinar (Bourne 1986: 94). After release in 1954, she became active in the Civic Resistance and the 26 July Movement (also becoming a fiancée of Montané), but, with Haydée, effectively established the Movement while Fidel and the other leaders were still imprisoned. Finally, she became part of the Rebel Army. After 1959, despite having no significant posts, she long remained in the ruling Central Committee of the successive parties, and was still a sitting deputy in the National Assembly in 2013. Hence, her 'belonging' to the inner circles was attributable to the Moncada episode and fleeting service in the *Sierra*.

Another exception, further down the hierarchy, was Fernando C. Vecino Alegret, who, after 1959, served in several lesser posts but was also on the post-1965 party's Central Committee, eventually becoming Minister of Higher Education until 2009. Therefore this confirmed what was observed in the last chapter: namely that, outside the 'core', there were several other key players in the wider 26 July Movement, whose later survival in positions of influence or authority resulted partly from their urban activism and apparent dedication to the cause, but was usually enhanced by some action in the *Sierra*.

### Ex-guerrillas and the military

Sierra 'service' was thus usually the deciding factor for inclusion. Interestingly, however, that experience seems to have marked several activists in one particular way: rather than basing their subsequent political career on it, they remained in the FAR, as serving soldiers, even though some also occasionally occupied political posts. One such was Leopoldo Cintra Frías ('Polo'), who rose through the office of General of Corps and head of the Western Army to become Minister of Defence from 2011, elected to the party's Political Bureau and also to the Council of State.

Another was Sergio del Valle Jiménez, who, after graduating from Havana medical school, joined the guerrillas, becoming a captain and eventually Camilo Cienfuegos's second in command in Las Villas; he then went on to become Commander-in-Chief of the air force from 1959 to 1961 (Suchlicki 1988: 289) and Chief of Staff in the army. More than Cintra Frías, he straddled the military and political worlds, being Minister of the Interior in 1968–79 (ibid.: 289; Thomas 1971:

1255) and then Minister of Health (Bourne 1986: 298; Habel 1991: 69), although this is contradicted by another version that sees him as always being on the Central Committee and Bureau from 1965 (Suchlicki 1988: 289).

A third was Jesús Montané Oropesa. Like Santamaría and Fidel, a member of the Ortodoxos, he was involved in both the Moncada (as already seen, being one of the few involved in its planning) and the *Granma* expedition, and was part of the 'headquarters' in Mexico (Thomas 1971: 894). After the disaster of Alegría de Pío, he was captured and eventually sentenced to six years' imprisonment. Hence, for the rest of the rebellion, he remained on the Isle of Pines until his release on 1 January 1959. He was then immediately named civil governor of the island (Buch and Suárez 2009: 40), and, thereafter, remained a loyal member of the inner circle, taking a leading role in the FAR (after studying in the new Ñico López Party School until 1961). This included being on the General Staff (Almeida Bosque 1988: 105; Thomas 1971: 836) and Minister of Communications (1963–73).

Sixto Batista Santana, a much lower-ranked guerrilla than Montané, also remained in the FAR throughout the following five decades, joining the party's Central Committee in 1975 and the Secretariat in 1988 (Suchlicki 1988: 23), therefore remaining at the centre of power.

Service in the Sierra in some form or other therefore remained a badge of honour and, sooner or later, of office too, often in the military; this was something that especially applied to those in the Sierra del Cristal Second Front. The 'military' also then extended to the police and security forces, as they were at that time answerable to the Rebel Army (and thus to Fidel, as Commander-in-Chief) and not to the Ministry of Government (i.e. Interior) (Thomas 1971: 1071); in fact, within a month, fifteen of Havana's nineteen police stations were in the hands of the Rebel Army (ibid.: 1071).

Rogelio Acevedo, for example, one of the Rebel Army's youngest captains before 1959, was given the task in 1960 of leading the newly formed militias (ibid.: 1268), and was one of those on the Communist Party's first Central Committee in 1965 (ibid.: 1268), while Joel Iglesias (despite being only twenty years old in 1959) was appointed head of the Tenth District Havana police in 1959 (ibid.: 1340), going on to be given responsibility for organising the new Pioneros mass organisation. Similarly, a young Abelardo Colomé Ibarra (who would become a key political actor later) took charge of the military Campamento de Managua in 1959.

One outstanding example of this military pattern was Efigenio Ameijeiras, who remained at the centre of political decision-making for some time after 1959, despite being considered by some observers as a talentless but loyal opportunist (ibid.: 1320). His pedigree was ostensibly strong: a *capitán* on the *Granma* and eventually promoted to *comandante* under Raúl in March 1958 (Ameijeiras Delgado 1984: 21), he became head of the new revolutionary police force, the PNR (Abreu Cardet and Coredero Michel 2009: 29) on 1 January 1959; since he was still in Oriente, he finally took up the post on either 5 January (Buch and Suárez 2009: 49) or 7 January (Thomas 1971: 1071). He became Deputy Minister of the Armed Forces, but, in 1966, lost his place on the new party's Central Committee after only one year (ibid.: 1453). Information about him beyond that date becomes unclear; one version has it that he was briefly imprisoned (ibid.: 1467), although that is doubtful as, in 1984, he published his guerrilla memoirs without a problem. However, if his imprisonment were true, it suggests that guerrilla service even overrode some misdemeanours (unless serious), although it does raise the question of whether he enjoyed a special position in memory of two of his brothers who died in the rebellion (one at Moncada and the other in police custody in 1958). Efigenio, in fact, named his Sixth Column after one of his brothers, Juan Manuel, and the Revolution then named Havana's newest hospital after both.

The extraordinarily close correlation between service in the Second Front and a post-1959 role in the defence and security apparatus itself forms an interesting sub-plot to the wider narrative, in two respects. Firstly, given the fundamental importance of that apparatus to the Revolution's survival, especially in the early decades, loyalty and trustworthiness were crucial attributes to consider when appointing personnel; in this regard, it has always been clear that both the internal cohesion of the Second Front and its more coherent level of politicisation created a pool of talent on which the leaders could thereafter draw to staff an area of responsibility on which everything depended. Secondly, for all that the institutional structures of the emerging state might be weak or disjointed, the Revolution's leaders always knew that the defence and security apparatus was one area (and the only such area) where inefficiency could not be tolerated and where the combination of efficiency and ideological commitment could prove crucial to survival. Therefore, that apparatus's continuing reliance on the veterans of the Second Front tells us much about that guerrilla organisation's internal characteristics.

Another Cristal veteran who subsequently had a politically significant role, albeit briefly, was José A. Naranjo Morales. An ex-DR guerrilla, he was part of the steady radicalisation in May 1959 when he succeeded Luis Orlando Rodríguez as Minister of Government (or Interior) (ibid.: 1224–5), later becoming Minister of Food Industries (1967–76). Finally, the case of José Ramón Balaguer Cabrera is worth mentioning: promoted to *comandante* after the victory, he became Chief of Sanitation for the FAR in 1965, after which he worked his way up through the FAR, graduating from the School of War Studies and the Soviet Graduate School of Marxism (Suchlicki 1988: 20). However, his star really rose after 1975 (see later). In all, the political and military importance of Second Front service was demonstrated by the fact that nine ex-Second Front people were members of the 1965 Party Central Committee (Thomas 1971: 1198).

While some rose to political significance, however, others from the Second Front remained in the FAR. One was Calixto García Martínez, a veteran of all three key moments (albeit at the Bayamo attack rather than Moncada itself) and one of the eventual Sierra *comandantes*. He remained in the FAR, becoming a Brigadier-General (Almeida Bosque 2008: 380). Another of the December 1956 'few', Universo Sánchez, also remained quietly in the FAR (Thomas 1971: 1088).

From all this, we can deduce that, regardless of talent or proximity to decision-making, participation in the Sierra campaign, at some stage, was always a passport to continued respect (if not actual power or influence). As we have seen from these cases, it certainly became a badge of loyalty and reliability, almost a qualification for being assigned to a key role, locally or nationally, in the fluid years after January 1959. It was as though, as radicalisation accelerated, definitions changed and certainties became weaker, the one thing on which the leadership could rely was the legitimacy bestowed by the Sierra experience. The fact that, for some more lowly ranked ex-guerrillas, this experience qualified them for power and influence and brought them into one of the inner circles only after some years, rather than immediately, confirmed that, even much later, this 'badge' was still powerful and a sign of trust. Indeed, in some cases, as we will see, the implication was that at that later stage they were considered more inherently trustworthy than many younger 'politicians', who could never aspire to the same level of legitimacy, having never been steeled in the 'fire' of battle, and never having shared the radicalisation and the comradeship of the *Sierra*.

However, when deciding on national or even international roles, the Sierra experience was not necessarily enough: sometimes, what was needed additionally was either the supplementary legitimacy of participation in either the Moncada or *Granma* episodes, or clear evidence of outstanding political or intellectual quality or, alternatively, unfailing loyalty or proximity to one or more of the leaders. Certainly, the composition of the genuine 'inner circle' of both the early months and years and also the later decades makes it clear that, while *Sierra* service was an entry pass to trust and promotion, often other experiences and qualities were required for real power and influence: all of those whom we can easily define as part of that 'inner circle' demonstrate this clearly.

**Leading veterans?**

Of these, undoubtedly the most popular was Camilo Cienfuegos Gorriarán, one of the most charismatic and well-liked of the new leaders in early 1959, whose death (presumably in a plane accident, although no wreckage was ever found) on 28 October 1959 was mourned nationally. Because of that mysterious early death, he has often been seen (outside and inside Cuba) as a possible 'lost leader', since, until then, he had been visibly a close confidant of Fidel and, as one of the guerrillas' few early *comandantes* of 1956–57, one of the closest to power and decision-making; at that time, neither Guevara nor Raúl had been elevated to leadership status. Moreover, the lack of evidence for his death, and the circumstances before his flight back to Havana, have often led to speculation and conspiracy theories about his disappearance, although most serious historians of the process acknowledge the complete lack of evidence of any suspicious purpose (Anderson 1997: 451; Bourne 1986: 191).

After leading his northern column westwards successfully in late 1958, in parallel with Guevara's southern advance, and entering

Havana with Guevara on 2 January, he immediately, as planned, took control of Batista's old military headquarters at Campamento Columbia in the west of the city (while Guevara occupied the imposing Cabaña fortress to the east of Havana bay). Based there, he was one of five *comandantes* identified as being close to Fidel, constituting the command apparatus of the Rebel Army (Thomas 1971: 1043), the others being Raúl, Guevara, Valdés and Almeida. In January 1959, he was then designated Army Chief of Staff, a position that made him integral to the FAR's early construction. After disbanding Batista's security apparatus on 18 February 1959 (Buch and Suárez 2009: 86), he was also crucial to the establishment of the new security forces, with Guevara, Valdés, Raúl and the PSP's Víctor Pina (Anderson 1997: 385). Moreover, he also seems to have been part of the small Cojímar group, in early 1959, discussing with the PSP plans for further radicalisation, so he was far from marginal or opposed to the leadership's revolutionary plans or collaboration with the PSP.

It was, in fact, in his military capacity that he was sent by Raúl (then FAR head) to remove Huber Matos from his command (Klepak 2010: 60); Matos was then arrested once Fidel and others arrived on 20 October 1959. After that, Cienfuegos remained in Camagüey to take over Matos's duties as military governor of the province, including management of the ensuing collective resignation of the whole provincial executive of the 26 July Movement (Thomas 1971: 1245). It was then, during the flight back to Havana a few days later, that he disappeared.

Besides the brevity of his post-victory activism and the uncertainty surrounding his death, plus a reputation as having no clear political views (ibid.: 1247–8), one of the problems with assessing Cienfuegos's importance is the almost complete dearth of biographical details. Although there is ample evidence of his personal loyalty to Fidel, and of the latter's particular affection and respect for him, he seems not to have been part of all of the 'inner circle' activities of the early months (apart from Cojímar), although his army role was absolutely fundamental to the Revolution's consolidation. This gave rise to the later rumours that he was one of the anti-Communists in the 26 July Movement ('Benigno' 1996: 75), although what we know of his pre-1959 political past tends to contradict this. One, otherwise uncorroborated, account even suggests that he was a 'closet Communist' until late

1958 (Szulc 1986: 378), while a very partisan biography sees him as an anarchist (Franqui 2012). One significant role that he did play, however, was in the Revolution's early external profile: in March 1959 (when he was still head of the army), he was active in the creation of the Movimiento de Liberación Dominicana, designed to overthrow Trujillo in the Dominican Republic (Abreu Cardet and Coredero Michel 2009: 28), the first expression of the Revolution's later active insurrectionary internationalism.

Another ex-guerrilla who was clearly significant in this respect was Ramiro Valdés Menéndez. Because of his full involvement in all the key episodes of the insurrection and also because of his evident abilities, by 1959 he was one of the five *comandantes* 'close to Fidel', and was party to the PSP-linked Cojímar discussions at Fidel's villa (Anderson 1997: 384). In April 1959, Raúl asked him to lead the new security apparatus (G2) under the FAR (Thomas 1971: 1213). It was that association that almost certainly led to the later tendency to see Valdés as pro-Moscow and 'hard line', running the G2 'probably under Russian supervision' (ibid.: 1321), despite the fact that he essentially built up a corps of G2 leaders from the previously anti-Communist DR, with people such as Julio García Oliveras, José Abrantes and Carlos Figuereido (ibid.: 1321). One observer characteristically describes him as 'an unabashed admirer of the Soviet Union' (Szulc 1986: 378), without specifying when or on the basis of what evidence. Certainly, Valdés's subsequent trajectory continually confirmed his centrality to decision-making and influence.

The third ex-guerrilla of particular importance after 1959 was Pedro Miret Prieto. Immediately after 1959 he was named Deputy Minister of Defence (Suchlicki 1988: 189), and in mid-1959 he replaced Sorí Marín as Minister of Agriculture (ibid.: 189; Thomas 1971: 1225), retaining that post until it disappeared in 1961, when he then re-joined the Defence Ministry. His closeness to the top leadership was therefore never in question, although some have seen him as a reluctant supporter of the increasingly close PSP and Soviet links – he and López Fresquet were identified as the only two in the audience not to applaud Soviet Foreign Minister Mikoyan at the 'auditorium of Havana' (ibid.: 1265) – which, if true, may explain his continual occupation of deputy posts, rather than being given full ministerial responsibility.

Finally, among the ex-guerrillas, Guillermo García stands out, but, being neither a Moncada nor *Granma* veteran, more for his historical place in the guerrilla insurrection, again perhaps explaining his continual occupation of posts lacking major responsibilities or power. Like many former guerrillas, after January 1959 he remained in the FAR, where he was a *comandante* until 1966, after which (for 1967–70) he was designated to lead the Oriente section of the newly created Communist Party.

## Women in the inner circle

When examining the cases of those whose revolutionary 'curriculum vitae' qualified them for 'inner circle' membership (or maybe membership of the next 'layer' outside that), the cases of the three most prominent female guerrillas are especially interesting. At one level, there is no good reason to separate these three from their male counterparts, except that, firstly, the guerrillas themselves originally did so, excluding women from guerrilla activity (although not the Moncada attack) in the first few months, and then later relenting and allowing the formation of a special female group, the Mariana Grajales Platoon. Secondly, some historians have since tended to relegate them to 'also-ran' status; Thomas, for example, seemed to suggest that their inclusion in the various 1960s Party Central Committees came about because they were, respectively, Fidel's secretary (Celia Sánchez), Raúl's wife (Vilma Espín) and Hart's wife (Haydée Santamaría), with the only identified female member of those Committees at that time, Elena Gil, playing a role typically assumed to be female, as secretary to Dorticós (Thomas 1971: 1432). Generally, therefore, women's contribution was for some time systematically undervalued by even the most astute observers.

Yet their biographies reveal a somewhat different picture: of three women justifiably at the centre of things and enjoying an evident influence in their own right, rather than as adjuncts to their spouses or bosses. The most obvious case in this respect (because she was the only woman member of the Tarará group, despite having no specialist agrarian expertise) was Vilma Espín.

After 1959, she became prominent: on 23 September 1960, on her own initiative, she was allowed to found the women's organisation the FMC, whose National Executive, interestingly, included Guevara's wife, Aleida March, as treasurer (Bell Lara et al. 2007: 269). In that role, she clearly remained central to much of what was going on, as had been the case before 1959; indeed, the FMC (along with the CDRs) became the most powerful and influential mass organisation at a time when (as already outlined) those bodies became fundamental to citizen socialisation and the spreading of the Revolution. Certainly, the organisation played a crucial role in many of the early social reforms, bringing women into the workplace – including the spread of crèches (*círculos infantiles*) and other mechanisms to allow them to work – retraining prostitutes for 'normal' life, launching programmes of sexual education (Kirk 2011), facilitating the diffusion of contraception and legalising abortion, but it also generally made women's social liberation and integration into the evolving process a clear priority.

The second case is that of Celia Sánchez, generally known in most of the literature on the Revolution as Fidel's closest confidante from the late 1950s. Hence, from January 1959, staying by Fidel's side, she remained an integral part of the decision-making group for all of the Revolution's important moments, strategies and plans. In fact, there was serious discussion among the 26 July leaders in January 1959 of naming her as the first Minister of Education, until Fidel opposed it, preferring her to remain in her already crucial role in the Movement (Buch and Suárez 2009: 53). Thereafter, that was precisely what she did, becoming both 'personal manager' and record keeper, and also working hard 'to complement Fidel in his areas of weakness', executing details of the 'grand plans' but also protecting him; she 'continued to serve as manager, wife, secretary, confidant, adviser, and protector rolled into one' (Bourne 1986: 200).

In April 1961, it was her Havana flat that served as the nerve centre of the leadership's defence operations against the Bay of Pigs invasion (Anderson 1997: 508), and, in March 1962, she also took over the key role of secretary to both the presidency (by then occupied by Dorticós) and the Council of Ministers (Alvarez Tabío 2004: 278), later undertaking the same role in the post-1976 Council of State (having been elected to the new National Assembly as a deputy for her native Manzanillo). Another indication of her centrality was that she was also on the Central Committee of the new 1965 Communist Party. More significantly, however, she remained constantly by Fidel's side, evidently having his ear throughout, and more evidently executing his orders: she was with him, for example, at the symbolic signing of the first agrarian reform (in the Sierra in May 1959) and during his historic UN visit in 1959 (ibid.: 287). Certainly, her death (from cancer) in 1980 seems to have had a profound effect on him (Bourne 1986: 294–5), even, according to some reports, slightly impairing his judgement. In all, her importance should not be ignored, and it is clear that, despite any sexist or even sensationalist tendencies to downplay her role, she was always central to the political process, and not just to Fidel's personal entourage, someone on whom Fidel relied for her political judgement as much as her indefatigable loyalty. One journalist described her as 'unquestionably ... the most important woman – and very likely the most important human being – in his life' (Szulc 1986: 7). After her death, her support and advisory role was, at a much less significant level, taken over by people such as José Miguel Miyar Barruecos (known as 'Chomy'), whose formal position after 1980 was secretary to the Council of State.

The third of these female activists, Haydée Santamaría Cuadrado, was also no shrinking violet or mere adornment after 1959. In fact, partly based on her special place in the post-January vanguard, she asked for, and was given, the right to open the Casa de las Américas cultural centre, formally within the Ministry of Education, although enjoying considerable autonomy. There, although commentators implied that she was included in the inner circle only because of her marriage to Hart, by then Minister of Education (Thomas 1971: 1466) or as a cultural apparatchik, her leadership of the Casa was in fact always imaginative, aesthetically sharp, and even protective, as in the Casa's record of sheltering some of those marginalised in the 1968–76 period ('Benigno' 1996: 36), enabling the centre to retain a high degree of independence for many years. She committed suicide in 1979, according to one version because of growing official concerns about her supposedly lavish lifestyle (ibid.: 36), but there is no real corroboration of that. Beyond that detail, however, Santamaría's long-lasting position of respect remained an example of the enduring legitimacy of those in the Revolution's 'historic core'; while she may not have enjoyed the daily political clout of, say, Ramiro Valdés or, indeed, her own husband, she nonetheless continued to be considered integral to the process's destiny. As one unidentified writer observed in the 1960s, 'because she was in the

Revolution from the Moncada days, nobody can argue with her about whether something is Revolutionary or not' (Sutherland 1969: 22).

## The *Llano*

All three women were, of course, more part of the *Llano* than the *Sierra*, which confirms that, while membership of the guerrilla group was the main passport to trust and high influence, an equally proven and significant participation in the urban underground, throughout the struggle of 1955–58, could also count for much, albeit occasionally tempered by ex-guerrillas' suspicions.

The two outstanding examples of this trust were Armando Hart and Osvaldo Dorticós. Hart's protagonism (where he showed real influence on decision-making) really came after 1976, so that contribution to the process will largely be dealt with in Chapter 5. However, in the early years, he was central to many of the changes as Minister of Education (1959–65), overseeing the seminal 1961 literacy campaign, the nationalisation of all schools, the major and contentious university reform, and the creation of experimental schools. Since all of the rebels believed firmly that education was central to the Revolution's plans and ultimate success, by giving Hart control of that area the leadership clearly indicated their collective trust in him and their recognition of his qualities. If his contribution during this period has been largely overlooked, that is possibly because, unusually, he remained in the same post for some time. However, even after leaving that post, in 1965 he became organisation secretary for the party Central Committee, a key role in cementing the party's centrality to political power and linking the leadership with the grass roots. Then, in February 1967, he wrote a significant article in *Granma*, critical of the tendency towards 'bureaucratism' in the Soviet system, read by many as a warning shot to any (most obviously those formerly in, or around, the old PSP) still hoping to emulate the Eastern European models (Karol 1970: 296).

Osvaldo Dorticós Torrado has also been somewhat misunderstood. On the one hand, he has often been dismissed as a tool of the radicals, principally because of the image in some of the early literature and media reports that he was conjured up, as a forty-year-old Cienfuegos lawyer (head of the National Lawyers College), to replace a supposedly principled, liberal and resistant Manuel

Urrutia, as a more compliant president on 17 July 1959 (Thomas 1971: 1234), or alternatively that he was always part of the plot. The latter possibility was seemingly 'proven' by the fact that, like Raúl, he had much earlier joined the JS, the PSP's youth wing (Buch and Suárez 2009: 225). While one account suggests that he subsequently went on to join the PSP itself in the 1940s, acting as Marinello's private secretary at one time (Thomas 1971: 1085), another later and much more detailed Cuban account of his personal history makes no mention of that at all (Buch and Suárez 2009). Given the Revolution's history and the official attitude to the PSP's historical role, this would be a strange experience to ignore, if true. Nonetheless, his JS membership and service to Marinello were enough to add grist to the mill of the image of an increasingly communist Revolution.

The reality was probably somewhat different. For a start, any membership of the PSP would have been brief; moreover, given the common pattern for former Communists to thereafter reject Communism, one might have expected him to oppose, rather than welcome, the growing alliance with the PSP, as with Franqui. Whatever the case, his commitment to the 26 July pole of the rebellion was clear: in July 1957, he was asked (by País) to set up and lead the Cienfuegos branch of the new Civic Resistance Movement (ibid.: 228), since he lived and worked there. He was then imprisoned briefly after the 26 July-linked Cienfuegos military mutiny of 1957 (Suchlicki 1988: 92), and then he joined the Movement itself, becoming its Cienfuegos coordinator in April 1958 and even sending a contingent of volunteers in 1958 to join Guevara's westward column (Buch and Suárez 2009: 232; Suchlicki 1988: 92). Arrested briefly once again in late 1958 (after returning from a meeting with Guevara in the Sierra del Escambray), he fled to Mexico on his release in mid-December, returning after 1 January 1959 to take up the post of Minister of Justice (Suchlicki 1988: 92). Hence, he was far from unknown within the Movement, although perhaps less known to the Cuban public, to the extent that some rebels had doubts about his acceptability to Cubans if appointed President (Buch and Suárez 2009: 144), and he was far from just a sympathetic observer.

As President, his importance became much greater than is often imagined, as he played a significant role in defining policy and direction. In 1959, as Minister of Justice, he was directly responsible for drafting 'revolutionary laws' (ibid.: 129), and he seems to have played a special role in developing Cuba's foreign policy, being given substantial freedom to negotiate bilateral relations with other countries (Balfour 2009: 113). His May 1960 tour of Latin America has also been seen as the first step in Cuba's new insurrectionary Latin American policy (Thomas 1971: 1285), while his November 1966 visit (with Roca) to Vietnam was probably significant in cementing the growing relationship and identification with a fellow embattled country. In March 1961, he took over the organisation of ORI from the disgraced Escalante (ibid.: 1379). Karol described him as being clearly au fait with Marxist ideas in the late 1960s, suggesting a deeper radicalism than the image of compliant pragmatist suggests (Karol 1970: 356); Karol even argued that, with Guevara's departure and death, he became the non-PSP radicals' 'top theorist' (ibid.: 357).

Dorticós and Hart, however, seem to have been the only highly placed people from the urban movement who were unquestionably influential; others seem to have enjoyed prominence more sporadically, although they were never dispatched to the 'outer limits'. One such was Marcelo Fernández Font; Fidel asked him to be Minister of the Economy (*Hacienda*) in the first government, but he declined, preferring to remain as national coordinator of the Movement (Buch and Suárez 2009: 57). However, perhaps because of his pre-1959 politics and his absence from the Sierra, or because he was not part of the group mainly driving the changes, he seems to have retained a less radical position on the Revolution after 1959; in fact, he reportedly led a group in the 26 July Movement planning to ask Fidel in 1959 to reaffirm his opposition to Communism (Thomas 1971: 1281).

A similar story can be told of Enrique Oltuski Ozacki. Given his political and professional credentials and experience, he was a logical choice to become Minister of Communications in the first government, but seems to have been demoted later in the same year (possibly as a result of PSP pressure, given his previous and – according to some – perhaps still evident anti-Communism). After that, despite previously arguing with Guevara over the PSP's role and Guevara's radical ideas on land reform (Buch and Suárez 2009: 352), he went to work under Guevara in the new Ministry of Industry (ibid.: 361), perhaps given Guevara's growing pattern of giving refuge to those who had crossed the PSP, which he increasingly considered sectarian (Anderson 1997: 607).

The final such case is that of Faustino Pérez. As with Fernández Font, he was an obvious person to enter the first 'coalition' government, becoming Minister of Confiscated Property. From that point on, however, his political position became less clear. In November 1959, along with Manuel Ray, he resigned, allegedly over his concerns arising from the Matos affair (ibid.: 453; Thomas 1971: 1251). Certainly, he dropped out of view until April 1961, when he played a major role in repelling the Playa Girón invasion (directing operations alongside Fidel) and, in October 1962, he was part of the small group of ex-guerrillas that Raúl took with him to Santiago to prepare for the worst during the impending Missile Crisis (Thomas 1971: 1408). Shortly afterwards, moreover, he led troops in the long counter-insurgency operations in the Sierra del Escambray (Buch and Suárez 2009: 323).

## The PSP after 1959

*The mavericks* Since one thing that, in the literature, has always characterised discussion of the *Llano–Sierra* tensions was the role of, and attitude to, the PSP, this brings us logically to consider PSP membership of the emerging 'inner circle'. We start, however, with a slightly different category of PSP member, namely those inside the party who always enjoyed a special place within the rebels' 'inner circle', separate, and often disconnected, from their party colleagues.

Of these, the most outstanding was Alfredo Guevara. An anarchist in his youth as a dock worker, alongside Lionel Soto (Guanche 2013: 1), he joined the JS and then the PSP, but, more importantly for this narrative, he was also a close student colleague of Fidel from 1945 to 1948 (also accompanying him to the same Bogotá student congress in the latter year, where they were swept up in bloody street protests). Thomas, in fact, describes him as a 'Communist leader in the University of Havana' (Thomas 1971: 814), and, as a young activist, he was imprisoned, and even tortured, a few times (Guanche 2013: 4). His friendship with Fidel was certainly significant, since it led to a JS request in March 1952 for him to approach Fidel to try to persuade him to return to the university and organise a broad opposition front there (Szulc 1986: 54).

After 1959, as we have seen, he was curiously part of the Tarará discussions (although he was no expert on agrarian reform), and hence evidently part of at least one form of the emerging 'inner circle'. However, it was in the cinema where he made his permanent mark. Already a cinema enthusiast in the 1950s (attached to the Tiempo Nuevo group, which was largely composed of radical film-makers and enthusiasts), he asked for, and was permitted to create, a new cinema institute (ICAIC), which took shape in March 1959. That institute was certainly central to the Revolution (being one of the first national institutions created after the victory): not only did it become a powerful base from which Guevara could influence and define cultural policies, but, echoing both the Soviet and the Mexican experiences of the 1920s, it also played a fundamental role in mass political socialisation. In this task, the ICAIC increasingly found itself in opposition to the more liberal cultural supplement *Lunes de Revolución* between 1959 and 1961, a difference of opinion that culminated in the controversial ICAIC decision not to distribute a short film, *PM*, which had been made under the magazine's auspices, an event that soon became a *cause célèbre* and resulted in three large June 1961 meetings of worried intellectuals with Fidel and other leaders.

More interestingly, the ICAIC began and remained outside the control of the new National Cultural Council (CNC), which was, from the outset, run by a group from the PSP and associated with rather orthodox Soviet ideas on culture. Indeed, it remained substantially autonomous until the mid-1980s, when Guevara fell from grace somewhat after a dispute about cultural policy. Until then, he used that autonomy to protect some intellectuals and artists marginalised in the new process. This was especially true of a group of young musicians and singers in the new 'protest' song movement, which became, under his wing, part of the ICAIC. Overall, his inclusion in the Tarará discussions but divergence from the orthodox Communist thinking of the CNC raise the possibility that he was allowed that autonomy precisely because, firstly, he asked for it and seized the opportunity (as did Santamaría, with Casa de las Américas) and, secondly, because he offered an attractive form of 'communism', being a radical Marxist but dissenting from the orthodoxy that Moscow and the PSP represented. He died in 2013.

A less prominent, but similar, case was that of Antonio Núñez

Jiménez. His role in the development of the Revolution was unusual in that, although he left his post at the University of Las Villas to join Guevara's guerrillas very late on, on Christmas Eve 1958 in fact (Thomas 1971: 1027), he clearly enjoyed some influence after 1959, and continued to enjoy the respect normally accorded to a guerrilla veteran. One explanation may be his former friendship with Fidel and membership of his group of like-minded politically aware students when they began to study in Havana (Bourne 1986: 38); another, more convincing, is that he soon developed a close friendship with Che Guevara, the latter probably also attracted by his unusual combination of radical ideas and maverick Communism (Núñez Jiménez 1959) – he had been a PSP member, but seems to have left some time before 1958 (Thomas 1971: 1215). Hence, he was included from the outset in the Tarará discussions and made a fundamental contribution to the fact and nature of the controversial agrarian reform of 1959, perhaps even drafting the law itself (ibid.: 1215). Immediately after that, he was named executive director of the agrarian reform organisation, INRA, with Fidel formally its president (Núñez Jiménez 2005; Thomas 1971: 1217), until he was 'dismissed' after criticisms of expropriations (Thomas 1971: 1376). Anderson dismisses him as 'general factotum for Fidel' (Anderson 1997: 404), but his contribution seems to have been more important than that and, anyway, he was always closer to Guevara and to his arguments about economic policy (confirmed in an interview in 1994). In addition, in December 1959, he was entrusted with a significant mission to Europe, seeking $100 million in loans (Thomas 1971: 1257); again, in spring 1960, he visited Moscow, developing the new relationship (ibid.: 1280); and, in 1961, his declaration of Cuba's solidarity with the Algerian National Liberation Front (ibid.: 1317) seemed to herald a new Cuban foreign policy aimed at the colonial and ex-colonial developing world. After this, he retreated into the background a little, becoming president of the National Commission of the Academy of Science (1962–72), but then he gradually took up cudgels for the environment, building on his specialist knowledge and affection for Cuba's flora and fauna, an area in which he came into his own much later in the 1990s.

*The orthodox Communists* These two were, however, somewhat maverick PSP members. As for the party itself, and its main leaders or activists who played a role early on, their identification is slightly muddied by two key factors. Firstly, much of our early information about the PSP is based on rumour or defectors' accounts, neither especially reliable for seeking the truth, particularly as they mostly emanated from those who had opposed the PSP's entry into the rebel alliance and subsequently sought to present an image of the PSP's subversion and infiltration. Secondly, clandestine activity had long bred a need for internal PSP discipline, hiding any real divisions within the party. Thus, for example, for some time we only knew from reports that, before 1959, it was the younger members of the PSP (citing especially Alfredo Guevara and Lionel Soto) who favoured closer links with the rebels (ibid.: 923).

Among those main leaders, the one with the greatest notoriety was Aníbal Escalante Dellundé. Although (Cuban) history remembers him as a devious and even sinister plotter, he was actually a respected intellectual, with a significant and revered past and position within the party before 1959. One of the earliest members of the original Cuban Communist Party, he went on to become aide to the party's general secretary (Jorge Antonio Vivó) in the early 1930s (Suchlicki 1988: 100) and edited the party newspaper, *Hoy*, from 1938 and throughout its pre-1959 years (ibid.: 101), even keeping that post after January 1959.

After 1959, he seems to have been instrumental in unifying the party leadership in their otherwise divided approach to, and opinions of, the 26 July Movement (Anderson 1997: 399), and, as we have seen, he was one of the three PSP leaders taking part in the early Cojímar discussions about fusing the revolutionary groups (ibid.: 384). Most importantly, it was he who played the most pivotal role in the creation of the first step towards a single party (the ORI); he was designated its national organising secretary and therefore was responsible for merging the three revolutionary groups. He did this with characteristic efficiency, soon establishing an ORI headquarters in 100 of Cuba's 126 towns (Thomas 1971: 1373), mostly using PSP facilities and staff. We know, of course, that his final version of the new National Directorate saw him far exceed his brief, which led to him being criticised publicly by Fidel and dispatched to the Socialist Bloc and diplomatic duties.

Despite this ignominy, however, it is perhaps significant that he was not punished with anything more severe than temporary 'banishment', from which he returned as early as 1964 (being then given enough space and leeway to plot, again, with other PSP colleagues – from around 1966 – to seek to prevent the Revolution from continuing its increasingly unorthodox path). Hence, several conclusions emanate from his personal biography: that he was respected and influential in 1959–62 says much for both his recognised talents and power in the party, and also for the rebel leaders' willingness to go along with someone of his apparent pedigree. The fact that he was pilloried publicly in 1962 again says much about the leadership's evolving attitude to orthodoxy in the Communist movement, and perhaps also about its determination to make clear, at home and abroad, that the Revolution was 'theirs' and not the PSP's. Equally, however, the lightness of his punishment, the ease with which he re-entered the political world, and finally the freedom to operate again as he did, all speak volumes for the degree of tolerance within that system (for those on the 'inside', however flawed or 'sinful' they might be), the relative chaos or fluidity that allowed him to conspire again, at quite a high level, and the caution within the leadership about being seen to punish the PSP and ex-PSP people more than was politically wise, until Escalante's second conspiracy was seen as one step too far.

Unlike the role played by Escalante, however, there is no doubt about the significance of the contribution of Carlos Rafael Rodríguez. Already more respected and trusted by the rebels than other PSP leaders, after 1959 he continued to urge the PSP to support fully the 26 July Movement and especially Fidel's leadership. That stance and his willingness to go along with Fidel's radicalism did not, however, endear him to his colleagues, and, in April 1959, a reformulation of the PSP's Secretariat saw him dropped (ibid.: 1208), and a May 1959 PSP meeting (to decide on relations with the rebels) found him on 'the right' of the leadership (ibid.: 1222). At the PSP's Sixth Congress (1961), he argued that Fidel should be accepted as the leader and guarantor of 'maximum unity' (ibid.: 1292).

In 1960–61, he was also instrumental in shaping the new university reform, and, in 1961, and more significantly, he took over the direction of INRA from Núñez Jiménez, thereupon occupying the highest position given to a PSP leader to date (ibid.: 1376), holding it till 1964 (ibid.: 1454). During that time, INRA was converted into a ministry in 1963, giving him the unique position of having had ministerial posts under both Batista and Castro.

However, alongside Rodríguez, in terms of seniority and trust both within the party and within the rebel alliance, was his fellow leader, Blas Roca. After the Escalante affair, Roca retained a crucial role, helping to coordinate the various manifestations of the emerging single party. However, while his background gained him respect in some 26 July quarters, it also aroused suspicions; moreover, it is not impossible that some of the doubts about him were the result of social snobbery and even racism, since he was an undeniably popular *mulato* working-class stalwart in a decidedly white middle-class leadership. Indeed, it is similarly not impossible that those same Roca characteristics contributed to the tendency in much of the non-Cuban literature on the Revolution (and in many partisan émigré accounts) to depict him, rather than the more urbane and educated Rodríguez, as the *éminence grise* of the PSP–26 July relationship, as the Stalinist organisation man, the hardliner and the (implicitly less intelligent) ultra-orthodox Moscow loyalist; certainly, he seems to have been firmer and less flexible than Rodríguez, but, although politically astute and even calculating, he appears to have been prepared to defend the PSP's identity in the early months, even accusing Fidel on one occasion of endangering the Revolution by tolerating an anti-Communist campaign (ibid.: 1220).

After 1959, while holding on to the party's identity, he also proved crucial in opening, and keeping open, serious initial discussions with Moscow; in March 1960, for example, he went to the Socialist Bloc, immediately after the CIA had been given the go-ahead to run the Bay of Pigs invasion force (ibid.: 1271). However, Roca seems to have miscalculated in 1961, leading a PSP group whose approach to the impending United States-backed invasion was to welcome it for its capacity to turn Cuba into the US Hungary, thereby gaining international sympathy but committing Moscow to nothing. Khrushchev's unexpected commitment to guarantee Cuba's defence, however, led to a shift, following which Roca accepted that Moscow's support meant that, despite his remaining doubts, the Revolution was permanent, and that greater cooperation should result (ibid.: 1290).

Those doubts seem to have been present all along, about the

political identity of the 26 July leadership and also about the Revolution's potential survival and its capacity to become a genuine and recognisable revolutionary process, or at least one that his orthodox interpretation of Marxism could accept. Hence, he argued in 1961 (at the PSP's own Sixth Congress) that Cuba should not go down the road of rapid radicalisation and should, instead, keep some private enterprise and even a national bourgeoisie (ibid.: 1291).

The final major PSP protagonist in the early decade was, like Roca, a long-standing stalwart of Communist activism, Lázaro Peña. Originally a Havana tobacco worker who became a union activist, he had joined the Communist Party in 1930; after that he was imprisoned repeatedly but steadily gained a reputation as a fearless and efficient organiser, and was eventually instrumental in the creation of the newly permitted CTC in 1939, becoming its first general secretary. In 1947–48, as part of the United States-backed Latin American drive against Communist unions, led in Cuba by Prío, the then Auténtico Minister of Labour, the party's influence in the CTC was broken by strong-arm tactics. After Batista's coup, in 1953 Peña left Cuba for Mexico, and thence went to Moscow, returning finally to Cuba in mid-January 1959 (ibid.: 1083). However, by 1961, he was again general secretary of the new revolutionary version of the CTC, the CTC-R, keeping that post until at least 1968 (when he was succeeded by Miguel Martín). Given this role, there is little doubt about the importance, albeit in a limited dimension, of his contribution to the process of change in Cuba (Miranda Fernández 1984).

*Lesser PSP players* However, in post-1958 Cuba, the PSP was by no means limited to the four main national leaders: a cast of lesser, but nonetheless significant, party members was increasingly visible in a variety of crucial roles and institutions, some less Moscow-loyalist than Roca but others as disciplined as the party preferred them to be. As we have already seen, one such was Lionel Soto Prieto, a former student colleague of Fidel from 1946 (although in the Faculty of Philosophy and Arts rather than Law), who was already one of a group of more radical students (Bourne 1986: 38) and a PSP member when they met, having joined the university branch in 1947 and becoming its leader until 1952 (Batlle Reyes 2008: 149). He was already well placed within the party itself, becoming its international secretary – reportedly in 1945 (Suchlicki 1988: 265), although this does not match the other dates we know for him.

. Soto's specific contribution to the rebellion after 1956 seems to have been his work within the PSP to change the party's attitude to the insurrection (ibid.: 265). In this, he should be considered along with another of Fidel's ex-student friends, Flavio Bravo (see below). After 1959, Soto was therefore well placed to enjoy considerable trust among the rebel leadership. In March 1960, he was responsible (with two others) for running the new Universidad Popular (significant in spreading the word for the Revolution); then, in December 1960, he was given a similarly significant responsibility, running the new political education schools, the EIR (that being the first major appointment for a PSP member: Thomas 1971: 1314), thereby helping to shape the radicalism of the emerging cadres of the single party. In 1968, he seems to have been demoted as part of the collateral damage from the 'microfaction' affair (the 'second Escalante affair'), and to have been given agricultural work (Suchlicki 1988: 265), although there is no evidence of Soto's involvement with Escalante's conspiracy.

Bravo was also of some significance around this time. Having joined the old Communist Party in 1937 and becoming a founder member of the JS in 1944 (Rojas Blaquier 2010: 132), he was clearly identified as a Communist. Nonetheless, he remained friendly with Fidel, meeting him a few times in Mexico after 1955 (Bourne 1986: 129), and being sent by the PSP to try to persuade Fidel to postpone the planned invasion (Szulc 1986: 285). After 1959, he was influential in building links between the PSP and the Rebel Army and in organising the new militias (Rojas Blaquier 2010: 133), and, in 1961, he was on hand enough to play a role, as a *comandante*, in resisting the Bay of Pigs invasion (Bourne 1986: 38).

There were several other PSP members of some importance. These, for example, included José Matar, who was given the significant responsibility in 1960 of coordinating the new CDRs (Thomas 1971: 1322); he later became ambassador in Hungary, until, in 1968, he too was demoted in the wake of the same 'microfaction' affair. Another was José Ramírez, who, like many other radicals who had been part of Raúl's Second Front, went on to run the new small farmers' mass organisation, the ANAP, from 1961 (ibid.: 1330), yet another crucial role given to a PSP member. Ladislao González Carbajal was in a slightly different position, since, despite being a high-ranking PSP activist (elected, for example, to its Central Committee in 1959), he had joined the guerrilla struggle, becoming part of Guevara's column in Las Villas (ibid.: 1337) and he thus enjoyed the ex-guerrillas' special respect. After 1959, he was appointed to run the Oriente provincial JUCEI (Coordination, Execution and Inspection Board, a local government structure). Yet another was Dulce María Escalona, who became Deputy Minister of Education in 1961 (ibid.: 1340), a post from which, it was alleged by those fearing a Czech-style Communist takeover, she, rather than Hart, actually ran the ministry. Finally, one should not forget César Escalante, Aníbal's brother, who survived the purge after the PSP's 1962 debacle and who, until his death in 1965, remained on the National Directorate of the new PURSC; from reports and interviews (in 1994), it seems that he never shared Aníbal's orthodox reading of the Revolution and was closer to Carlos Rafael Rodríguez's approach, which probably explains his survival.

In this group, the name of Armando Acosta also stands out. After joining Guevara's column in late 1958, he became what was described by one biographer as Guevara's 'commissar' in Las Villas, and certainly a close aide to Guevara (Anderson 1997: 384). After January 1959, for example, he was entrusted with the political education classes for the rebel troops in La Cabaña, thus, like Soto in the EIR, helping to shape the early radicalisation of at least some of the ex-guerrillas (ibid.: 385). Another one close to Guevara was Francisco García Vals, although he did not join that entourage until after 1 January 1959; nonetheless, despite not having fought in the insurrection, he curiously was appointed as lieutenant in La Cabaña, becoming Guevara's executive assistant (ibid.: 405). More significantly still, it was in his Cojímar house that the early 1959 meetings of PSP leaders took place (ibid.: 405); later, in May 1959, he accompanied Guevara throughout his three-month tour of fourteen developing countries (ibid.: 428). Also close to Guevara was Alfredo Menéndez, a sugar economist who joined Guevara's column in Las Villas, remaining with him thereafter. Like García Vals, he too accompanied Guevara on his travels in May 1959; in fact, he reportedly used that opportunity to execute the highly significant responsibility of starting crucial negotiations with the Soviet Union on sugar sales (ibid.: 428–9).

Yet the PSP story does not end there, as mention should also be made of some party members who, although not high-powered or nationally influential, did nonetheless play crucial roles in the educational and cultural spheres. The best known was undoubtedly Juan Marinello, the long-standing party member and former leader, who had long been a well-respected intellectual. Not only did he and Severo Aguirre constitute a delegation to Moscow in January 1959, which, while formally attending a Communist Congress, briefed Moscow on the Revolution and on the PSP's decision to support the rebel leadership (ibid.: 413–4), but also, in 1960, he was named rector of the reformed Havana University, thereby demonstrating a high degree of trust in his ability to shape Cuba's youth elite for the future.

If Marinello was the best known, other PSP activists became the most notorious, namely the two who, after 1961, dominated the new CNC, using their positions to try to shift the Revolution's cultural policy in a more orthodox, and even Stalinist, direction. These were the husband-and-wife team of Joaquín Ordoqui (one of the oldest party members, since 1927) and Edith García Buchaca (ex-wife of Carlos Rafael Rodríguez); between them they sought to resist and marginalise the influence of the *Lunes de Revolución* 'pole' of the new cultural apparatus (Kapcia 2005: 131–3; Kumaraswami and Kapcia 2012: 78–80) and even to overcome the influence of the ICAIC in the new cinema policy (Pogolotti 2006). While their influence remained limited to those areas of culture under CNC control, it nonetheless left a legacy within the institution that later allowed Luis Pavón and others to enact the *quinquenio gris*, the period of discrimination against selected Cuban writers and artists. However, although Ordoqui eventually rose to become a Deputy Minister of the Armed Forces, in 1968 it was revealed that, in 1955–57 in Mexico, he had protected the then JS member Marcos Armando Rodríguez, who had informed Batista's secret police, the SIM, about the remnants of the DR group in hiding in a house in Humboldt Street in Havana, following the attack on the presidential palace. As a result, Ordoqui was 'kept under house arrest indefinitely' (Thomas 1971: 1467–8) with García Buchaca, until released in 1973 (Mesa-Lago 1974: 21).

In the world of culture, mention should also be made of a handful of PSP members who played prominent, if not always influential, roles in the broader definition and character of the evolving revolutionary culture. The most notable was Nicolás Guillén, the long-established and internationally known *negrista* poet who was chosen to lead the new UNEAC in 1961, but who, in 1968, showed enough influence and access to the leadership to present UNEAC's concerns about the UMAP camps and then get them closed. Others were Mirta Aguirre, influential among new writers at Havana University (Kumaraswami and Kapcia 2012: 24), and José Antonio Portuondo (a critic who soon led the prestigious research centre, the Institute of Literature and Linguistics). One might also mention the novelist Alejo Carpentier, who (once a member of the Communist Party) led the new National Publishing House in 1959.

In this catalogue, there was also one further activist whose PSP links may well have helped him to survive in a series of posts that required a high level of trustworthiness. This was Camilo Cien-fuegos's brother Osmani (often spelled Osmany). Apparently in touch with the PSP in the months before the *Granma* invasion (Thomas 1971: 1050), he became a JS member until, in January 1958, he joined the 26 July Movement. However, after being imprisoned frequently, he finally left for Mexico, remaining there until January 1959; hence, he was neither a participant in the Sierra, nor a fully fledged PSP member. Despite this, and perhaps helped by his relationship to Camilo, he was given significant posts from early on, becoming head of army education once Raúl took charge of the FAR (ibid.: 1198), and then, in November 1959, taking over from Ray as Minister of Public Works (ibid.: 1251). While still a minister, he then led a key militia battalion in the Playa Girón campaign, relieving the local peasant militia that had been the first line of defence (ibid.: 1362), a performance that significantly raised his profile (ibid.: 1377). As a result, he then joined the Central Committee of the new 1965 party (Suchlicki 1988: 61).

What is incontrovertible from this long list of activists is that, whatever doubts and tensions reigned, the PSP contributed a signifi-cant number of key players to the early processes of radicalisation, helping in different ways to shape the structure and definition of the early Revolution. Some fell foul of those tensions, but others survived and continued to play key roles, that survival resulting either from the need not to alienate the PSP or Moscow unnecessarily or from their proximity to, and respect from, either Fidel or Guevara.

## The Directorio Revolucionario

What, though, of the third element of the rebel alliance, the DR? Although several DR members were incorporated into various new institutions, not least the security apparatus, there was only ever one leader who proved to be nationally significant, Faure Chomón Mediavilla. Generally somewhat neglected by the literature on the Revolution, and dismissed as either irrelevant or an opportunist turncoat for having apparently overcome his previous anti-Communist beliefs in order to remain in the system, becoming 'doubtless through opportunism ... the most zealous philo-Communist of all' (Thomas 1971: 1313), he seems to have undertaken some critical responsibilities at various times.

His pre-1959 pedigree was considerable. In 1957, he was second-in-command in Carlos Gutiérerrez Menoyo's group for the palace attack, being sheltered afterwards by Felipe Pazos (ibid.: 930); as we have seen, he then returned in 1958 to lead a guerrilla struggle in the Sierra del Escambray. There, it was he and Rolando Cubela who negotiated a cooperation agreement with Guevara and Valdés in late 1958 (ibid.: 1017), a decision that proved fundamental to the DR's incorporation into the revolutionary alliance.

As the DR's main remaining leader after 1957, his politics began to radicalise (he had always been closer to Echeverría's politics than to those of Gutiérrez Menoyo), making his adaptation to the radicalisation process after 1959 perhaps less surprising than some allege (material from a 1994 interview). Certainly, he is described as moving 'sharply to the left' after January 1959 (Anderson 1997: 465), and, on 13 March 1959, at a commemoration of Echeverría, he asserted that the DR was further to the left than the 26 July Movement (Thomas 1971: 1203); while this might have been rhetoric, it suggests a willingness to go further along the road towards a radical definition.

Hence, although his dispatch to Moscow in May 1960 (as the Revolution's first ambassador) might have been seen as removing him (as a former anti-Communist) from the political scene, his role in representing the increasingly unorthodox Cuban leadership to an increasingly exasperated and suspicious Moscow should not be ignored; it is unlikely that the revolutionary leadership would have entrusted a key post for liaison with their new, and fundamental, allies to someone unreliable or marginalised. Therefore, although

Chomón's associate, Cubela, was probably dispatched to Prague (as a relatively low-ranking military attaché) to remove him from the scene, Chomón's appointment probably reflected the opposite, namely a degree of faith in his abilities and usefulness, rather than any desire to sideline him. In fact, he had already been chosen by Raúl, in May, to lead a somewhat informal FAR delegation to Moscow to discuss military relations with their Soviet counterparts. Curiously, that group consisted almost entirely of ex-DR people and one from the PSP (Buch and Suárez 2009: 413), suggesting not only a degree of trust and importance but also a desire not to send a misleading message to the Soviet government; it was later that a formal delegation went there.

Chomón's position seemed to be confirmed when, in March 1961, he returned to Cuba, becoming Minister of Communications for 1962–63 (Thomas 1971: 1379) and then Minister of Transport (1965–70). It is, of course, possible that he was actually withdrawn, to express Cuban anger at the Escalante and PSP machinations (assuming that they had a direct line to Moscow), or, alternatively, as the missile arming of Cuba was under way, that the leadership wanted a more senior representative in Moscow to keep channels as open as possible. Interestingly, in 1964, it was Chomón who was chosen to provide the evidence against Marcos Rodríguez, Fidel thereby making a clear statement about the DR having a greater right to historical legitimacy than the by now highly suspect former PSP.

### 'Independent' radicals

Chomón, however, was not alone in leadership circles in being from neither the PSP nor the 26 July Movement (although he did boast guerrilla credentials), for there was one other 'independent' who clearly did not owe his position to either the Sierra experience or the PSP's authority. That person was Raúl Roa García, unexpectedly appointed Foreign Minister in June 1959, who went on to play a highly significant role in shaping Cuba's foreign policy, and thus defining its external profile at a time when that profile assumed a greater importance than ever before.

Roa was by no means an unknown. Long recognised as a leading Cuban intellectual, with a prominent past as a political activist (being active in the rebellious Ala Izquierda Estudiantil – Student Left Wing –

in the 1930s' insurrection against Machado), by the 1950s he was a well-respected university teacher, exercising an influence on radical students (Guanche 2013: 3). There was also a curious dimension to his political past: under the Auténtico governments, he served as director of the Department of Culture (Ramos Ruiz 2006). Finally, after 1952, having written criticisms of Batista and fleeing to Mexico in 1953 – where he seems to have had some slight contact with Fidel and the other rebels, having sent them books before their release from prison (Szulc 1986: 261) – he returned to teach at Havana University in 1955.

He was also no political ingénue. On this, Suchlicki seems mistaken when he says that Roa adopted Marxism–Leninism only after 1959 (Suchlicki 1988: 243), since he was clearly a Marxist long before that and there is no evidence that he became a 'Leninist' after 1959, only that he did not oppose the Revolution's new direction (by no means the same thing, as we have seen) and agreed to represent Cuba abroad. In fact, Roa had been a maverick Marxist in the 1920s and 1930s, and was certainly very close to other student and intellectual radicals, such as Mella, Rubén Martínez Villena and Pablo de la Torriente Brau, all associated with or active leaders of the Communist Party (Thomas 1971: 1225). Roa did in fact join the party in 1927 (Suchlicki 1988: 243), being arrested in 1930. At some undefined point after that, he left the party, however, and by the 1950s was 'estranged' from it (Thomas 1971: 1225); indeed, in 1956 he wrote a fierce denunciation of the Soviet Union over Hungary (Bourne 1986: 192), which may later have contributed to the Soviet Union's refusal to invite him to visit Moscow until as late as 1971, i.e. ten years after his appointment as Foreign Minister (ibid.: 193). In 1956, he joined the Civic Resistance movement (Suchlicki 1988: 243), thereby nailing his colours to the mast of the rebellion. Immediately after the rebel victory, he was named Cuba's ambassador to the Organisation of American States (OAS), but then, in May, he replaced Agramonte as Foreign Minister.

What this past and also his appointment and continuing position as Foreign Minister all show was a confirmation of Fidel's preference for radicals who had, and even still, refused to toe the orthodox Soviet line; in fact, Roa had potentially blotted his copybook some time before with the 26 July Movement, when, in Mexico in 1955, he apparently refused an invitation to meet Fidel on the grounds that, as a former teacher when Fidel was a student activist, he had associated him with the *bonchismo* of that time (Bourne 1986: 192). Hence, the rebels' continuing loyalty to him perhaps confirms his importance, and even his influence, since Fidel would not normally have forgiven that, unless he respected a person for their qualities or advice. In fact, shortly after his appointment as Foreign Minister, in 1959 he went on record at the UN as aligning Cuba more with the Third World than with the USSR, saying that 'Cuba refuses to choose between capitalism, which starves people to death, and communism, which solves economic problems but suppresses liberties that are so dear to mankind' (ibid.: 207). Once again, the fact that he remained Foreign Minister for twenty-five years (until 1976) says much for his position of respect.

Indeed, his surprise appointment seems to have arisen from the rebels' awareness of the need for Cuba to have a sophisticated but politically reliable representative in the world's forums; this undoubtedly contributed to the tendency for observers to ignore his contribution, dismissing him as either a lightweight or an opportunist. One historian, for example, saw him as opportunistically subordinate to Fidel and the other leaders, and even argued that the PSP's Ramón Calcines (chair of the ORI Foreign Relations Commission) was the real de facto Foreign Minster behind the scenes (until dismissed after the 'microfaction' affair in 1968) (Thomas 1971: 1468), while another described as 'sphinxlike' his rapid conversion to a movement that was closely working with the PSP (Anderson 1997: 435).

However, he was no lightweight. For example, a January 1960 visit to Asia and Africa, specifically to invite several leaders to a planned conference in Havana, indicates a significant level of responsibility. That month was evidently crucial for defining Cuba's new external profile, since Dorticós went to Latin America, Cuban–Soviet relations were established, and Fidel's first Declaration of Havana was issued, offering Cuba's Revolution as a model for Latin America to throw off dictatorship and achieve real independence. In 1972, it was also Roa who negotiated the anti-hijacking deal with the United States (Suchlicki 1988: 244). He remained central to decision-making bodies, serving on the emerging party's Central Committee and the governing Council of State until 1976, then becoming a vice president of the new National Assembly (ibid.: 244).

**The apostates**

The question of Roa's support for the Revolution and of his past doubts about Communism raises a final consideration in this 'catalogue' of activists in the early decade: the need to consider, briefly, the contribution, role and fleeting importance of those who played significant roles early on, either before 1959 or immediately after the victory, but who then became disenchanted, moving into active opposition. Their initial inclusion and then exclusion also tell us something about the motivations behind the shaping of the 'inner' and 'outer' circles, and behind the notion of 'inclusion'.

Of these, perhaps the most interesting case, standing a little apart from others in this category (since he did not conspire against the Revolution for long but simply left Cuba), is that of Carlos Franqui. In some ways, he is one of the more intriguing of the early leading activists. On the one hand, after joining in 1954 (Llerena 1978: 23), he clearly enjoyed considerable power and authority within the 26 July Movement from 1955 to 1961, being part of the Movement's National Committee in 1955, helping to run the Havana underground and also editing the Movement's newspaper *Aldabonazo* – the original name of the newspaper for its first issue, after which it became *Revolución* (Oltuski 2000: 94) – until he was forced to seek exile in Costa Rica in 1956 (Karol 1970: 40; Thomas 1971: 868). On his return to Cuba, he went to the Sierra in 1957, where he ran both Radio Rebelde and the newspaper *Revolución*, continuing the latter responsibility after 1959 (Martínez Victores 1978). However, his political views have not always been easy to define.

With an evident working-class pedigree (he was the son of a Las Villas peasant), he joined the Communist Party in 1941 and soon became a party organiser (aged twenty); however, he was expelled from the party in 1947 for contravening party policy. He next appeared as one of the plotters for the abortive 1947 Cayo Confites expedition against Trujillo (Karol 1970: 121). Curiously, although he seems to have remained both suspicious of, and disliked by, the PSP, unlike many ex-Communists he was slow to become noticeably anti-Communist and seems not to have shared some activists' growing doubts and complaints about the PSP's rise during the early years; indeed, according to one account (Thomas 1971: 1281), he dissuaded Fernández Font from asking Fidel to publicly oppose Communism.

Yet, equally curiously, few critics of the Revolution have criticised him for remaining relatively silent about the Revolution's leftward shift and collaboration with the PSP. That silence was relative: in 1959–60, *Revolución* often voiced criticisms of the PSP; for example, on 8 March 1959, Roca was criticised for 'seeking to divide the movement' and on 15 May 1959, the PSP was described as 'deviationist' (ibid.: 1219) and 'divisionist' (Scheer and Zeitlin 1964: 116).

In fact, though, despite this relative silence, he did seem to become increasingly disenchanted and, once *Revolución* was merged with *Hoy* in 1965 (to form *Granma*), he then simply left active politics, dedicating himself to developing the arts. He was then eventually given special (albeit unwritten) leave to depart Cuba quietly with his family, almost because of his non-participation in opposition activity inside Cuba and also because of his *Sierra* past. Even outside Cuba, he remained for a while less actively critical of the Revolution than many others: it was as late as 1968 that he publicly condemned Cuba's somewhat conditional support for the Soviet invasion of Czechoslovakia, after which he did indeed start to voice trenchant criticisms and write about his experiences and his negative opinions (Franqui 1976; 1980).

Another in this group was Rolando Cubela (occasionally and confusingly spelled Cubelas, even in Cuban books). Formerly a DR activist, he initially served the new Revolution faithfully, being crucial in the radicalisation of the University of Havana in 1960 (while still serving in the FAR), along with José Puente Blanco (also ex-DR), Angel Quevedo and Omar Fernández, later Minister of Transport (Thomas 1971: 1286). After serving as military attaché in Prague for a while, he then became attaché in Madrid; there he began to cultivate links with a leading exile, Manuel Artime, and, with him, planned to assassinate Fidel. Discovered and tried, he was sentenced to twenty-five years in prison in 1966 (ibid.: 1467). Artime himself (having fought in the Sierra from December 1958) had served briefly under Sorí Marín in the Ministry of Agriculture, but began conspiring from as early as March 1959 (ibid.: 1276) and eventually became part of the Bay of Pigs invasion.

Another activist-turned-early dissident was David Salvador. A former sugar worker and labour activist in Las Villas, he joined the Communist Party (1939–46) but then successively joined both the

Auténticos and Ortodoxos, as well as Aureliano Sánchez Arango's 'Triple A' organisation after 1952. Later, he became the 26 July Movement's national trade union organiser and even, briefly, its national coordinator (ibid.: 872). However, his involvement in the failed general strike of April 1958 (he, together with Faustino Pérez, Ray and two other, more symbolic members – the evangelical minister Fernández Ceballos and a doctor, Eladio Blanco – comprised the strike committee), along with the fact that he openly blamed the failure on what he saw as the PSP's lack of support (even hinting at their sabotage), probably contributed to his subsequent marginalisation, even before he began to take issue with the PSP's increasing role after 1959 and then to conspire against the leadership. In late 1960, he was arrested while trying to escape from Cuba and (in 1962) sentenced to thirty years' imprisonment.

The most complete case in this last group was Manuel Ray himself, who, more than any other person, moved from a powerful post as head of the urban underground during the insurrection to an increasing dissidence, critical of what he saw as creeping Communism and resigning as Minister of Public Works in November 1959 in protest at Matos's arrest (ibid.: 1251). He immediately returned to his former career at the University of Havana, but soon began organising opposition from mid-1960, founding the Movimiento Revolucionario del Pueblo (ibid.: 1276, 1286). He was duly arrested but escaped from prison and Cuba, to join the 'exile' opposition and the planning of the Bay of Pigs invasion, although he immediately broke with the majority of exiles.

Perhaps the saddest case was that of Humberto Sorí Morín. A former Auténtico, he joined the Civic Resistance and eventually made his way to the Sierra, where he became administrator in the rebels' headquarters, the *Comandancia* (ibid.: 1044), but, surprisingly, with the rank of *comandante*. On that basis, he was named Minister of Justice in the new government, and then Minister of Agriculture, theoretically overseeing the agrarian reform. However, by then, he had become increasingly disenchanted with what he saw as the drift to Communism, and had begun to plot with Matos and others while still in his ministerial post. After his resignation (June 1959), he intensified that activity, and then, after leaving for the United States, returned secretly in 1960 and continued to plot. Eventually he was imprisoned and, during the Bay of Pigs invasion, was shot by firing squad. His is perhaps the saddest case of the apostates since, unlike Cubela, Salvador and Ray, who all became active and knowing conspirators while in significant and trusted positions, Sorí Marín seemed to be always marginal to real decision-making, and reacting to, rather than shaping, both events and his own shift in loyalties.

What this last group, however, tells us about the nature of 'inclusion' and 'exclusion' is interesting. For, despite these eventual dissidents' presence in the Sierra at some stage, only Cubela actually took part in the fighting, the others' service as 'guerrillas' being limited to political or administrative duties in the relative safety of the rebels' 'liberated territory'. As a result, they did not quite qualify for the status of 'heroes' to the extent that the majority of the ex-guerrillas subsequently did, and their arrival in the Sierra was also relatively late. In this sense, most were actually considered more part of the *Llano* than the *Sierra*. Yet, Franqui apart, what they all had in common was their readiness to conspire actively and, in some cases, to take up arms against the Revolution, thus being seen as 'traitors' to the growing sense of 'revolutionary togetherness' that the process engendered. Even a 'hardened' ex-guerrilla such as Cubela was therefore eventually deemed beyond the pale. Even so, it is interesting that, firstly, only Sorí Marín was actually executed (and that seemed to be more of an exemplary retaliation for the Playa Girón invasion) – the others who remained in Cuba serving long-term prison sentences – and, secondly, that they were treated more harshly than Escalante, who had also clearly conspired against the leadership and the whole ex-guerrilla rebel movement. In the latter case, of course, three things weighed in his favour: firstly, he had not taken up arms or even threatened to do so; secondly, he was not an apostate to the same extent as the others (who had 'sinned' more than he had by betraying their recent heritage and the shared and perceived heroism of the struggle); thirdly, realpolitik determined that executing a PSP member was perhaps at that stage a step too far, while the full and trusting cooperation of both the PSP and the Soviet Union was required. Indeed, Escalante was only eventually imprisoned when he ignored that leniency and, when post-1960 Cuban–Soviet relations were at an all-time low, he proceeded to conspire actively again.

**Inner and outer circles**

What this detailed discussion tells us, as it traces the formation of, and changes within, the 'inner', 'intermediate' and 'outer' circles during the months of intense and rapid transformation of 1959–62, is that, while the 'core' of the circles remained largely unchanged (with the death of Cienfuegos perhaps removing one protagonist from that core), the other circles responded dramatically to the changing context. For, as the process of revolution deepened and accelerated, and the resulting tensions and differences both shaped and, in turn, were shaped by the definitions of the process, these developments all changed the personnel in, and people's claims to belong to, any of the three circles. Most significantly, it was the ex-PSP activists who made their way steadily into all three circles, until the crisis point of March 1962 was reached, after which only Rodríguez and Roca remained, probably conditionally and for pragmatic reasons, inside or on the edge of the new 'inner circle'. Equally, some members of, or people close to, the 1958 'inner circle' found themselves marginalised, demoted or expelled, depending on the extent of their opposition to, or doubts about, both the radicalisation and the pre-1962 collaboration with the PSP, and also, of course, depending on what they actually did to manifest that opposition. But even some of the silent but loyal participants at the top found themselves occasionally on the edge of the 'inner circle' at best, due to not having shared either the Moncada, *Granma* or Sierra experiences, or because of their association with the increasingly suspect *Llano*.

That, however, would change for some of them, as the following years saw an intensification of the ex-guerrillas' hegemony within the Revolution, but also of the distrust between the 26 July Movement and the PSP; hence, some of those 'on the edge' would soon find themselves brought back into the fold, as an expression of the new 'Cuban' Communism that resulted after 1962.

# 4 | THE YEARS OF 'REVOLUTIONARY' FLUX: 1963–75

Several factors separated the 1959–62 period from the radical years that followed. Not only was the direction of the Revolution after January 1963 much clearer (following the defining moments of Playa Girón, the 'Escalante affair' and the Missile Crisis), with the ex-guerrillas' vision and personnel firmly in control, but also the mood and nature of the evolving revolutionary state were noticeably different. On the former, instead of the euphoria and confusion of the early months, the next twelve years were characterised by a growing mood of defiance, determination, defensiveness and enforced togetherness, faced with the reality of isolation, siege and mass emigration, but with a deliberate acceleration of the process of change. It was this mood and those imperatives that helped to redefine the three circles of influence, with the 1959 criteria of trust (Moncada, *Granma* and *Sierra*) becoming once again paramount, but, this time, with the *Llano* back in favour and generally preferred to the (by now much less trusted) ex-PSP activists.

In fact, that message was clearly sent in 1963 to both the PSP and Moscow, arising less from the Escalante affair than from the fallout from the Missile Crisis, after which both the PSP and Moscow were tarred with the same brush of unreliability and insufficient revolutionary commitment, in the ex-guerrillas' eyes. In April and May 1963, the first post-Crisis Cuban delegation to Moscow included only one PSP member, Rodríguez (as we have seen, always the closest in the PSP to the guerrilla rebels), but included many from the formerly 'suspect' *Llano* contingent, as though to make a point to both Moscow and the PSP about their greater reliability. For example, Faustino Pérez and Fernández Font were included, as was Ameijeiras, almost 'brought out of oblivion' to make that point (Karol 1970: 284). Pérez then went on to be named Minister of Hydroelectric Works in 1967, a sign of trust.

**The changing state**

However, while individuals (and their history and qualifications) had counted for much in 1959–62, the changing nature of the state now made them less significant than before and less significant than groups now were. This was essentially because a state of some sort was beginning to emerge, although the nature of the state was still contested, liable to change and often undermined by the ethos that increasingly reigned within the leadership group, not least the spirit of 'anti-institutionalism' that grew up rapidly in response to the perceived PSP 'threat' of March 1962, reflecting a fear that institutionalisation might create a vehicle for another attempted 'coup'. This emergence of the new state really occurred at two different levels and in different ways.

At the top, in response to Girón and the Missile Crisis, a structure of defence and security had rapidly been constructed, based on Cienfuegos's early efforts but then enhanced under both Raúl and Valdés; hence, a 'manager' state might still be inchoate, with ministries still being poorly formed, treated marginally or acting like 'permissive spaces' (not least during the 'Great Debate'), but a powerful 'defender' state of some sort was now visible. Meanwhile, at the bottom, local activism and the emerging mass organisations had steadily constructed grass-roots networks and structures of participation, supply, socialisation and mobilisation. Thus, by 1963, 'the state' was familiar enough to most Cubans: at one level, it either meant 'benefactor' or 'defender' (of social gains and sovereignty) or, to those who contested or feared the Revolution's direction, it meant repression and control; at another level, it meant that the systems of social involvement and delivery on which the reforms depended and through which popular support was channelled worked well, bringing a sense of loyalty to those mechanisms.

Crucially, however, it was at the intermediate levels that a state was much less visible, more fluid and ultimately still subject to challenging and confusing change. That included the emerging systems of political involvement, other than the growing network of CDRs. In fact, one thing that separated 1959–62 and the following years in this respect was the character of the planned, united 'single party' for which the ORI had been preparing; for the whole Escalante affair had created real fears in the 26 July Movement about the wisdom of continuing with that party, and certainly about giving it any clear power.

In that sense, the issue about the 'affair' had been one of control and leadership, rather than of ideological or political definition. Indeed, this was soon confirmed, as the ORI was replaced late in 1962 by the promised United Party of the Cuban Socialist Revolution (PURSC). Interestingly, this party's national committee more or less repeated Escalante's contentious National Directorate. It counted eleven ex-PSP members, but also only twelve, and not the earlier planned fourteen, from the 26 July Movement, and included only one DR member (Thomas 1971: 1454). However, crucially, the eleven in the PSP contingent included several who were known to be more favourable to the 26 July position than Escalante had been, and others whose loyalty was not in doubt. Hence, although the overall composition might look like a retreat from the post-Escalante stance or, alternatively, as though it confirmed 'creeping Communism', in fact it confirmed two other things. Those were, firstly, the unquestioned leadership of the process by the 26 July leaders, and, secondly, the more radical direction now being followed.

### The new radicalism

That radical direction was evident from the outset, and, indeed, had already been signalled in 1962. That was the start of the so-called 'Great Debate', stimulated by a severe economic crisis in 1962–63. Although that crisis could be attributed to a conjuncture of several factors – the disruption of the Cuban economy's long-standing links (supply, markets, investment) with the US economy, the costs of the massive social revolution under way (exacerbated by the rapid loss of the professionally trained middle class, with the resulting expense of replacement), the inability of the private sector to play its part in the UN ECLA-style mixed economy of 1959–61, and overambitious and unrealistic economic plans from 1961 – it provided enough food for thought to generate a reassessment. This was coupled with a sense of anger and mistrust about the advice emanating from both the PSP and the Soviet Union (following the 1962 internal and external political crises), which instinctively guided the leadership away from those formerly attractive and easily understood models.

A range of orthodox and unorthodox leftist economists and

socialist thinkers, from Cuba and the outside world, was therefore invited to engage in an open public debate in the pages of specialist or often somewhat obscure theoretical journals about the question of whether an underdeveloped economy such as Cuba's could, or should, seek to achieve socialism, rather than (as Moscow preferred) settle for the state-led capitalist development that Cuba's supposedly semi-feudal economic character, according to an orthodox reading of Marxist theory, demanded. As this very peculiar debate coincided with a steady rethink in what was emerging as the 'New Left' in the United States and Western Europe, the time was right to capture some of that novelty of thinking and put it to use in Cuba; certainly, once the so-called 'school' of dependency theory began to emerge in Latin America and bases such as *Monthly Review* from the mid-1960s (with its questioning of the basic premise about the region's 'feudalism'), it resonated well with the outcome of the debate in Cuba.

On one side of the debate was Guevara, most eloquently and passionately taking the lead in arguing for the desirability and possibility of achieving communism in Cuba, without passing through the 'necessary' stages of late capitalism and socialism; in this he was supported by many on the unorthodox 'New Left'. Ranged against him was an array of orthodox Communists (led, in Cuba, by Carlos Rafael Rodríguez), but also less Marxist economists, whose vision of a socialist economy assumed a slower pace of change and a need for Cuba to specialise, not least in its 'comparative advantage' of sugar (rather than going down Guevara's preferred road of rapid industrialisation in a state-controlled system). The latter group included the Cubans Alberto Mora and Fernández Font, as well as the Belgian Charles Bettelheim (Martínez Heredia 1989; 2010).

The outcome, as already observed, was something of a compromise, but what became known outside Cuba as the 'moral economy' (because it argued for moral, i.e. non-material, incentives for the workforce as a means of escaping the vicious circle of capitalist consciousness) began in earnest from about 1966. This stressed voluntarism, mass labour mobilisation and ideological commitment rather than material rewards (which were unavailable anyway, as a result of the US embargo and COMECON's persistent refusal to allow Cuban membership), and reached a peak in the March 1968 'Revolutionary Offensive', which, most spectacularly, nationalised all the remaining non-agricultural enterprises in Cuba (approximately 55,000 of them) – this was essentially all self-employed artisan, services and retailing activity. The real culmination was supposed to be the new, ambitious target of harvesting 10 million tonnes of sugar in 1970 (Cuba's previous record harvest having been around 7 million tonnes). Designed to be the boost to end Cuba's enslaving dependence on sugar exports, generating capital to invest in a more industrial future, free of debts to the Soviet Union, this drive was stymied from the start by inefficiency and a dangerous lack of infrastructure, machinery, oil and capital. It therefore failed: despite famously producing a record crop of around 8.5 million tonnes, it almost destroyed the rest of the economy and the system as it took a costly toll.

Politically, the new radicalism was visible in a domestic resistance to institutionalisation and an external commitment to supporting revolution in the Third World and carving out a position separate from both superpowers. The anti-institutionalism that developed arose partly from a nervousness about the vulnerability (to another attempted takeover) of a monolithic structure, partly from a growing distaste for a Soviet-style bureaucratisation – indeed, there was a sustained anti-bureaucracy campaign during this period – and partly from a faith in the power of mobilisation. The latter was one conclusion that was undoubtedly drawn from the astonishing success of the 1961 literacy campaign, but it also reflected the whole emphasis on the power of 'subjective' conditions to overcome objective ones, driven in part by Guevara's theoretical position but also by many of the rebels' Sierra experience and their resulting instinctive preference for action over words.

One outcome of this was the curious matter of the single party that eventually emerged in 1965 from the ashes of the scheduled PURSC. While its name – the Cuban Communist Party – seemed to locate the Cuban version of Communism firmly in the Soviet camp, in fact it did precisely the opposite; for, while the ruling parties of the Bloc, apart from the Soviet Union's, had to give other names to their parties (United Workers' Party, Socialist Unity Party, and so on) rather than Communist Party, since they were only supposedly 'people's democracies', on the way to communism, the Cubans decided to flout that convention and reinforce the point made during the Great

Debate. Even then, however, this new party was totally dominated by the ex-guerrillas, the so-called 'new communists', leaving the ex-PSP in the cold to a large extent. Moreover, despite being created in 1965, the party did not hold a National Congress until 1975, thus perpetuating an existence on only two levels: the broad leadership (the Central Committee and so on) and the grass-roots *núcleos*, with little in between. Despite appearances, therefore, the new Cuban system bore little similarity to the Socialist Bloc.

Abroad, though, the Cuban challenge to the Soviet Union was even greater, for the Cuban government now used the space and pretext provided by the outcome of the Missile Crisis – which had guaranteed freedom from US invasion but also revealed the limits of active Soviet support and reliability – to embark on a policy of active protagonism in the newly emerging 'Third World'. This meant courting new independent governments in Africa and Asia and their growing international organisation, the Non-Aligned Movement (NAM), but also building links with anti-colonial rebels in existing colonies. Hence, close links were built with countries such as Algeria and Vietnam, but also steadily with India and other leaders of the NAM.

But it was in Latin America where the new strategy really flourished. Guided by Guevara's ideas and essentially announced by Fidel's January 1962 Declaration of Havana, but also working through a special unit within the Ministry of the Interior, the Cuban government took the policy to new levels of activism by encouraging armed revolution throughout the continent, most of which, after all (except for Mexico and Canada), had decided in early 1962 to exclude Cuba, participate in the US embargo and seek the end of the Revolution. Therefore, for most of the 1960s, Cuba became the place where scores of guerrilla groups from throughout the region were trained, funded and armed, all following Guevara's ideas (especially based in the countryside) and most of them challenging the supremacy on the left of the established Communist Parties. Indeed, the new strategy, while directed against 'US imperialism' and following an explicitly anti-imperialist agenda, was also a direct challenge both to Soviet ideas of peaceful coexistence with the United States and to the Soviet reliance on words (of support) rather than actions. Thus, when the Soviet-organised Tricontinental Conference was held in Havana in 1966 (to attract Third World radicals to Moscow's leadership, rather than China's), the Cuban hegemony was evident in the conference's public slogan, which was a clear dismissal of the Soviet position: 'The duty of the revolutionary is to make the revolution.'

That strategy, of course, produced few immediate results, apart from the death of Guevara in 1967, the rise of a militarism that talked of long-term militarisation to defeat the guerrilla threat, and the shift from a rural-based phase to a newer concept of urban guerrilla warfare. The reasons were clear: the inapplicability of Guevara's ideas, the greater preparedness of both the United States and the newly US-retrained armed forces, the reluctance of the Communist Parties to become involved, denying the guerrillas vital urban support networks, and the inexperience of many of the would-be guerrillas. Longer-term outcomes were, however, different: not only did many such groups survive, to recover and emerge more successfully (for example the Nicaraguan Sandinistas) or more visibly (in Central America, Colombia and Peru) in the 1970s and 1980s, but also a generation of new leftists was created, eventually becoming the core of the 'pink tide' of the 1990s and 2000s. But the strategy had another value: it created a new foreign policy that reaped dividends later (in terms of sympathy, recognition and support) through the 1970s policy of 'internationalism', reinforcing the togetherness and militant ethos of the 'embattled enclave' and establishing a clear distance from both superpowers.

The first seven years of this period were therefore far from predictable but clearly followed a new pattern of action and thinking, and a new direction, guided by an ethos that had been hinted at in 1959 but distracted in 1960–62. This was shown by the character of the new party in 1965 (in the midst of the falling-out with Moscow): the nine-person ruling Political Bureau contained no PSP members at all, consisting of the two Castros, Guevara, Valdés, Almeida, Hart, García, Del Valle and Dorticós (Thomas 1971: 1454). The larger (but less powerful) Central Committee showed more PSP influence: PSP members in this body were Roca, Rodríguez, Acosta, Severo Aguirre, Bravo, Calcines, Joel Domenech, Fabio Grobart, Secundino Guerra, Luzardo, Isidoro Malmierca (a former PSP member and ex-head of the JS who became part of the new security apparatus and then first editor of *Granma* in 1965), Marinello, Miguel Martín, José Matar Franye, Milián, Peña, José Ramírez, Ursinio Rojas, Clementina Serra and Lionel Soto (ibid.: 1454). Certainly, there were more PSP representatives than the fourteen veterans of the Moncada or the *Granma* landing (ibid.: 1455) or the DR's four – Chomón, Abrantes, García Oliveras and Naranjo Morales (ibid.: 1455) – however, the PSP still numbered only twenty, compared with sixty-four from the 26 July Movement (ibid.: 1454).

In fact, from 1962 to at least 1968, relations between the PSP and 26 July/DR remained strained, the former being essentially 'on probation'; indeed, after 1962, Roca was content to argue that Escalante (who had once, before 1959, been powerful enough to replace him as general secretary of the party during Roca's absence in the Soviet Union, for medical treatment) had used his control of the party to build up a base (Batlle Reyes 2008: 99). Meanwhile, this was all complicated by the emerging Sino–Soviet split, with Roca and others remaining predictably loyal to Moscow, but with Guevara (and possibly the PSP's Rodríguez) being much more openly sympathetic to Mao and the Chinese model (Thomas 1971: 1315). The terms of that 'probation' were acted upon in 1968, when Escalante was again condemned publicly.

Having returned to Cuba in 1964, and been given the deliberately demeaning post of farm administrator (ibid.: 1468), Escalante had proceeded to conspire with other ex-PSP people (like him, disaffected by their subordination to the ex-guerrillas). These were especially Matar and Calcines, but also thirty-four others, all later accused of being actively opposed to Cuba's Latin American policy and the 'moral economy', of considering Fidel mad and uncontrollable (and therefore appropriate to be removed), and of passing documents to the Soviet Union. This was his 'sin', of forming a 'micro-faction', for which he now stood trial, being condemned to fifteen years. Revealingly, the fallout from this latest scandal was considerable: forty-three people were arrested, of whom thirty-five were eventually sentenced and imprisoned, nine were expelled from the party, and two people resigned from the Party Central Committee (Domínguez 1978: 162).

### The new inner circle

*Veterans of the Second Front* At this stage, in examining the nature of the new 'inner circle', it is interesting to note that the Sierra del Cristal veterans tended to enjoy a special place in the new structures and policies. It is interesting because one common way of characterising the post-1961 Soviet–Cuban relationship was to attribute the closeness of those links to Raúl, as well as to the PSP. However, during a period when former PSP members were clearly out of favour and when it seemed that the ideas that held most sway were Fidel's preference for mobilisation, an insurrectionary foreign policy and Guevara's views, those associated with Raúl before 1959 were clearly in positions of authority. This, therefore, is a useful reminder of the need to avoid readings of 'factions' and assuming any Fidel–Raúl split or tension; the influence of the ex-Cristal people actually corresponded to the more radical positions that they had long adopted and that the whole process was now espousing.

One of the most prominent of the Sierra del Cristal veterans was Ramiro Valdés. Having been closely associated with the creation and development of Cuba's new security operation, it was logical to find him appointed Minister of the Interior. In that position, he became the single most important Cuban in the formation and control of all of the internal intelligence services, at a time when the 'siege' was at its most intense and the mood of defensiveness most powerful. It was that mood that created the notorious UMAP 're-education camps' of 1965–68, which, it is often alleged, were set up at his behest (although there is no conclusive evidence of that). Although the camps continued to exist after 1968, they were no longer punitive and were geared more towards mobilising the labour of young Cubans, associated with the new Youth Labour Army (EJT). In either 1968 or 1969 (Suchlicki 1988: 288), Valdés lost that post; whatever the precise date, either this may possibly have been connected with the 1968 'micro-faction' affair or, more credibly, it was because of Valdés's perceived proximity to the Soviet Union. Both, however, are pure speculation: with regard to the former possibility, Valdés was never associated with Escalante (and, given his loyalty to the *Sierra* group and to Fidel, was never likely to conspire against the leadership); and, on the second point, he remained firmly in the 'Cuban' rather than 'Soviet' camp. The chances are, in fact, that neither was true, not least since in 1970–71 he became Deputy Minister of Defence, directly under Raúl (ibid.: 288), and responsible for the 'Construction Sector', and then, from 1972 to 1976, he was Deputy Prime Minister (ibid.: 288).

Whatever the case, it is clear from his presence at so many crucial meetings, from his official posts and from his survival that Valdés was always at the centre of important discussions, wielding considerable influence throughout those radical years. It is also clear that his talents were appreciated by those around him.

Two other veterans of the Second Front now also came into their own: Jorge Risquet and Manuel Piñeiro. Risquet had been a PSP member at some time between the late 1940s and the 1950s, according to one account (ibid.: 241), but, in most other accounts, he still belonged to the party in the late 1950s; however, he joined the rebels in the Sierra 'in the late 1950s' (ibid.: 241) as part of Raúl's Second Front. There, Raúl eventually gave him a key role, in charge of political education in the Sierra del Cristal (ibid.: 241; Thomas 1971: 1431); this indicated a high level of trust – and, according to some (probably exaggerated) versions, ensured ideological uniformity in the group (Szulc 1986: 358). In 1959, as a *capitán*, he then became head of the Department of Culture in Santiago, which effectively meant that he had responsibility for education in the whole of Oriente. In 1967, he went on to become Minister of Labour; in that post, he showed real drive and some considerable autonomy in the fight against bureaucracy, in the drive to bring women into the labour force, in rationalising the distribution of labour in favour of agriculture, and in labour reforms seeking to give workers a greater say in workplace-level decisions (Suchlicki 1988: 241–2). Eventually, he was the main person responsible for the notorious 'anti-loafing' law of 1971 (ibid.: 242), which effectively criminalised wanton unemployment.

Piñeiro (better known as 'Barbarroja' or 'Redbeard') had previously studied in the United States, at Columbia University, until mid-1953, when he returned to Cuba, joining firstly the DR and then, in 1957, the 26 July Movement. He became the Movement's organiser in Matanzas, until he finally joined the Sierra rebels in June 1957 (ibid.: 218), eventually becoming *comandante* under Raúl. In January 1959, he was given control of the Moncada barracks and then overall military command of Oriente province (ibid.: 219), a position from which he exercised what was called 'revolutionary justice', i.e. with some ruthlessness (ibid.: 219), but his willingness to work with the local PSP led to a certain amount of tension with some rebels in Oriente. In mid-1959, he was moved to Havana, where he became part of the FAR General Staff, but then, in March 1960, he was named Deputy

Chief of Security Police (Thomas 1971: 1273), effectively becoming Valdés's second in command in what emerged as the G2 organisation.

In fact, as a key player in the Ministry of the Interior, he seems to have had responsibility for counter-subversion; in 1961, he became head of the externally focused DGI security forces (Suchlicki 1988: 219), responsible for foreign intelligence. It was from that position that he achieved notoriety, becoming crucial to Cuba's whole Latin American strategy from 1962 (after Cuba's expulsion from the OAS, which really launched the new strategy in earnest) until 1968, directing a 'Liberation Department' under the Deputy Minister's office of MININT (Anderson 1997: 533, 759).

It seems that, after 1968, he encountered some difficulties because of the failure of the guerrilla strategy and also because of Soviet pressure to control the DGI's overseas activities. However, probably as a reflection of the Cuban leadership's determination to continue the Latin American fight regardless of Moscow's qualms, these insurrectionary projects were then moved to a new Department of the Americas of the Communist Party's Central Committee, therefore remaining protected and under the leadership's close control (Suchlicki 1988: 219).

While others who shared these activists' Second Front past did not achieve these heights or centrality to decision-making, that past clearly stood them in good stead, as they tended to be used, as loyal and reliable servants, in administrative but also politically significant roles. Jorge Serguera, for example (having acted as a lawyer for some of the *Granma* survivors), became one of the judges at the January 1959 Santiago trials of known *batistianos*, and then, as Judge Advocate of the army, he tried and sentenced Huber Matos. After a stint as a military commander in Matanzas, and then a brief sojourn as Cuban ambassador in Algeria (Thomas 1971: 1255), Serguera was finally given the crucial post of running Cuba's radio and television in 1968, directly answerable to the Party Central Committee and ensuring that those key media remained faithful to the 'party line'. Alongside him, eventually, was Jorge Enrique Mendoza, an ex-Ortodoxo law student who became a reader on Radio Rebelde in the Sierra and then a captain in the guerrilla forces (Martínez Victores 1978); in July 1959, he was appointed head of INRA in Oriente province and then occupied a similar post in Camagüey (specifically in order to overrule Matos's anti-PSP delaying tactics in the province). Finally, in 1967, he became editor of the new unified party newspaper, *Granma* (Thomas 1971: 1241).

*Other 26 July Movement players* However, political influence was not limited to the Second Front veterans, for many of those associated generally with the guerrilla experience, regardless of where they served, continued to enjoy access to decision-making circles or, in some cases, began to do so. Among those who had already been influential in the early years was Pedro Miret. For, whatever doubts there may have been about his commitment to the form of the steady radicalisation before, he was now clearly part of the inner circles of power, being named a member of the new party's Central Committee in 1965. In 1966, he became a Deputy Minister of MINFAR (the Defence Ministry), and from 1969 to 1973 he was Minister of Mines and Metallurgy, then going on to be Deputy Minister of Basic Industries (Suchlicki 1988: 189). More significantly, throughout the following period (the one usually associated with the rehabilitation of the old PSP people and great proximity to the Soviet Union), he remained clearly central to decision-making, being a member of the party's Secretariat and Political Bureau from 1975, and also of the newly created Council of State (ibid.: 189) as one of its vice presidents. Hence, any previous doubts about his attitude to the PSP and Moscow did not seem to prevent this centrality, confirming the continuing primacy of the previous badges of influence.

A similar pattern was seen with Dorticós, who clearly enjoyed real influence during this period; for example, while still serving as President, he was also given responsibility for the Ministry of the Economy (1964–76, taking over from the politically 'suspect' Regino Boti) and also, even more significantly, for the planning agency JUCEPLAN (ibid.: 92). Then, like Miret, even during the supposedly 'Sovietised' years after 1975, he remained of some, if somewhat re-duced, importance. With the change in institutional structures after 1975–76, including the creation of the People's Power electoral system, he was replaced as President (formally, of the Council of State) by Fidel Castro, but he remained one of the Council's and Cuba's vice presidents. Later, in 1980, he became Minister of Justice, a post in which he remained until his death by suicide in 1983.

Marcelo Fernández Font was, as we have seen, of direct significance during this period, not least because of his participation,
against Guevara's arguments, in the 1962–65 Great Debate. Whatever
doubts he may have entertained about the increasingly radical direction of the Revolution in 1959–62, he nonetheless sided with the PSP's
more orthodox arguments in the debate. Moreover – doubts aside,
even during that debate – he succeeded Guevara as President of the
National Bank (1963–64), clearly therefore remaining a trusted figure.
This apparent contradiction in his political position led one historian
to see him as either excessively loyal to Fidel or simply an opportunist (Thomas 1971: 1281), although Thomas went on to admit that
what he called Fernández Font's long-established 'anti-Americanism'
(i.e. Cuban nationalism) was powerful, and probably influenced his
willingness to cooperate with the radicalisation, despite any doubts
he may have had. That does indeed seem to make some sense, since
Thomas's account (typical of many in the first decade or so of the
Revolution) reflected the common tendency to focus so much on
the role of, and attitudes to, the PSP that the underlying nationalist
impetus of the process, and thus of participants' commitment to
it, was neglected. There seems little doubt that Fernández Font's
personal loyalty to Fidel may well have been simply part of a wider
loyalty to 'the Revolution', as a nationalist project. Interestingly,
despite his membership of the 'losing' side in the Great Debate, he
became Minister of Foreign Trade in 1964 (taking over from Alberto
Mora, another in that camp), holding the post until 1980, when
he was finally succeeded by another long-serving minister, Ricardo
Cabrisas (until 2000).

During this more radical period, it was not only the 'old' and
trusted combatants who rose to, or continued to enjoy, positions of
influence. José Llanusa Gobel had, before 1959, remained a largely
unnoticed member of the 26 July Movement in the United States
(until, in early January, he flew to the Sierra with Haydée Santamaría); in fact, he was much better known as a sportsman, being a
member of Cuba's national basketball team in the 1940s and 1950s
(and even competing in the 1948 London Olympics). Yet, curiously,
on 1 January, he was named the new mayor of Havana (albeit with
the new title of 'Commissioner'). He kept that position until 1961,
when his background led to him becoming president of the new

Cuban sports institute, INDER, where he oversaw Cuba's rapid (and ideologically driven) shift from professional sport to amateurism, which also, in the process, established the basis for Cuba's subsequent, and very successful, push for sporting excellence from the 1970s. However, his position was strengthened considerably, as, in 1965, he succeeded Hart as Minister of Education (until 1970), also being named as a member of the party's first Central Committee and even being described as one of Fidel's closest collaborators in the late 1960s (Karol 1970: 382). Interestingly, in 1968, as Minister of Education, he chaired the highly heterodox 1968 Havana Cultural Congress (ibid.: 382).

*The PSP survivors* Of course, since this period was characterised by the undercurrents and resentments created by the 1962 differences with the PSP and Moscow, the really interesting survivors within any of the circles of power were those connected to the PSP. In this respect, not only did Carlos Rafael Rodríguez's own personal position seem unaffected by the fallout from those episodes (although, being editor of *Hoy* from 1961, he was decidedly identified with the PSP), but, as with Fernández Font, it did not prevent him from adopting a very open opposition to Guevara's arguments during the Great Debate. This was almost certainly because of the ex-guerrillas' residual respect for his continually emollient and conciliatory attitude to the 26 July Movement and Fidel's position, but also due to his hitherto sympathetic attitude to the guerrilla strategy. In fact, during all the 1962 arguments and crises, he remained trusted by the ex-guerrillas, being therefore a vital link between Havana and Moscow and also a key conduit for repairing the damage of the Escalante affair of that year. In all, throughout the confusing 1960s, he remained a reliable member of the leadership, one of only two PSP leaders within the 'inner circle' of the new post-1965 party. The others in the old PSP leadership, however, continued to remain on the edge of power and influence until the 1970s.

Therefore, what this account of the different personalities of 1953–75 tells us is a good deal about the patterns that were emerging, and continually developing, inside the Revolution's groups of activists and public or political actors. For this period, in particular, showed patterns of 'inclusion' and 'exclusion' of individuals emerging more clearly, enabling us at this stage to develop something of an initial typology of groupings of those individuals, based on the idea of concentric circles of power, influence and respect; in other words, we can now start to put flesh on the bones of the already repeatedly mentioned 'inner circles'.

As we have seen, from 1958, all the evidence pointed to the existence of a fairly solid, definable and largely unchanging 'inner circle', those who – quite apart from Fidel, Raúl and Che Guevara – were most powerful and even to some extent autonomous, closest always to real decision-making, and clearly exercising some influence on those around them, on decisions, and even on the process's direction and policies. What still largely qualified them for inclusion in this 'circle' was their personal history of involvement or association with all three 'historic' episodes – the Moncada (or Bayamo) attack, the *Granma* expedition, and the guerrilla struggle in the Sierra, preferably from late 1956 – or at least with any two of them. In fact, there may even have been something of an internal hierarchy, distinguishing three-episode stalwarts from two-episode veterans, although there is no evidence of punitive treatment for anyone lacking the 'third'.

What characterised these people was the unquestioning trust that those around them and the leading three continued to have in them: they were always seen as politically reliable, were known to be loyal (to 'the group', forged during the insurrection itself, and therefore also implicitly to the essential idea of 'the Revolution'), and had been 'steeled' in the Revolution's battles. They also acted with considerable authority and autonomy in their chosen area or, indeed, in several areas, and their judgement was always trusted and their advice often sought. The members of this circle were obvious: people such as Camilo Cienfuegos (early on), Valdés, Celia Sánchez, Espín, Miret and perhaps (though that was debatable for the first period) Hart.

### The intermediate and outer circles

Outside this 'inner' sanctum was what we might call an 'intermediate circle', which then, at the end of the 1960s and in the early 1970s, was the home of two classes of activist. Firstly, it included those whose 'historic' claim to 'revolutionary' status was based on only one of the three historic episodes (typically service in the Sierra, or in the march west in late 1958). Secondly, it included former members of both the PSP and the DR who could boast a proven record of loyalty, faith in the 'mission' of the 26 July Movement and rebellion – which was always the core of the Revolution's 'idea' – and who had demonstrated reliability, effectiveness (if not efficiency) and flexibility as political actors.

These people were seen by those above them in the hierarchy as every bit as reliable as the 'inner circle' but not as authoritative (they tended to have narrower responsibilities, albeit ones where they could often exercise considerable autonomy) and rarely was their advice sought, except in very specific and specialist areas. Unlike those above them, for whom the question of forgiveness never arose, these people's past qualified them to be easily forgiven later, in the event of their incompetence in office or even for any doubts expressed privately about the Revolution's post-1959 direction (not least the growing proximity to the PSP), although they were never forgiven for outright opposition and conspiracy, which were the greatest 'sins' of all. However, Escalante's membership of this circle was demonstrated by the remarkable tolerance shown to him after 1962, when he was not cast into the 'outer darkness' (until he became seen, after 1968, as a 'serial offender') but rather was consigned to a period of supposedly reflective temporary banishment.

Hence, as we will see later, those who lived for several decades more, and remained politically active (or at least prominent, even if their actual activism was increasingly rhetorical or symbolic), were rewarded for their loyalty and faithfulness by being permanently kept 'inside' the circles, if not necessarily still part of the 'inner circle'. Indeed, examining the membership of the National Assembly of 2013 and even the party's Central Committee of 2011, we can find some of those people (now well into their seventies and eighties and long since ceasing to be politically active) still playing a formal role, theoretically at the 'centre' of political life.

This intermediate circle included people such as the honoured 'veterans' Melba Hernández, Guillermo García, Haydée Santamaría, Montané, Ameijeiras, Piñeiro, Chomón and Bravo, but also included *Llano* veterans such as Franqui (until around 1962), Faustino Pérez, Oltuski, Fernández Font, Dorticós and Hart. Then there were the ex-PSP contingent: Rodríguez (who occasionally was let into the 'inner circle' but always provisionally and conditionally), Roca, (briefly)

Aníbal Escalante, Núñez Jiménez and Alfredo Guevara. It also included the special case of Roa.

Finally, authority in the collective leadership of the period was also visible in what we therefore call the 'outer circle'. This comprised those with some historical proof of loyalty to the 'mission', usually based on their (probably brief) membership of the pre-1959 guerrillas or second-rank but reliable and adaptable protagonism in the *Llano*, or because they were trustworthy 'recruits' to the struggle immediately, or soon, after the victory of January 1959 (mostly ex-PSP at levels below the main leaders). These people rarely exercised real power at the 'centre', but rather wielded it in very small spaces where they could indeed be very powerful. They were seen more as high-profile 'subaltern officers', eminently usable (and trusted to get on with the job without close control or invigilation), and, in fact, could be rested when their immediate tasks were completed (or when they had blotted their copybook in some form or another), but were assumed to be available to be called upon when needed, in different circumstances. They too could be forgiven for misdemeanours or incompetence, but only up to a point, never quite enjoying the leeway of those in the 'intermediate circle'.

The cast in this circle is vast, consisting of the many individuals who crossed the national stage at some point in the confusing early 1960s, i.e. people such as Joel Iglesias, Serguera, Soto, García Buchaca and even Peña (although it is arguable that his power base in the CTC qualified him for 'intermediate circle' status, albeit that he displayed little authority beyond that field, and died in 1973).

This pattern of 'inclusion' only ever applied to questions of leadership, power or influence. However, it did have much wider implications for the long-term interpretations of 'loyalty' within the system, since it was premised on the underlying and overwhelming importance of 'loyalty' – to the 'the group', 'the Revolution' and the 'nation' – which overrode any number of failings, sins and doubts. This will be discussed further in Chapter 6.

## 5 | THE STABLE YEARS: SYSTEMS, INSTITUTIONS AND BUREAUCRATS: 1975–86

### Contested institutionalisation

Most histories of the Revolution tend to label the post-1970 years as the years of either 'institutionalisation' or 'Sovietisation'. The former follows both Mesa-Lago (1974) and also the Cubans' own eventual designation; the latter is based on the fact that, following the disastrous sugar harvest of 1970 and the reassessment that followed, Cuba finally (after having asked to join in the early 1960s and been refused) was accepted into COMECON in 1972, and then, from 1975, began to adopt Soviet-style political structures. This included, in 1975, the final convoking of the new (post-1965) party's First Congress; the adoption in 1975 of a more orthodox and Moscow-approved economic strategy, under Carlos Rafael Rodríguez and Humberto Pérez González, the 'losers' of the 1962–65 Great Debate; and, in 1976, an apparent copy of the Soviet Union's pyramid electoral structure (with indirect election of a twice-yearly National Assembly) in the People's Power system.

This interpretation is not totally inaccurate: COMECON entry did in fact mean that Moscow considered that Cuba's economic policies were no longer as maverick and heretical as they had been in the era of the 'moral economy'. In addition, the ex-PSP dominance of that strategy confirmed something of a shift internally, towards Moscow's and the former PSP's preferences and away from the ideas of the 1960s – indeed, People's Power was substantially modelled on the Soviet system. Nonetheless, it is also misleading, glossing over some significant differences between the new Cuban orthodoxy and the supposed models, differences that suggest that 'Sovietisation' was not always more than skin-deep (Fitzgerald 1988).

For one thing, the conventional reading tends to overlook the gap between the crisis (1970) and the First Congress and the start of the new electoral system (1975–76), and usually even takes the turning point back as far as 1968, when Fidel's apparent endorsement of the Soviet Bloc's invasion of Czechoslovakia was seen as emanating from a new subservience to Soviet wishes. However, that misreads the complex set of considerations that actually motivated the Cuban position in 1968, not least since that year saw a low point in Soviet–Cuban disagreements over the need for armed revolution in Latin America, with public criticism of the Venezuelan Communist Party for its un-revolutionary position and suggestions that the Bolivian Communists' failure to support the guerrillas there had partly contributed to the death of Guevara. In fact, not only did Fidel's endorsement of the invasion include an oblique and tongue-in-cheek hope that the Soviet Union would also intervene to prevent any Cuban movement towards capitalism (thus implicitly criticising the Soviet climbdown in October 1962 when it did indeed have that chance), but Fidel's view on the Czech reforms was actually fully consistent with his global position at that time. This was because, if the Soviet Union was being criticised by Havana for being insufficiently revolutionary in the global struggle against imperialism, then Dubček's hints about leaving the Warsaw Pact were an even greater betrayal of the necessarily united front against that same imperialism. To Cubans (who saw themselves as being on the front line of that struggle since 1961), such a move was dangerous in the extreme, and, if the Soviet Union had not resisted it, it would have had enormous implications for the Cubans. Moreover, what is always presented as Fidel's endorsement of the invasion actu-ally turns out to be something less when one examines the wording of his statement: although he accepted the 'necessary evil' aspect of the invasion (given that the struggle against imperialism overrode everything else), he actually described it as a flagrant violation of sovereignty, using the statement as an opportunity to remind Moscow of its obligations to hold the line against reforms leading to capital-ism and also to support Cuba (implying that it had not done so in October 1962) if Cuba were ever invaded (Balfour 2009: 90).

Beyond that, however, the five-year gap also suggests that all was not well inside the Cuban leadership; while 1970 was indeed recognised as a crisis point, the fact that it took five years to set up the new systems suggests that 1970–75 was one of the Revo-lution's periods of argument and debate, essentially between the radical-Guevarist-*fidelista*-nationalist position of the 1960s and the more orthodox-Soviet-PSP position of 1962–65, between the same two competing discourses of socialism and revolution that had been battling away since 1960. The new systems that were set up included the economic model; COMECON membership, after all, was both essential by then as a result of the crisis, and also contingent on some sort of adaptation to orthodox models, so the fact that it came in 1972 was not perhaps as significant a climbdown as it seemed.

There is growing evidence of the continuing survival of the radical position and continuing resistance to the required orthodoxy, albeit not in the fundamentals of the economy or in the formal political structures (Clayfield 2013). Thus, for example, People's Power included some features not characteristic of the Soviet model (notably the six-monthly 'rendering of accounts' feedback, required of all delegates and with the resulting threat of their recall and rejection), building more on the Cubans' own experiments in local participation – notably local power – than on Eastern European models. Equally, People's Power never replaced the characteristic CDRs, which continued in place: although they may have lost some of their immediately political role, their existence and growth meant that they were still a key element of mass involvement, socialisation, dissemination and debate. Again, the essentially Guevarist voluntarism of the 1960s also survived in the continuing notion of *trabajo voluntario* (voluntary labour), linked to the CDRs, and the construction micro-brigades. Finally, the creation of the Centre for Martí Studies in 1977 was an explicit exaltation of the national(ist) dimension of the Revolution, since a nationally important research centre had been dedicated to someone whose profile only really fitted into orthodox Communist interpretations as a member of the 'progressive bourgeoisie' but who had not only clearly inspired and guided most of the 1953–58 rebels but still dominated Cuban thinking into the 1970s, despite 'orthodoxy' (Kapcia 2000: 196).

Nonetheless, the simple fact that, after 1975, a more stable set of state structures (and thus a more recognisable stable state) finally took visible shape inevitably had an effect. At the same time, a larger, and thus eventually more bureaucratic, party emerged (membership rising from revealingly approximate figures of around 45,000 in 1965 and 100,000 in 1970 to the much more accurate 202,807 in late 1975 and 434,143 in 1980: Azicri 1988: 79; Gonzalez 1979: 6), strengthening both the Cuban state and the party, centralising and either weakening or eliminating the hitherto characteristic plethora of semi-autonomous spaces. In some areas of Cuban life and the system, this tendency was beneficial – most notably, in culture and the arts, where the new Ministry of Culture (from 1976) created an evidently more permissive atmosphere and opportunities than the previously restrictive and even repressive *quinquenio gris*, under the always problematic CNC, had done. Thus institutionalisation here actually meant greater freedom, and, paradoxically, it was during the 'interregnum', when the debate was under way, that the most Stalinist approach to culture was adopted. However, in other areas, the resulting proximity to Moscow and Communist orthodoxy brought Cuba closer to Soviet models and the Socialist Bloc: in education, Eastern European textbooks became the standard in many disciplines (philosophy, linguistics and economics, for example); in the military, Soviet training became fundamental to the newly restructured FAR. All told, this led to a greater sense of conformity, alongside the rise in living standards and material satisfaction.

Nonetheless, the gap between 1970 and at least 1972 (and probably beyond) means that we should see the years between the problem *zafra* and 1975 as either transitional or, given the Revolution's trajectory as one of continual cycles of crisis–debate–certainty, as yet another period of debate, responding to the larger crisis of 1968–70 (rather than to the harvest alone). In that case, it is logical that not only would the participants of that debate – or at least the discourses – be largely the same as in 1961–65 but also that many of the 'key players' of the 1960s would continue to play critical and possibly influential roles in those years and beyond. However, given the steady process of consolidation and institutionalisation, and given the reduced role for individuals and the greater role of systems and party bureaucrats, especially from 1975, it was also inevitable that any such players would be less autonomous than in the earlier context of the weaker state. The exception, of course, would be those who were increasingly protected or privileged, or even made more powerful, by the steady shift after 1972–75, i.e. those associated with the old PSP, those close to Moscow's preferences and ideas, and those preferring – and prepared for – a stronger party.

*The 'new' party and the circles of power* Indeed, if we look at the composition of the upper echelons of the party, which finally had its First Congress in 1975, we can detect the shifts in personnel, and thus in perspective. However, while that was true of the new Central Committee (expanded from the nineteen of 1965 to 112), it is interesting that the leadership group (housed in the Political Bureau) showed little difference from the one created in 1965: namely, it was still clearly oriented towards the 26 July Movement, that contingent including Fidel and Raúl, Almeida, García, Valdés, Del Valle, Dorticós, Hart, Antonio Pérez, Risquet and Raúl García, while only four of the old PSP were there – Rodríguez, Roca, Milián and Malmierca (Suchlicki 1988: 208). In that respect, therefore, the old 'inner circle' was largely intact, extended to include only a handful of the more trusted, or powerful, members of the intermediate circle, but not enough to change the balance of power in the group. In fact, while the old eight-man Bureau was expanded to include the new influx of ex-PSP leaders, two former 26 July people (Miret and José Ramón Machado Ventura, another newly rising activist, an FEU activist before 1959 and then part of Raúl's Sierra del Cristal column) were also now members, maintaining the 26 July Movement's domination (González 1979: 7). Even so, there was something of a shift, inasmuch as, alongside those among the ex-guerrillas who were always more willing to cooperate with, and even occasionally follow the advice of, the Soviet Union, the newcomers would eventually prove to be as supportive of 'institutionalisation' as Raúl and Valdés.

Nonetheless, such shifts can also be exaggerated, since, after the first People's Power elections of 1976, the leading bodies of party and state were still overwhelmingly in the hands of former 26 July Movement people. In the newly elected Council of State, for example, twenty-one of the thirty-one members were from that stable (ibid.: 13). Indeed, that same pattern continued at the 1980 Second Congress, when the Bureau was expanded to sixteen members, accommodating Osmani Cienfeugos and two relatively 'orthodox' activists, Julio Camacho and Jorge Risquet. The inclusion of Cienfuegos was interesting; he had already possibly been able to benefit from his brother's memory, and, despite his former PSP membership, he had been included in outer circles of authority, having contributed enough to the pre-1959 *lucha* to qualify him for 'honorary' ex-guerrilla status, and, in addition, this past seemed to allow him to continue enjoying that respect and authority after 1975. Hence, although he might have been technically in the ex-PSP category (i.e. the old inter-mediate circle), he was also clearly considered someone who could qualify as part of the new 'inner circle', almost uniquely. Risquet's star was also undoubtedly in the ascendant, which almost certainly reflected the new legitimacy of the old PSP and the new détente with Moscow; by the late 1980s, he was Secretary for Foreign Relations in the party's Central Committee, a role in which he played a major part over Angola and especially in the final negotiations with South Africa and the MPLA (Movimento Popular de Libertação de Angola/ Popular Movement for the Liberation of Angola) (Habel 1991: 133).

In other words, a mixture of realpolitik (vis-à-vis the new, post-1970, Cuban–Soviet relations) and the shift in the competing discourses of the Revolution meant that the definitions of 'inner', 'intermedi-ate' and 'outer' circles were now less fixed than they might have been in the 'siege mentality' of the 1960s, but they were still largely recognisable. The shift mentioned above was essentially towards either an acceptance of greater 'orthodoxy' (in the 1959–65 sense of the term, i.e. defining positions according to the perspectives of, and in, the Soviet Union and Cuba's preferred path to 'socialism') or a necessary process of consolidation and institutionalisation, which really meant, among the ex-guerrillas who adopted that new perspective, a preference for 'participation through structures'. As a consequence, the group at the top now included more adherents of an argument that had seemed less convincing or enjoyed less credibility or legitimacy in the 1960s, or at least those whose views had hardened in that direction, although they did not necessarily correspond to what casual and journalistic observers were wont to term 'hardliners'.

*The question of factions* Indeed, this raises again the question of supposed 'factions', for the 'new' patterns of the late 1970s enhanced the old tendency to read the institutional and personnel changes and the shifts within all the leading bodies as illustrative of the growth of clearly identifiable factions. One such factional reading was offered by Edward González, specifically to account for the shaping of Cuban foreign policy. He saw three 'tendencies' in contention. The first was the Pragmatic Economic tendency, led by Carlos Rafael Rodríguez but supported by Fernández Font, Marcos Lage (the then Minister of

Sugar) and Héctor Rodríguez (then chair of the State Commission for Economic Collaboration), and consisting essentially of former PSP members and those opposing Guevara in the Great Debate. The second was the Revolutionary Political tendency, seeking revolutionary gestures abroad and clearly led by Fidel. The third was the Military Mission tendency, led by Raúl and MINFAR (González 1979: 17–22).

While this categorisation was not without its value (not least in distinguishing between Fidel's and Raúl's agendas and preferred manners of operation, while still seeing a cohesion or convergence between their positions and goals), it did seem to fall into two familiar traps. Firstly, as already observed here, the notion of factions in the Cuban leadership was already an unstable basis for building a theory, given the crossover between supposed groups on different issues, but also due to the underlying loyalty to the essence of the 'core' principles and people. Secondly, the distinction between supposedly 'revolutionary' and pragmatic motivations was also already questionable, even though Mesa-Lago had only recently proposed something similar as an overall explanation of the development of economic and political decision-making (Mesa-Lago 1974). This was because already one could detect any number of apparently ideologically driven decisions that turned out to have clearly pragmatic purposes and benefits, and vice versa (Kapcia 2011). Moreover, the other dimension to the inadvisability of talking in terms of factionalism is that, much of the time, those reading Cuba in that way were often applying paradigms borrowed from other contexts (most notably the 'Kremlinological' interpretations of Soviet or Eastern European politics) and saw the underlying, and surviving, 26 July–PSP tensions in those terms. As we have seen, while not without some value, that reading oversimplified the reality of patterns within the governing circles, not least because the borrowed dichotomy of 'hard line' and 'reformist' changed over time. Before 1962, the PSP and possibly Raúl were fitted into the category of 'hardliners' and the 26 July people into the 'reformist' camp; however, as the Revolution radicalised, the terms were reversed, with the PSP and 'allied' politicians being presented as the pragmatic reformers and the former guerrillas as the hardliners, a dichotomisation that curiously survived well into the 1990s (with those arguing for adherence to a Soviet model being seen as more 'sensible' than the ageing ex-guerrillas) and into the

2000s, when a pattern emerged in media-speak that saw the older ex-guerrillas as de facto hardliners.

Finally, on this issue, one of the most important question marks against this factionalist reading was that the separation of military and party was often a clumsy assumption, which continued to dominate outside thinking about the FAR (and MINFAR) for some time afterwards. Although this tendency had its roots in readings of Latin American politics, as well as in some interpretations of the rise of the military as a separate and powerful force in the Soviet Union, in great part it arose from Cuba's Angolan involvement. Not only was that involvement massive and successful (bringing enormous prestige to the FAR), it was also the first large-scale conventional deployment of Cuban troops (apart from the brigade in Syria in 1973), making the FAR seem like a conventional armed force. Thereafter, therefore, commentators began a process of always referring to the FAR as something separate from the rest of the political system, with its own agenda, its own sense of difference and its own legitimacy. As González put it in 1979, the FAR–MINFAR was 'the most important elite grouping within the new Cuban leadership', something that he saw then as crucial in building a 'Fidelista–Raulista' coalition (González 1979: 13).

The reality, in fact, was much more complex, as one study has demonstrated convincingly (Klepak 2010), not least because the supposed differences and previous competition between Fidel and Raúl were almost certainly more imagined than real. That said, however, it was clear that individual achievement in the Angolan episode could be a significant boost to a Cuban political actor's profile and promotion. When González talked of Colomé Ibarra's rise as attributable to his 'acclaimed' role in leading troops in Angola (González 1979: 13), there may well have been some truth in that: until then, although he had played crucial roles in the security apparatus, he had not been so visible publicly. Equally, the promotion in 1976 of the previously unnoticed Fernando Vecino Alegret to the key post of Minister for Higher Education may have had something to do with his perceived inherent trustworthiness as a FAR man.

## Return of the PSP?

The inapplicability of the term 'hardliner' for this period is best illustrated by the most obvious example of the more 'orthodox' pole within the new group, namely Carlos Rafael Rodríguez. Although he proved to be much closer and more loyal to Soviet precepts and models than, say, most of the ex-guerrillas, he had long shown himself to be genuinely flexible and ready to accept, and work with, the 26 July Movement, about which the rest of his party was cautious at best. Hence, although he now rose to greater prominence and influence than before, it did not necessarily herald a 'harder' line.

That prominence arose principally from the fact that, after 1972 and Cuba's entry into COMECON, he became the architect of the new economic institutionalisation process, which saw a return to a more Soviet-style orthodoxy. In fact, he had actually started that process in 1970, when he was appointed president of the Council of Ministers' National Commission for Economic, Scientific and Technical Collaboration (González 1979: 7; Suchlicki 1988: 245), essentially making him a key link to Moscow and economic orthodoxy. In 1971 (or 1972, according to some commentators), he also became Deputy Prime Minister and then, after 1976, vice president of the Council of State (until his death in 1997), but he also led the Ministry of External Organisations.

Mention of Rodríguez, however, brings into focus the parallel case of Roca, the other pre-1959 PSP leader who, since 1959, had worked most closely with the ex-guerrillas. Already a constant within the upper echelons of all the different 'party' formations from 1961 (ORI, PURSC and PCC) and a member of the Secretariat from 1965 to 1980, he became even more prominent and influential during this time. His importance had theoretically already been evident in 1965, when he was asked to chair the commission to write the Revolution's Constitution (Suchlicki 1988: 36), but that body was then relatively powerless, so his position there may in fact have been almost an indication of his 'penance' rather than his influence (Domínguez 1978: 308). However, after 1975, this role became more important, his contribution probably giving the eventual document its close resemblance to the Soviet charter. Hence, even before the 'new' Revolution began to take shape after 1976, he was already more powerful. From 1976 to 1981, he served as president of the new National Assembly, only eventually retiring through ill health in 1986.

Another such ex-PSP activist was Arnaldo Milián Castro. Evident in many of the early moves to link the PSP and the 26 July Movement, he nonetheless had not enjoyed a particular prominence in leadership circles. However, he now became an evidently trusted member of the new Communist Party's Central Committee and Bureau (1975), as well as of the Council of State, taking the role of Minister of Agriculture from 1980 until his death in 1983.

*Culture and institutionalisation* It was actually in the world of culture where the potential for easy, not to say simplistic, readings of 'factions', 'hardliners' and *fidelista* tendencies, after a watershed in 1970, broke down considerably. For, as already observed, while the supposedly Sovietised 'institutionalisation' process began after 1975, in culture something similar seems to have begun in 1971, or at least in 1968. In the latter year, after the January 1968 Havana Cultural Congress had seemingly nailed Cuban cultural colours firmly to the mast of a militant 'Third Worldism' in terms of the role of culture in a revolution, and also of the revolutionary Third World intellectual, a cause célèbre emerged when an already 'problematic' and would-be dissident writer, Heberto Padilla, was awarded the UNEAC prize for poetry (while another 'problem' writer, Antón Arrufat, was awarded the theatre prize). Because UNEAC disagreed with the jury's choice, the organisation inserted a disclaimer in the duly published work (which included some politically risqué content and expressions), condemning the book for its counter-revolutionary tendencies. Three years later, Padilla was at the centre of a worse storm when he was detained by the security forces and, after a few days, issued a notorious *autocrítica*, in which he publicly identified several other colleagues as sharing his doubts and tendencies. This was immediately followed by an international furore, as several formerly sympathetic European and some Latin American leftist intellectuals protested at what they saw as Stalinism and a shadow of old Soviet show trials; their protest, however, led to a fierce riposte by Fidel, the subsequent rapid retraction by some Latin American-based signatories of the protest letter, and the decision, at the last minute, to convert the planned April 1971 Congress on Education into the Congress on Education *and Culture*. That Congress turned out to be a militantly revolutionary forum, taking up the theme and tone of the 1968 Cultural Congress but angrily enlisting culture and all intellectuals in a 'serving' role within a more narrowly defined militancy (Kumaraswami and Kapcia 2012: 28).

This, however, was not Stalinism, whatever its appearances. For the years after 1966 had seen a steady 'Third Worldisation', not Stalinisation, of Cuban cultural attitudes and then policies, into which this new militancy and narrowness fitted. Hence, the 'sins' of the 'deviant' and problematic Cuban intellectuals were not so much their bourgeois attitudes (the classic Stalinist accusation) as their Western attitudes, copying European cultural models rather than focusing on the Third World. In this respect, the militancy was not that of the old CNC (under the ex-PSP activists) but that of the ex-guerrillas. For, in 1971, Luis Pavón Tamayo – an ex-guerrilla who had spent the 1960s editing the FAR magazine, *Verde Olivo*, and also writing poetry – was surprisingly appointed to lead the CNC (until 1976). In that role, together with Armando Quesada, he unleashed the *quinquenio gris*.

However, Pavón's role showed not only the need to distinguish one kind of 'hardliner' (i.e. 'revolutionary', based on a guerrilla ethos of sorts) from another (based on orthodox and possibly Stalinist Communism), but also the need to remember that, in the fluidity of the Cuban state at that time, what he was able to achieve in the CNC was limited to that institution and did not necessarily spill over to other areas. Therefore, although we can detect the development of the 1971 'line' as early as 1966, that year also saw the publication of Lezama Lima's *Paradiso*, an experimental and homoerotic novel that scarcely qualified as socialist realism. The following year, 1967, saw the creation of modernist and avant-garde architecture in the new Higher Arts Institute in Cubanacán, in the western suburbs of Havana, but also the staging of the avant-garde Parisian 'Salon de Mai' exhibition (in which the now somewhat marginalised Franqui was involved), while 1968 (the year when Padilla's troubles sharpened) saw the closure – not the opening – of the notorious UMAP camps. So there was no single policy for the whole area of culture, let alone in other fields.

Of course, this all brings into focus the case of Armando Hart, under whose auspices (as the new post-1976 Minister of Culture) Pavón's 'reign of terror' was ended. Given his past in the Catholic-oriented MNR and his associations with the *Llano*, his was hardly the type of ministerial appointment that one might have expected from a more Stalinist or 'hard-line' leadership; yet it was Hart who not only engineered the end of the cultural repression but also successfully rebuilt relations between the leadership and a somewhat cautious, if not frightened, cultural community.

This process of contested institutionalisation began to end in the early to mid-1980s; until then, the 'institutionalisers' never quite had it all their own way – the ex-guerrillas, although their influence was weakened or diminished, still numerically held sway within the key areas of power, such as in the party's upper echelons. But by the 1980s, the world had changed, as had Cuba.

## The changing world and changing Cuba in the 1980s: a new crisis

Externally, the United States changed gear in its Cuba policy. From 1976, the Carter administration's moves towards détente had produced a partial diplomatic recognition – with the opening of 'interest sections' in third-party embassies, always seen as a first move towards eventual full and normal relations – and also a new freedom for Cuban-Americans to visit their families on the island. However, from 1981 the new Reagan administration ended the former Republican administrations' tolerance of a steady deterioration of the embargo. Instead, the new administration now based the Latin American dimension of its global strategy of reheating the Cold War on an identification of Cuba as the 'source of the problem' in the region and therefore sought to end that 'threat'. The result was an increased level of hostility, seeking to isolate Cuba once again (with some success under the following Bush administration, when Cuba's ally, Nicaragua, and trading partner, Panama, were eliminated from the scene in 1989–90). Despite the partially rhetorical element of this new policy, many Cubans chose to see it as a real threat, leading to a new defensiveness in Cuba, and, in 1981, the re-creation of the long-defunct militias, this time as the new Territorial Militia Troops.

Meanwhile, the internal crisis of succession and the power vacuum in the Soviet Union (following Brezhnev's death in 1982), which caused its own problems for Cuban policy-makers and for those arguing for a continued close relationship with the Soviet Union, resulted in 1985 in the rise of Mikhail Gorbachev. That reality presented all manner of threats and dilemmas for Cuba: not only did Gorbachev's determination to make good US–Soviet relations a cornerstone of Soviet foreign policy have serious implications for the extent of Soviet commitment to Cuba, but also his equal determination to cut Soviet spending at home and abroad had a particular dimension for Cuba, namely a promise to end Cuba's privileged status within the Soviet trade and aid regime once Cuba's debts to Moscow were due for repayment (from the late 1980s). Thus, Cuba faced the stark reality of a more rampant and determined United States at the same time as the Soviet Union was removing most of the safety net under Cuba's economy and military capacity.

On top of this, the early 1980s saw a double crisis inside Cuba. On the one hand, economic weaknesses began to become evident after the post-1975 reforms and growth, while, on the other, a deep political crisis began to emerge. The economic crisis was no simple matter, for it involved both internal systems and external relationships. The domestic economy had really never recovered from the shocks of, firstly, the rupture with the United States in 1960–62 and, secondly, the trauma and chaos of the 1968 Revolutionary Offensive and the costs of the all-out effort relating to the 1970 harvest, plus the inherent inefficiencies of a rigidly centralised system of targets, production and distribution. Hence, while the 1970s reforms achieved some degree of decentralisation, the basic inefficiency remained, with its implications for the resulting black market and the soaring costs of low productivity. On the external front, quite apart from the now worrying relationship with the Soviet Union, the post-1975 opening up to the world economy and the world credit market (both of which Moscow and the post-1972 reformers had urged) now proved to be costly. To an unprecedented extent, Cuba now found itself vulnerable to the fluctuations of commodity prices and interest rate rises, and therefore part of a wider Latin American problem, with a growing debt to Western debtors and exposure to price changes.

The political crisis was also partly related to the post-1975 changes, as the new emphasis on limited consumerism and increased material incentives, together with a partial decentralisation of decision-making and operation and the opening of the party to encourage its growth, had all fused to create unprecedented opportunities for patronage, privilege and small-scale corruption. Those who held local or institutional economic power or party influence had a new context in which it was now more possible than before to take advantage of that power or influence. Hence, local or intermediate party secretaries, for example, could use their position to acquire much-valued and envied material goods, better housing or services, just as had already happened in many Eastern European societies or in the Soviet Union. Meanwhile, further up the system, managers could wield their power as patronage. While this was hardly corruption on, say, the Mexican scale under the Partido Revolucionario Institucional (Institutional Revolutionary Party) after 1976, it nonetheless had clear implications: not only did it offend the core principles of a revolutionary process with its genesis in the anti-corruption Ortodoxos and with an initial legitimacy in its visible emphasis on morality and *martiano* purity, but it also risked undermining that continuing legitimacy in a system where a high degree of equality had more than compensated for the material shortages. Quite simply, the leadership could not afford to allow corruption, or its implicit inequality, to become a major and visible problem, especially in a small population where inequality was difficult to disguise. Hence, corruption once again became an emblematic issue, as powerful as the related 'bureaucratism' had been in the 1960s; in fact, that previous campaign had also implicitly been against such corruption, *burocracia* also acquiring a further meaning as 'nest-feathering'. Indeed, when Ameijeiras was sacked in March 1966 (from his post as Deputy Minister of MINFAR and from the Central Committee), it had been for having created a patronage network below him, confirming that even low-level corruption was one 'sin' that could override the power of the Moncada–*Granma*–*Sierra* heritage. A few years after the 1986 turning point, the import-ance of this issue would be made all too clear, when the scandal of General Arnaldo Ochoa broke in July 1989, with his trial, sentence and execution in August.

## Changes to the circles of power

Both dimensions of the mounting crisis, therefore, were evident to party members and leadership alike by the early 1980s, leading to a growing debate inside the leading circles. The evidence of this debate came not in the usual pre-Congress discussions (the 1980 Congress had occurred and the next one was not due until 1985) but rather in an inconsistency of policy that revealed tensions at the top and a battle for hegemony. One clear example was the change to the policy (in 1980) to allow private farmers access to a new expanded consumer market beyond the state-run purchasing system (the *acopio*), a policy that was then reversed in 1986, in response officially to grass-roots complaints about marketeering, profiteering and the rise of a 'middle' peasant, but also in response to the dislike of the idea in one section of the leadership. A similar process happened with the limited freedom to acquire new housing.

Those quasi-debates, however, began to emerge more fully in the run-up to the 1985 Congress. Here, the evidence was clearer in the decision to postpone the Congress, without explanation, until February 1986, and then in the curious nature of the eventual gathering. For, when it did finally take place, the session was abruptly suspended until later in the year (the date as yet undefined), with delegates being given clear instructions to return to their *núcleos* and discuss issues again, with both the party grass roots and 'the people'. This was also, clearly, an encouragement for them to rethink their attitudes to proposed changes and even to make any changes deemed necessary to local and provincial delegations to the next reconvened session. As the next chapter will make clear, it was during that second session that a new shape to the lower levels of the leadership began to emerge.

In the meantime, however, the lack of a Congress was used by the leadership as an opportunity to make changes at the top, some of them evidently already under way. This applied especially to the person who, besides Rodríguez, had been most closely associated with the post-1975 economic reforms, the Moscow-trained economist Humberto Pérez. As Minister of the Economy (1976–83) and therefore also head of the new economic structure (the Economic Management and Planning System, or SDPE), he had enjoyed considerable influence in reshaping the successful new economy, and in bringing Cuba closer to Socialist Bloc practices and needs. Indeed, his success gave him greater power and authority for around a decade, but he finally fell foul of the shift in thinking around 1984–85 and was removed unceremoniously and publicly from his posts in 1984 (although he remained vice president until 1986). Officially, his removal was for 'shirking his responsibilities' (Habel 1991: 89), but in fact it was simply for having played a leading role in the latest period of post-debate consolidation, i.e. 'institutionalisation'. In other words, as the multi-layered crisis developed, he was dispensable, especially as he was not as 'protected' as those from the former PSP and other pro-Soviet activists who had been his patrons and had supported him. Hence, because his rising star shone only briefly and he lacked the historical legitimacy of older 'orthodox' people, he was simply removed.

However, that same shift cautiously away from the Soviet Union also seems to have briefly caught out a genuinely historically legitimate stalwart, Ramiro Valdés. As we have seen, he had always been an integral part of the 'inner circle', close to all decision-making and with a powerful base in the growing Interior Ministry apparatus. Indeed, in 1970–71, he had been moved to Defence, becoming Deputy Minister directly under Raúl (Suchlicki 1988: 288), to whom he was always close politically, sharing his preference for structures and organisation, and almost certainly sharing his preference for closer links with the Soviet Union. There, he became responsible for the construction sector of the ministry.

A year later, his centrality seemed to be confirmed again by his appointment as Deputy Prime Minister (until 1976) (ibid.: 288). That said, however, it should be observed here that this post made Valdés (as one of eight Deputy Prime Ministers) part of what soon became a characteristic of the governing system: multiple vice presidents. Since there have usually been at least six such posts at any one time, usually only one or two post-holders have had any real power or prominence, the other posts being reserved for 'parking' those historically significant leaders who, in some form or other, have been deemed to have failed or who, because of oscillating debates and internal arguments, are temporarily deemed appropriate for marginalisation until needed again, but whose historical legitimacy has to be recognised somehow. Thus, for example, others at that time included Guillermo García, but also more activist and more significant leaders such as Flavio Bravo, who had enjoyed a comeback after 1975, having been influential in the 1975 negotiations with Agostinho Neto to arrange the dispatch of Cuban troops to Angola (Valdés 1979: 98). In fact, he eventually went on to preside over the National Assembly.

In the case of Valdés, however, his trajectory from the late 1970s seemed somewhat unclear politically; while he seemed to be demoted briefly (a recurring pattern throughout), serving in a string of relatively junior posts, he also became one of the vice presidents of the newly created Council of State in 1976, and, in 1979 – although one source incorrectly gives 1981 (Suchlicki 1988: 288) – he regained the crucial post of Minister of the Interior. However, the 'mystery' about him continued, as, in 1985 (confirmed at the contentious 1986 Party Congress) – i.e. at the formal start of what would become known as 'Rectification' – he was once again demoted from both the ministry and the Political Bureau (Bourne 1986: 298; Habel 1991: 69). Since this was some years before the Ochoa affair of 1989 (which provoked a drastic clear-out of the MININT and security apparatuses), it was unrelated to any other scandals, processes or incidents, and it puzzled observers. One historian attributed it to his supposed opposition to Fidel's new entente with religion, in response to the rising popularity of liberation theology in Latin America (Bourne 1986: 298); another attributed it to his 'being suspected of excessive allegiance to the Soviet Union' (Habel 1991: 98); and still others, in Cuba, have explained it as being due to his own preference for taking a long 'sabbatical'. The most likely explanation seems to be that his proximity to Moscow (and the Soviet, and East German, security apparatuses) made him curiously both 'protected' and suspect, and his star rose or fell in accordance with the balance of arguments within the leadership.

But the apparent vicissitudes of Valdés's position were no simple matter; while he may have been demoted for one reason (still not entirely clear), Humberto Pérez had been demoted for being too closely and prominently associated with a 'failed' or contested (and unpopular, within the leadership) strategy from 1972, making him a casualty of 'war'. What remained true, however, as will be seen in the next chapter, is that the most powerful argument for keeping Valdés 'inside' was his undoubted membership of the 'historic' core of the 'inner circle', a pedigree that, as we have seen, enabled him and others to 'sin' or fail repeatedly, without real sanction or disappearance from the corridors of power. One of the interesting aspects of his demotion was that he was replaced as Interior Minister by another ex-guerrilla whose profile had remained relatively low until then (having served for a while as one of Fidel's bodyguards), namely José Abrantes Fernández (often wrongly spelled Abrahantes in the literature).

Valdés was not alone in (however erratically) rising up the structures of power and influence during this period, for the hegemony of what we might call the orthodox discourse within the Revolution was not associated exclusively with the former members of the PSP or with those who had 'lost' the arguments of the 1960s, especially the Great Debate. Inevitably, the strengthening of the PSP argument affected the levels of influence that those associated with that 'pole' could exercise in the system after 1975. Of course, people such as Lionel Soto were bound to be prominent in the new ordinance, if only because, as a former PSP member, he was trusted by his former comrades and also trusted by those around Fidel; hence, he was now reinstated. After serving as ambassador to the UK (1973–76), he then enjoyed an influential position in the offices of the Party Central Committee, as Director of Foreign Relations from 1978 to 1981, and then with responsibility for the Committee's special Economic Commission (Suchlicki 1988: 265). From 1983 to 1986, he held the trusted position of ambassador in Moscow. However, as we have seen, this prominence was neither surprising nor out of character for someone in his position.

During this time, there was still evidence of the Soviet connection playing a part in bolstering a political career, as illustrated by the case of Carlos Aldana, whose star had risen dramatically in the late 1980s. Helped by Moscow's patronage, he became secretary (i.e. head) of the Ideology Department of the Party Central Committee, a position from which, after 1985, he supported Gorbachev's reforms. He thus felt able to address those younger party members and those in the UJC whose frustrations with the seemingly ossified Cuban leadership led them to welcome a Gorbachev-like approach to Cuba's system.

Another politician seemingly protected in this period was Jaime Crombet. Like Ricardo Alarcón de Quesada (see Chapter 6), an 'adolescent' (rather than a 'child') of the Revolution, he had risen up through the appropriate ranks, treading a familiar path: firstly as President of the FEU (1962–63), then First Secretary of the Havana UJC (1964–66), then national UJC First Secretary (1966–72). He then entered, and rose within, the senior party, from 1972 to 1983, this being interrupted by brief tours of perhaps significant ambassadorial and political duty in Angola. Finally, he occupied the key post of secretary to the party's Central Committee (1983–90), as well as becoming a vice president of the Council of State (1990–93) and later presiding over ANAP. There is no evidence of him taking a protagonist role in anything, and his performance fits much more with that of a 'safe pair of hands', as one of the so-called 'Soviet-trained' generation, although he actually trained in Cuba. His activism tended to fade after 1993 and he died in 2013, a year after retiring through ill health.

However, the overall pattern of personnel changes in this pre-Congress lull was one of reinforcement of the ex-26 July Movement contingent in the inner circles. One such 'reinforcement' was Osmani Cienfuegos, brought in from the (relative) cold. As we have already seen, in the preceding decade or so he had already been Minister of Agriculture, Minister of Construction and Minister of Transport, and also, from 1976, had occupied the somewhat powerless post of secretary to the Council of Ministers (ibid.: 61) – it was with Carlos Lage's appointment to that post in 1992 that the role became much more important and powerful. Now, however, Cienfuegos was promoted to run a special 'Central Group' (consisting of vice presidents and some key ministers), charged with 'correcting' the failings of the SDPE plans and restructuring them to follow new guidelines (Habel 1991: 90). Therefore, for all that he might have been viewed as part of the 'hard-line' elements of the debates in the 1960s (given his PSP links), he was now clearly seen by Fidel and those around him as a reliable person to take up the principles of 'Rectification'. This was confirmed by his promotion to the Political Bureau in 1986, after the Congress. Part of the explanation may have been his association with the decidedly non-orthodox foreign policy of the late 1960s, for he had led the Havana-based OSPAAL international network of radical Third World movements from 1967, and (from 1966 to 1973) had been head of the party's Foreign Affairs Committee (Suchlicki 1988: 61). It was, in fact, in that latter capacity that he became the de facto first Minister for Tourism (INTUR then belonged to the Foreign Ministry), a post in which he would be confirmed as a full minister after 1990, when tourism was expanded, and where he remained until 1998.

Cienfuegos's position confirmed that previous membership of the 26 July Movement, rather than specifically being a guerrilla veteran, was now sufficient to count for inclusion. In fact, this was confirmed further with the return of Faustino Pérez, who, after being somewhat marginalised in the 1960s and early 1970s (serving, for example, as ambassador in Bulgaria from 1973 to 1977), returned to take up a potentially significant position as liaison between the government

(Council of Ministers) and the new People's Power structures, including the National Assembly (Buch and Suárez 2009: 323). He kept this post until he died in 1992. Pérez, of course, was in a stronger position than Cienfuegos, given his 'historic' credentials (*Granma* and the Sierra). However, his association with the *Llano* and his evident early doubts about collaboration with the PSP seem to have made him more marginal than others early on. Yet his survival tells a story of sorts: while one way of viewing his survival was to describe him as an almost opportunist 'inveterate survivor' (Anderson 1997: 758), his loyalty to the 26 July Movement, which probably caused problems in the early 1960s, almost certainly counted in his favour in the 1980s.

Personnel shifts were being made even before the postponed Third Party Congress (in February 1968), and by the middle of the year it was clear that a major shift within the leadership, and thus also in the character of the various ruling circles, was under way, although the changes were evidently still resisted by those who had wielded power and influence in the post-1975 years. It was also clear that, while, at one level, this was simply a continuation of the competing discourses within the revolutionary coalition, by now the crisis that had generated this latest cycle of debate had acquired more serious dimensions, with the threat implied by Gorbachev, the seemingly growing problem of corruption and the spectre hanging over Cuba of a newly rampant United States. Clearly, therefore, the 1986 Congress was to be crucial in ways that the 1975 and 1980 assemblies had not been. While the abortive February session closed one phase (of institutionalisation), the reconvened session in December would be seen as launching another.

In that sense, therefore, the 1975–89 period had seen a break in the preceding pattern of inclusion, in that the traditional inner circle of 1959–75 had been partly reshaped. Although few, and certainly none of the old 'core' group, had been removed to the outer circles and no one had been expelled altogether, the balance of power within those various circles had indeed changed over the period. Simply, what we might loosely call the pro-Moscow element (incorporating the ex-PSP people and the new 'realists' and 'technocrats' who had either been trained in the Soviet Union or had come to appreciate and advocate a closer and even mimetic relationship with Moscow) had seen its power rise, backed as it was by external pressure from

Moscow and a sense of resignation among the insurrection veterans. Hence, although the latter remained numerically significant, and although the hold of Fidel on the reins of power and decision-making and the influence of the veterans' view of the 'Revolution' remained formally considerable, the reality was that Fidel's freedom of action had been circumscribed by the realities of Cuba's relationship with the Soviet Union, by the growing complexity of the newly institutionalised structures and the growing self-interest of a more bureaucratised system, and by a changing world scene. Certainly, while the inner circle remained unchanged in great part, the circles outside it had become peopled by those who sided with the 'new realism', reducing the overall influence of the veterans. The 1986 Congress therefore acquired a greater long-term importance than simply dealing with yet another crisis.

# 6 | THE RETURN OF FLUIDITY: 1986 TO THE PRESENT

## Explaining 'Rectification'

As was observed in the opening chapter, in most 'periodisations' of the Revolution's trajectory, the post-1986 years are treated as two, or occasionally three, separate phases: 'Rectification' (1986–89), crisis and Special Period (1990–2000, or, more commonly, through to the present day), and, sometimes, the Battle of Ideas (from 2000 and generally assumed to have ended around 2006–07). However, this chapter treats all three as part of the same process, or period, for three reasons.

Firstly, as already argued, 'Rectification' ('of Past Errors and Negative Tendencies', to give it its full title) is best understood not so much as a separate phase, but as a period of characteristic debate, albeit without a clear beginning but ending with a jolt, with the onset of the crisis provoked by the collapse of the Socialist Bloc in 1989–91. That is because its purpose and nature reflected more the 1962–65 or 1970–75 periods, of reappraisal, introspection and contestation, than the intervening periods of either crisis or certainty. Indeed, one might best see those years as starting somewhere in the early 1980s rather than in 1986, which is the date most histories record and which that year's Party Congress confirmed (although, given the tendency for such Congresses to legitimise and formalise after the event, one should always exercise caution when taking note of such declarations). After that, moreover, it becomes clear that, rather than starting the process of reappraisal, the 1986 event largely legitimised and institutionalised it, giving it the impetus of final consensus. In fact, that Congress's two separate sessions (February and December) effectively acted as a bridge between a period of intense and hotly contested debate and an ultimately abortive process of more positive debate, moving towards the kind of certainty that, in the past, had usually accompanied the effective hegemony achieved by one side of an argument.

Secondly, 'Rectification' hardly qualifies for the title of a 'phase', since the multi-layered motives for launching the strategy produced a variety of potentially contradictory, and certainly discrete, processes and policies. Besides being yet another (rudely abbreviated) period of post-crisis debate, it was also driven by a desire to reverse some of the policies and precepts that had governed Cuban policy-making since 1975 and, in so doing, to rescue something of the original Revolution, seemingly lost after the 1970 crisis and the resulting institutionalisation. In this sense, 'Rectification' was a return to some of the ideas and models of the 1960s, especially resurrecting the ideas and principles of Che Guevara (who had noticeably been overlooked, if not marginalised, after 1975) and simultaneously rehabilitating those activists formerly associated with him. Hence, it also provided an opportunity to restore some of those who had previously inhabited the inner circles but who had found themselves excluded or marginal in the more pro-Soviet years, and also, therefore, an opportunity to move away from those now questionable Soviet models to some extent.

Those models were now seen as questionable because, firstly, they had produced the new economic vulnerability from which Cuba now suffered and also the social and political 'ills' associated with materialism and consumerism. Secondly, they were questioned because of the implications for Cuba of Gorbachev's new policies. Therefore, while some of the new ideas might be presented as 'idealistic' or radical resistance to orthodox Soviet ideas, others were firmly rooted in a realistic desire to address the threat posed by Gorbachev; this was less the result of a deep-seated conservative suspicion of his modernising reformism (as 'Rectification' tended to be seen by the non-Cuban media at the time) than because he seemed to threaten the economic survival of the Revolution.

However, the third motive and strand of 'Rectification' came from a seemingly opposite position, namely a drive towards a much-needed economic efficiency and streamlining, potentially advocating policies that might eventually go in a different direction from an otherwise more 'Guevarist' process. Nevertheless, many of the economic strategies that began to be executed after 1986 turned out to be remarkably similar to those adopted after 1993 by the leadership and the party, with the result that there was a surprising lack of disjuncture between 'Rectification' (in some respects) and the economic reform policies eventually adopted to 'save the Revolution'.

In two ways, those apparently different motivations converged. Firstly, and especially as they came separately from the two leaders, Fidel and Raúl, they both focused on the urgent need to find ways of protecting and furthering 'the Revolution' as a process of nation-building, but now in a very different and newly challenging world. Hence, both the newly awakened 'Guevarism' and the resurrection of the 1960s, on the one hand, and, on the other, the would-be economic modernisation were driven by the same imperative, rather than (as was subsequently assumed) by the two contrasting motives of idealism and realism.

*The issue of corruption* The second way in which they converged was that they both targeted the problem of corruption, as both an unacceptable outcome of the new 'materialism' and bureaucratisation and as something that the Revolution could never accept on principle or for pragmatic reasons of credibility. Besides the increase in incidences of lower-level abuse of party office to gain material advantage, the mid-1980s saw some high-profile scandals: two defections – one of a deputy minister (Manuel Sánchez Pérez) to Spain, and the other (to the United States) of General Rafael del Pino, president of the Civil Aviation Institute – together with other similar cases confirmed how far up the system the cancer of corruption had spread (Habel 1991: 59).

In fact, although this issue had been one of the factors generating 'Rectification', it was not until 1989 that it was tackled via the remarkably, but significantly, high-profile Ochoa case. Given that profile, and the shock it delivered to many Cubans, the case merits discussion here, to reinforce the importance of corruption as an issue behind the new phase.

Because of his previously impeccable record and status (he was one of very few Heroes of the Revolution, named so in 1980), many assumed that the accusations against General Arnaldo Ochoa were false. Essentially, he was accused of abusing his privileged position (he oversaw the special, and secret, MININT unit set up to find ways of breaking the stranglehold of US sanctions) by allowing Colombian drug barons to overfly, and perhaps even land in, Cuba. The problem with this was that it threatened Cuban security by risking US action; after all, in December 1989, the Bush administration used a supposed drug threat to the United States to justify 'Operation Just Cause' against Noriega in Panama. However, the most common external interpretation was that this accusation was false and that he had in fact been tried and then executed either because he was leading a FAR faction or a pro-Gorbachev campaign against Fidel and Raúl or because, as a result of his leading role in the whole Angolan operation and subsequent military leadership in Ethiopia, he was becoming popular inside and outside the FAR, thereby threatening the leadership's position (Oppenheimer 1992: 102–4). However, it should be said that neither of the latter two conspiracy theories has yet thrown up any concrete proof, merely conjecture and hearsay, often emanating from somewhat unreliable and partisan sources. Moreover, the idea that a general who had been relatively junior in 1958 would seriously threaten the popularity or legitimacy of either of the two remaining 'historic' leaders of the Revolution was far-fetched. Similarly, the idea that Raúl, who was clearly well respected by most of the officer corps in the FAR (Klepak 2010), would be conspired against was also untenable. Hence, we have to accept (as most historians now do) that Ochoa's crime was neither conspiracy nor personal gain (interestingly, he was never accused of feathering his own nest or of gaining personally from that abuse) but, rather, the 'sin' of risking Cuban security and, more seriously, not acting against the rampant breaches of proper behaviour within his remit. Indeed, in the subsequent twenty-odd years, several ministerial casualties have resulted not from personal corruption but from failure to stamp it out in their area of responsibility.

The reason in Ochoa's specific case was clear enough: anything that might justify US action against Cuba was inimical to Cuban sovereignty. But the whole argument against corruption was both moral and practical: on the former, the Revolution had, after all, been fought in part to cleanse Cuba of a system whose corruption had been legendary, spectacular and shameful, a major cause of popular opposition (Vignier and Alonso 1973); on the latter, the leadership recognised (from its knowledge of Eastern Europe and the Soviet Union) that a small enclosed society such as Cuba could not afford the visible evidence of an unacceptable inequality in living standards, resulting purely from political authority and power. That was true in the 1980s, and partly drove 'Rectification', but it remained true, and became even more so, in the 1990s, once inequality reared its ugly head again.

What was also interesting was the fallout from the case, for not only was there a major clear-out of MININT, but the minister himself, Abrantes, was sacked, tried and sentenced to twenty years' imprisonment for abuse of authority, negligence in his duties, and improper use of government funds (he died in prison in 1991). Corruption was indeed being given a high priority by such public displays of official retribution. In this sense, Ochoa was clearly given such high-profile treatment, including being executed, as an example, albeit not necessarily (as often alleged) because of his threatening ideas (Oppenheimer 1992: 128–9).

## The Third Party Congress of 1986

However, as already seen, corruption was only one dimension to the larger crisis, which, formally, the reconvened Third Party Congress sought to address. This it did in two clear ways: by labelling the new strategy (following the familiar pattern of giving a formal title to a process and a momentum already under way) and also by making new personnel changes at all levels. The turnover of the party's Central Committee, for example, was substantial, with 37 per cent being replaced (LeoGrande 2008: 52), but the clear-out even extended to the levels above that. Moreover, below that level, the pattern was repeated, with 43.5 per cent of the municipal party secretaries appointed in 1985 being removed in, or by, 1987 (Domínguez 1990: 57).

Another leading activist dropped at the Congress (from the Political Bureau and also from his post as Minister of Transport, where he had been since 1979) was Guillermo García (Bourne 1986: 298; Suchlicki 1988: 115). Having long been one of the stalwarts of the *Sierra* group, he was a politician whose talents had been less visible over the years but who had been kept inside the governing circles through historic respect as much as through recognition of his specific skills; his post of vice president in 1976–79 therefore tended to be seen as attributable to historic recognition. However, García illustrates the complexity of the decisions to include someone within the governing circles: a consistent member of the Political Bureau from 1965 and

still in the National Assembly after the 2011 elections, he represents
an excellent example of the pattern whereby someone could be sacked
for ministerial ineffectiveness but still retain a place at the ideological table of the Revolution's inner circle, especially if that person
was an ex-guerrilla. This suggests that, at least under Fidel (even
if less so later under Raúl, who clearly downgraded people for not
doing their job properly), a given ministerial position could be seen
as transient and less important than the essential and longer-term
trustworthiness of having been one of the historic 'few'. Further out
in the system of 'circles' was the case of José Luis Padrón González,
who had clearly risen through the ranks, becoming head of INTUR
(the tourism institution, before it was made into a ministry) and
then going on to play a prominent role in the Angolan involvement.
However, he too was sacked in 1986 (Szulc 1986: 36).

There were also, however, two quieter but more natural political
disappearances: of Blas Roca and Carlos Rafael Rodríguez. In the case
of Roca, his retirement through ill health in 1986 possibly removed
the potential dilemma of a second high-profile sacking (after Valdés).
Although some commentators at the time speculated that ill health
was a pretext and that he had in fact been forced to resign, his
death in 1987 probably confirmed that such speculation was wide of
the mark and that the official reason was correct. Rodríguez, too,
succumbed to ill health in the same period, being sensitively and
quietly retired from active duties as his health deteriorated and until
his death in 1997.

As for those chosen to replace these casualties, few immediately
came into the limelight. However, that was partly because the process
of making personnel changes continued after the Congress, especially in the wake of the Ochoa affair. One notable introduction to
the governing circles was Colomé Ibarra, until then a lower-profile
activist within the rebel ranks. Having joined the 26 July Movement
in 1957 (at the age of seventeen) and having then become part of
Raúl's Second Front, he had remained in, or associated with, the
FAR after 1959. He served especially in the security services from 1963
(under Valdés and Piñeiro), in which capacity he was part of Guevara's
Latin American strategy. Although Suchlicki (1988: 66) records him
as having joined the PURSC in 1963, it seems highly unlikely that he
would have done that so late in the day, given his close association

with Raúl and the FAR, and also given that, in 1965, he was elected to the new party's Central Committee. In 1971, confirming his FAR connections, he became Deputy Minister of MINFAR (with special responsibility for security and intelligence), and in 1975 participated fully in the Angolan involvement (which 'helped him consolidate his position': ibid.: 66). Hence, by 1986, it was already clear that he was emerging as someone who had the potential to be influential; this was confirmed when he succeeded Abrantes as Interior Minister in 1989, in the post-Ochoa clear-out. Thereafter, he ran MININT effectively and successfully, skilfully resisting rising evidence of US-supported dissidence and remaining as both a loyalist and an effective political operator and organiser.

## The 1989–94 crisis and economic and political reform

However, whatever changes were made in either 1985–86 (during 'Rectification') or 1989 (after Ochoa), they paled into insignificance compared with the shake-up that followed the crisis of 1989–91, a far deeper and more traumatic crisis than that which had faced the leadership in the early to mid-1980s. This was because, on the one hand, the scale of the resulting economic collapse threatened both the very basis of the Revolution's existence (not least its carefully constructed edifice of social protection) and the survival of the state, which, as we saw in the Introduction, was forced into near bankruptcy, obliged to rely on local activism and even ad hoc measures to ensure that some sort of state structure continued. On the other hand, the crisis was political and deeply psychological: not only had the Revolution's global military carapace disappeared (and, with it, the US undertakings of October 1962, raising the frightening possibility of a US invasion, especially after the ease with which Panama was invaded and occupied in December 1989), but so too had all the ideological certainties on which Cuba's membership of a global socialist community and the population's faith in the long-term systems of social provision and security depended. Even the most loyal and faithful activists of the party and the mass organisations feared, in 1993–94, that the system was either on the point of collapse or in imminent danger of being overthrown by outside forces.

In fact, the scale of the crisis and the urgency of a response led, in 1991–93, to an unprecedented programme of economic reforms, which were debated, decided and then enacted in 1991–94, ultimately saving the system and setting Cuba on the road to a steady, if painful, recovery. The recovery was painful because of the depth of the collapse and the long-term nature of both the Special Period and the austerity that the measures brought.

However, that same scale and urgency also had another effect, equally unprecedented and equally disruptive: the recognition that urgent changes were needed to the political structures, and even perhaps to the political leadership, to help regain the ideological initiative among younger generations and sustain the morale of older Cubans, whose faith had been sorely weakened by the collapse of both the Socialist Bloc and the certainties inside Cuba. At one level, those reforms were effective – and often overlooked by those commentating on the Special Period. They included: the 1992 reform of the National Assembly (making it more directly elected and thus restoring some credibility to a body that had come to be seen as a meaningless rubber-stamping institution); the slightly more cosmetic rewording of the Constitution (to make it more *martiano*, and thus more implicitly 'Cuban' and less 'Soviet'); tolerance of religious believers as party members; and also the more structurally significant spreading of the previously experimental People's Councils from 1993 onwards. The latter were largely administrative in purpose (designed, in fact, to break through the supply bottlenecks that were hampering recovery and angering ordinary Cubans who had limited access to food and other goods), but they also filled a void that had existed since the foundation in 1976 of the municipality-based People's Power electoral and representation system. That void was at the level of the barrio – in other words, between the street-level CDRs (declining but still effective in many ways, especially during the years of hand-to-mouth survival) and the much more distant *municipio* (covering as many as around 65,000 Cubans in each district) – and that was precisely the area in which the councils operated.

The People's Councils also reflected the other fundamental political change (mentioned in the Introduction), one that is even more neglected by outside observers: the rise of a new grass roots-based 'localism'. This began in 1991 partly as a spontaneous development (by local party and mass organisation activists) and partly as a centrally decreed encouragement to such activists, essentially seeking to adapt urgently to the lack of resources and funds and also to the state's new weakness by reconstituting the state at the grass roots and rebuilding a damaged state structure from the bottom. This was the *comunitario* movement, which developed in many different ways (most visibly in things such as the reconstruction of buildings in Old Havana and Centro Habana, and in a new cultural focus) and which made as great a contribution to the 'saving' of the system as any of the economic reforms.

*The Battle of Ideas* However, as the economic reforms took hold and as so many aspects of the familiar Cuban systems changed as a result, many in the leadership and many activists lower down the system observed regretfully that some of the social and even ideological costs of those reforms were unpalatable, most notably the small but discernible rise of petty crime (and, more corrosively, the fear of crime), the return of an embarrassing level of prostitution (developing, and even tolerated informally, to meet the new tourist demand), a weakening of the sense of collective solidarity, and a worrying return of levels of inequality (with the effects of the dual currency and the influx of remittances). But they also rued the reality that the unprecedented nature of the reforms led to a great difficulty in adjusting the principles and ethos of the pre-1989 system to the new pragmatic demands. It was, in fact, that unease that generated, firstly, the new debate about the fundamental nature of 'the Revolution' and, in turn, the Battle of Ideas, responding to the underlying imperative to discuss the hitherto unthinkable, creating new spaces for debate in magazines, academic and research centres, and so on.

Hence, in 2001, the Battle was formally declared to have begun in 2000. It arose from the experience and enthusiasm of the massive nationwide campaign, from autumn 1999 to June 2000, to demand the return to Cuba of six-year-old Elián González who, taken by his mother on a boat across the Florida Straits (but without his father's knowledge and, of course, illegally), was then shipwrecked and rescued by the US Coastguard. Since his mother died in the wreck and he was found at sea, according to the 1994 migration agreements between Cuba and the United States (which distinguished between 'wet foot' migrants, who were stopped at sea by the US authorities, and 'dry foot' people, who reached US soil), he was duly processed to be returned to Cuba, which was where his father remained. However, his Florida-based relatives began a legal and political campaign to prevent that, generating in turn a massive and sustained campaign in Cuba for him to be returned. That campaign consisted of daily marches and rallies (largely led by the UJC and FEU, and even staffed by young Cubans), saturated coverage in the media, and a nationwide explosion of posters and hoardings.

While Elián's return owed more to the US government's determination to face down the (often violent) Cuban-American protests and execute their agreed legal duty, the campaign in Cuba was seen as a political success, not least because, after years of demoralisation and an absence of the old characteristic mobilisation, it had reminded Cubans and the leadership of the power of such mass and 'passionate' action. Hence, it immediately sparked a conscious effort to capitalise on that moment and on the energy of the young protesters; this was christened the 'Battle of Ideas', explicitly challenging the corrosive ideas of capitalism (which were seen as entering the body politic during the Special Period, and with the influx of the US dollar and foreign tourists), but also seeking to reinvigorate Cubans, and especially young Cubans, ideologically. The underlying motive was to try to repeat the energy and processes of the early 1960s, when such mass mobilisation had clearly worked and tackled so many deep-seated problems.

Therefore, the Battle enlisted the UJC as a new, powerful element of the leadership, and as a consequence that organisation gained in importance. However, the Battle also signalled that the pendulum of participation had again swung firmly away from the old emphasis on material rewards and formal structures (not least because, in the Special Period, such rewards were once again unavailable or expensive, and because the new and continuing poverty of the state apparatus militated against such structures) and towards 'participation through (passionate) mobilisation'.

## The changing state and the changing inner circle

The sequence of deep crisis and state austerity, followed by wholesale reforms (including the creation of a new class of petty traders and artisans – in many respects the genesis of a new petty bourgeoisie) and finally the destabilising effects of the new mobilisations all had a profound effect on the nature of the Cuban state. As already seen, and despite appearances to the contrary, the Cuban state and system had only ever been strongly institutionalised and centralising in the 'middle years' (1975–86), the fluidity of the early years of transformation and nation-building being more characteristic. Now, the post-1991 Revolution saw the state weakened beyond recognition and eventually reformulating itself. This redefined system saw the return of the fluidity of the 1960s, and with it the old pattern of spaces, bases and individuals, as the old continuum of individualism–collectivism (which had been in operation since 1959) now adapted to the new crisis, the new demands and the new world context.

Hence, the 1990s once again changed the nature of the governing circles. In part this was inevitable because of the process of ageing within the 'inner circle' (this period saw the retirement or death of some prominent activists of the earlier eras), recognition of which led to a drive to rejuvenate the governing circles by introducing a younger generation. However, the changes and their inevitability were mostly due to the scale and urgency of the crisis, and two Party Congresses (the Fourth in 1991, exactly as planned, and the Fifth, slightly delayed, in 1997) created both the necessary processes of debate before the Congress and the resulting legitimation of the outcomes. Revealingly, the Sixth Congress, due in 2002, was repeatedly postponed, indicating both a process of ongoing debate and heightened mobilisation, and a continuing weakness of the institutional apparatus of governance, political communication and involvement.

As a result of all these pressures and imperatives, the 1990s and 2000s saw a series of personnel changes that reflected the underlying debates, the new urgency and the recognition of the need for considerable, if not fundamental, change. In the new context, two distinct patterns of collective leadership now emerged.

Firstly, those advocating rapid and deep economic reform or greater political flexibility, in order to adapt to the crisis, were promoted and found support from Raúl and also a base for their ideas. Besides Raúl himself (who championed the unprecedented economic reform programme), a group of 'technocrats' – understood as mostly (relatively) apolitical academics or specialists – and other reform-minded political actors were brought into office to enact the reforms. Others in the leadership were persuaded that these reforms were essential to save something of the whole post-1959 revolutionary project. Secondly, however, almost as though to provide a balance to these 'reformers', there was an enhanced version of the post-1985 promotions: that is, a growing reliance on old stalwarts of the 1953–58 insurrection and guerrilla campaign, and especially on members of the original *Sierra* group, whose loyalty was unquestioned and who could be expected to provide either a brake on excessive reform (to avoid a repetition of Gorbachev's errors) or a guarantee to grass-roots loyalists that the baby was not being thrown out with the reform bathwater.

*The stalwarts* The latter included people such as Juan Almeida Bosque, one of the longest lasting of the Moncada, *Granma* and *Sierra* veterans. Usually dismissed by outsiders as an unthinking 'bit-part' player (although long considered by Cubans as one of the most respected and valued ex-guerrillas), his inclusion in the leadership circles had long been seen by some outside commentators as a sop to the colour question, almost as a 'token black'. One, for example, described him disparagingly as a man 'of limited intellect but loyal to Castro as a leader' (Thomas 1971: 1320). In fact, his biographical details suggest someone much more central to the whole guerrilla experience and someone whose qualities were far from invisible; indeed, Franqui included him as one of his 'twelve' iconic or representative 'heroes' (Franqui 1967). He was one of the many working-class participants in the Moncada attack (being a stonemason by trade), was then imprisoned with Fidel and others on the Isle of Pines, went to Mexico with Fidel, and became one of those arrested, in June 1956, with Fidel, Valdés and four others (Alvarez Mola and Ravelo López 2007: 10). He was then one of the rebels on the *Granma*, and in fact was named as one of the few designated *capitanes*, going on to become a *comandante* on 27 February 1958 (Almeida Bosque 2008: 10). This standing within the guerrilla group was then demonstrated when he was given command of one of the four new fronts created to take the guerrilla war outside the Sierra Maestra; Almeida's Third Front was given responsibility for surrounding Santiago, and one of his columns was led by Huber Matos (Aladro Cardoso et al. 2007: 190). In January 1959, he was one of five *comandantes* identified as being close to Fidel and essentially integral to the command apparatus of the Rebel Army (Thomas 1971: 1043), the others being Raúl, Guevara, Camilo Cienfuegos and Valdés.

In June 1959, Almeida briefly replaced the defecting Díaz Lanz as head of the air force (ibid.: 1230), but he remained in the FAR in a number of capacities. Moreover, throughout the formal changes from 1961 onwards, he remained in the Central Committee of whatever form the united single party took, over fifty years or more, until his death in 2011.

Now, in the new crisis, he rose to greater prominence, with the creation in 1993 of the first new mass organisation since 1962, the Association of Veterans of the Cuban Revolution (ACRC). This was designed to mobilise and retain the loyalty of the many FAR people made redundant by the savage cuts to the military budget in the face of the crisis (Klepak 2005: 61). The ACRC thus became, for a while, a potentially valuable mechanism for channelling the ex-soldiers' loyalty in ways that the newly instituted and problematic workplace-based party could not do. Until then, the ruling party had largely followed the model of the Socialist Bloc and based its local *núcleos* not in residential areas, as is usually the case with British or US parties, but rather in workplaces. Membership of the party depended on the recommendation and invitation of one's workmates; now, however, with unemployment becoming a reality for the first time since 1959, that approach made little sense and residential area branches were allowed to exist, in order to attract and accommodate people such as ex-FAR loyalists.

A more spectacular and significant rise, however, was seen in the case of José Ramón Machado Ventura. As already seen in earlier chapters, he had been of some importance in the early decades. Another veteran of Raúl's Sierra del Cristal column from February 1958 (having joined the guerrillas in September 1957), he was named Head of the Military Household of the Presidential Palace in early 1959, becoming the person directed to take over the palace from the disgruntled DR members (Buch and Suárez 2009: 53). Having previously graduated in medicine (in 1954), he was then appointed Director of Medical Services in Havana for 1959 to 1960, as well as being responsible for medical services in the FAR (ibid.: 349); on this basis, he was then, in May 1960, named Minister of Health (a post he held until 1968). Thus his inclusion in the new party's Central

Committee in 1965 was logical, but in 1975 he was promoted to the Political Bureau and, in 1976, to the party's Secretariat, as well as to the Council of State (Suchlicki 1988: 167). Interestingly, before that, during the years of relative alienation from Moscow, it was he who was chosen to act as Cuba's sole representative at the 1967 Moscow celebrations of fiftieth anniversary of the Russian Revolution, which the Cuban leadership otherwise boycotted in protest at Moscow's silence over the growing criticisms of Cuba from Latin America's Communist Parties (Karol 1970: 392). In the meantime, during his rise through the party ranks, he successfully ran the provincial Matanzas Party from 1971 to 1976, and then was promoted to run the more prestigious Havana Party.

However, despite these appointments and evidence of either considerable trust or clever positioning, he largely kept a low profile; he seemed to prefer to be seen as an efficient organiser (he was, after all, the Political Bureau's member responsible for party organisation from 1971 until the early 1990s) and a loyal servant. Given his (never completely proven) reputation for stolid resistance to some of the more ambitious reform measures, some began to argue that Machado Ventura also used this position to steadily take over the party after the 1997 Congress, when the five-yearly cycle fell into disuse, the scheduled Sixth Congress being repeatedly postponed (until it finally materialised in 2011, after Raúl's insistence against evident opposition). Those reading his activism in this way argued that he took advantage of the lack of formal structural accountability (which Congresses normally provide) in order to create a considerable space and opportunity to make the party his power base. In fact, the Congress's decision in 1997 to reduce the size of the Central Committee (from 225 to 150) may have helped any such plan. Later, his somewhat surprising election as vice president in the 2008 Council of State elections seemed to confirm his power, although it was quite possible (and even probable) that he was elected at Raúl's instigation, as an attempt to balance the warring groups, as a counterweight to an otherwise unfettered reformist constituency and also as something of a signal to those thousands of party members who viewed the reforms with fear or disquiet. Moreover, we should not forget the long-standing ties of loyalty within the ex-Second Front guerrillas, which in other areas still seemed to count for something, so the idea of a Raúl–Machado battle may have been at least partly exaggeration and supposition.

As for the other old Second Front stalwart, José Ramón Balaguer, he was another 'background' player who survived over the decades. He was repeatedly linked with Machado Ventura in the 1990s and 2000s and was seen as Machado Ventura's closest party colleague, until he was retired (on grounds of ill health) in 2010. As already seen, he enjoyed some low-level prominence in the 1960s, without being especially significant; indeed, he was promoted to the party's Central Committee only in 1975, but he was clearly of growing importance by then. He was named First Party Secretary in Santiago, a post that he held from 1975 to 1983, although, according to one source, he was removed in 1985 (Suchlicki 1988: 20). In 1991, however, he was rehabilitated, becoming a key member of the Central Committee, Political Bureau and also the Secretariat, confirming his new influence and authority. Then, in September 1992, when Aldana, now denied the protection of Moscow, was summarily dismissed, 'ostensibly for involvement in illegal financial dealings' (LeoGrande 2008: 55), it was Balaguer who was chosen to replace him as Ideology Secretary of the Central Committee. Subsequently, he proceeded, in alliance with Machado Ventura, to ensure party loyalty in the wake of the 1990s crisis and in the face of a reduced membership. He also became Minister of Public Health during this latest period, and, in July 2006, was still a key player, being named by Fidel as one of six ministers designated to take over his duties while he underwent surgery. Although Balaguer was demoted later, he retained a significant responsibility in the Central Committee, in charge of its Department for International Relations.

A less obvious stalwart, and something of a case apart, was José Ramón Fernández. Unusually, he was not an ex-guerrilla but rather a former Batista army officer who joined the Cienfuegos mutiny in 1957, and was then imprisoned on the Isle of Pines until January 1959. At that point, he was immediately designated military administrator of that island by the new revolutionary leadership (Buch and Suárez 2009: 40). He was later given a key responsibility for training the new militias, which he led during the Playa Girón fighting, taking over a large part of the campaign's operations. Although he served as Minister of Education (1972–76 and 1984–90) and was on the party's Central Committee from 1975 until well into the 2000s, even being one of the (symbolically important) vice presidents (1978–2012), he seems to have kept a relatively low profile over the decades, until he too was raised in importance during the early 1990s, once again as a trusted veteran, albeit not of the Sierra guerrilla campaign.

However, a much higher profile was enjoyed by the most signifi-cant 'stalwart' to return to prominence during these years: Ramiro Valdés. His sudden return to power and influence after 2005 surprised those who had assumed that his equally sudden and unexplained departure from power in 1985 had been the result of misdeeds or excessive closeness to Moscow. However, it became clear that, since 1985, he had actually been 'retraining' in information technology (as head of the Copextel enterprise), in order to take charge of Cuba's approach to the IT challenge and its opportunities. In fact, he then went on to become Minister of Communications in 2005, even be-ing promoted in 2011 to be one of a handful of 'super ministers', confirming both his importance within the leadership and, related to this, his loyalty and value to Raúl's reform programme. In other words, Valdés's latest rise proved the enduring value of that old 'core' experience (Moncada, *Granma* and Sierra) in allocating posts (and power) and in surviving previous demotions or marginalisation. For, after 2010, it was clear that he was now more important and influential than the official senior vice president, Machado Ventura, whom he might even have superseded in the event of Raúl's sudden demise. In reality, his trajectory confirms that, rather than being dropped and rehabilitated (which suggests a more fickle approach to appointments or a constantly contested battlefield), Valdés never actually left the real 'inner circle', but simply went through periods on its edges when he did not fill specific posts.

*'Specialists' and loyal servants*  However, if these ex-guerrillas repres-ented some sort of ideological certainty and guarantees, the other promotions in this new crisis represented something quite differ-ent: a commitment to necessary (and even unprecedented) reform, focusing on efficiency and streamlining, almost in the same way that the seemingly 'idealist' or 'ideological' strand of 'Rectification' had been accompanied by a parallel strand of 'realism' and 'reform' (all of these easily used terms being contestable in the face of a reality always much more complex than easy terminology).

The most crucial new appointment was that of José Luis Rodríguez García, the quiet academic economist who actually drafted the reform ideas and oversaw them all, successfully, as Minister of Finance and Prices (1993–95) and then Economy Minister, posts in which he enjoyed an evident freedom to think the unthinkable and enact his longstanding ideas. His importance was shown by his parallel nomination as one of the vice presidents, a position he held from 1995 to 2009. However, he was unquestionably a 'technocratic' (i.e. specialist) appointment and promotion, rather than a political one.

Less technocratic and more political were some new appointees who, though coming from clearly political backgrounds (local and provincial party leadership or a base in the mass organisations), were clearly brought to the fore during this period for their quiet efficiency and reliability. One evidently capable or reliable actor (since he survived the political tussling of the 1990s and the subsequent shift to a Raúl-led system) was Esteban Lazo Hernández. Like Almeida, he often tended to be dismissed by commentators abroad as something of a lightweight and, being black, as a 'cosmetic' appointment, but he turned out to be a significant survivor and someone evidently trusted to run an efficient and loyal (rather than overbearing) party.

Having been too young to participate in the insurrection (he was fifteen in 1959), he nonetheless joined the militias in 1961 (Suchlicki 1988: 158) and steadily worked his way up the system, becoming the Matanzas Party's leader and the youngest member of the Political Bureau in 1986. Once close to Machado Ventura, he then came to the fore when appointed to be Havana Party Secretary, following the 1994 disturbances, and remained an integral part of the leadership from then on. With the changeover to Raúl, his position was enhanced further, confirming his reliability and efficiency, and, in February 2013, he was elected as President of the National Assembly to replace Alarcón. While some observers took this to be an indication of a downgrading of the Assembly (i.e. continuing the assumption that Lazo was a lightweight or slavish opportunist), it seemed more likely that Lazo's appointment actually confirmed the opposite, namely his political significance, given that there had been many signs from 2008 that Raúl was shifting power and authority towards the People's Power system (and specifically towards the Assembly and the Councils of State and ministers), as a counterweight to a persistently recalcitrant party hierarchy. In fact, for a while it seemed that Lazo might well be destined for ultimate leadership of a post-Raúl party.

The other similar promotions were of two leaders of the CTC, appointed both because of the political importance of that particular mass organisation (especially with the post-1993 and then post-2008 economic reforms needing the support of, or at least agreement from, the unions) and thanks to their own political talents. The first was Pedro Ross Leal, a pre-1959 member of the PSP youth section (the JS) who became a founder member of the new party in 1965 and provincial party leader in Oriente, and thus was also on the Central Committee. After 1975, he became head of that Committee's Agricultural Department. After serving briefly in Angola, he was chosen in 1989 to lead the CTC, a position from which he was also elected on to the Political Bureau, the National Assembly and the Council of State. Despite this profile and his clear importance over many years, he was yet another politician frequently described abroad as having no great discrete significance, being seen as someone chosen to toe a party line inside a suitably compliant CTC. In fact, he was running that organisation when grass-roots workers' complaints began to be expressed about the austerity measures from 1990, and he therefore became, if not the architect, then the person who instituted and operated the workplace *parlamentos obreros* (workers' parliaments), which brought a welcome degree of consultation and even change over the reform proposals.

In 2006, as part of the shifts at the top, Ross (who was appointed to diplomatic posts abroad) was replaced by Salvador Valdés Mesa. Once again, his image abroad often suffered because he was head of an organisation usually dismissed as part of a party-controlled monolithic structure. However, after 2008, he evidently flexed the CTC's muscles; although supporting Raúl's reforms, he also was successful in defending the interests of workers in the face of the proposed drastic job cuts (initially supposed to be up to a million job losses in the first year of the programme). He won a significant reduction in both the pace and the scale of those cuts, as well as ensuring better guarantees of protection and consultation for those losing their jobs.

As something of a colophon to this discussion of external observers' tendency to overlook people such as Ross and Lazo (and, earlier, Almeida), it is as well here to briefly discuss Cuban attitudes to race since 1959. This is because it has been a highly contested issue since the mid-1960s, with, on the one hand, allegations of an institutional racism within the Revolution's (largely white) leadership and structures and, on the other hand, generalisations about the Revolution's exemplary resolution of 'the race problem'. Hence, it has often been difficult to separate truth from polemic and objectivity from a priori positions, although some notable exceptions have managed to bring a welcome calmness to the debate (De la Fuente 2001; Morales Domínguez 2013). This lack of clarity became especially evident as the post-1990 crisis and reforms took their toll, both seeming to penalise Cuba's black population disproportionately. This was partly because the emigrant population (the source of remittances after 1993) was, and still is, overwhelmingly white; therefore, remittances to relatives tended to contribute to a new inequality, putting more much-needed hard currency into the hands of Cuba's whites than into those of the black population. However, the situation also arose because the Revolution's leaders and activists pursued policies in the 1960s that seemed contradictory and even clumsily 'colour blind'.

One fundamental complication in any discussion of race in Cuba is, of course, the unreliability of official statistics, and hence the lack of a clear consensus on the size of Cuba's black population, both before and after 1959. Basically, because race definition before 1959 depended largely on self-identification (e.g. in censuses) and skin colour, but also because the characteristics of race mixing and intermarriage over centuries had produced a population that, by North American standards at the time, was substantially non-white, most pre-1959 statistics tended to under-represent the size of the black and *mulato* population. Post-1959 trends have not significantly altered that pattern and so official figures of between 12 per cent and 20 per cent of Cuba's population being black seriously underestimate the reality. In fact, one recent expert assessment puts the non-white population at around 60 per cent (Morales Domínguez 2013: 181).

However, beyond this revealing statistical uncertainty, the whole question was complicated in the 1960s by four factors. The first was the statistical effect of the emigration of the largely white elite and middle class, which increased the population's proportion of non-whites. The second was the system's curious policies towards the black population on the one hand, and Afro-Cuban culture on the other. In essence, the leadership's approach to racial inequality was, from the outset, to assume that it could be eliminated by legislative action (famously outlawing segregation of properties in 1959) and by social reform. Indeed, as reforms bit deep into the areas of housing (rents and rehousing), food rationing, land distribution and education, it was soon true that they all especially benefited the black population, which was generally at the bottom of the social pile. This therefore meant ignoring the question of race.

That deliberate neglect was driven by two considerations. Firstly, the rebel ideology's clear debt to Martí's ideas generally included a repeated citing of the *martiano* principle; this stressed the political importance of nationalists being neither black nor white but 'Cuban', generating one kind of 'colour blindness'. Secondly, however, as the more radical rebels began to gravitate towards Marxism, this meant a tendency to read Cuba's social patterns and problems in terms of class (rather than race) and also, taking note of Marx's own famous (but often misquoted) dictum about religion being the opium of the people, to consider Cuba's various Afro-Cuban religions to be both 'opium' and superstition.

That said, however, the third complicating factor was the determination of the Revolution's leadership from very early on to rescue and re-validate many aspects of Cuba's black past and heritage. This meant, for example, raising the profile of the once denigrated *rumba*, as well as creating a Conjunto Folklórico Nacional (National Folklore Ensemble) specifically to rescue, preserve and spread appreciation of Afro-Cuban culture in dance and music. It also meant encouraging historians to address Cuba's history of slavery, and supporting anthropological research into Afro-Cuban cultural practices and forms.

However, while the leadership was enthusiastic about creating an awareness of Cuba's black heritage, this approach often seemed to be limiting awareness of colour to a 'folklorisation' of blackness. Indeed, later in the 1960s, when Cuba welcomed many US Black Power activists to the island and happily reported on black protest and radicalism (and even black consciousness) in the United States, Cuba's leaders were decidedly cautious, if not fearful, about any incidence of a black consciousness inside Cuba itself. This leads to the fourth complicating factor – the overwhelming drive for national unity after 1961, which saw any special focus on one 'group' as potentially undermining that unity, deemed essential in the years of 'siege'.

All of this therefore led to a confused and even contradictory attitude to race; indeed, it actually led to an official silence about the question from around 1962 (ibid.). This lasted until after Cuba's involvement in Angola in 1975 (presented domestically and internationally as 'the return of the slaves'), which generated a reassessment of blackness and a growing intellectual and political awareness of not just a black heritage but also the residual racism inside some sectors of the Cuban population that still prevented the upper echelons of the political structures from reflecting Cuba's colour mix. It was that residual racism that resurfaced in the divisive conditions of the Special Period.

*The support group and its politicians* Whatever the motivations of appointing and demoting given individuals, this pattern arose from the leadership's recognition of the need to change politically, as well as economically, which led in part to a discernible degree of panic. The reaction was not unlike the one that (rightly, it turned out) produced the economic reforms, but, in the process, it led to some unlikely – and ultimately discarded – discussion of, for example, the need to allow foreign capital to own property and land. This response saw the introduction into the inner circle of a new generation of younger politicians (here, the term 'politician' turned out to be significant). Since, by definition (given their age), they could not count on the same pedigree as the old inner circle, their qualifications were largely based on any one of two criteria: either a record of effective leadership of the UJC or membership of a new body that had grown up, the *Grupo de Apoyo*. This 'Support Group', its full title being Coordination and Support Group (Szulc 1986: 35), was attached to, but significantly separate from, the inner circle.

The *Grupo de Apoyo* was a selection of the supposedly brightest and best young political activists whom Fidel had gathered around himself in 1983, before 'Rectification' set in, as a kind of 'kitchen cabinet' under the guidance of two trusted advisers, 'Pepín' Naranjo Morales and 'Chomy' Barruecos. This was a time when debates, and tensions, were evident after the crises of the early 1980s, and Fidel evidently felt that such a group (consisting of ten men and ten women) could be the basis of a new future vanguard, untainted by the old orthodox pro-Soviet ideas and loyalties, which were still evident in the upper reaches of the system. He saw this group as dynamic, forward-thinking and loyal, but, ultimately, the group turned out to be something of a law unto itself, structurally unaccountable to anyone other than Fidel. Whatever their underlying loyalty to Fidel, many ex-guerrillas or veterans of the 1960s transformations undoubtedly found this new untouchability galling, especially when one of those younger leaders, Carlos Lage Dávila (a former leader of the UJC), was seen to be spearheading the economic reform programme that so deeply troubled many of the supposed 'old guard'. In a sense, the *Grupo* was created to replace the old looser grouping of close confidants and advisers who had originally surrounded Fidel, namely people like Celia Sánchez, Montané, Luis Buch, Núñez Jiménez, 'Pepín' and 'Chomy', and the lesser-known 'all-purpose' secretary Conchita Fernández (Valdés 2008: 38).

If José Luis Rodríguez was a 'technocrat' rather than a politician, Lage was unquestionably more political, becoming rapidly the most significant and influential of those promoted from the Support Group, not least as he was allowed to turn the formerly subordinate post of secretary to the Council of Ministers into a genuinely powerful position, becoming the de facto 'Prime Minister'. From that position, he backed the economic reform programme, becoming the visible face of the whole strategy, with a growing reputation for both efficiency and forward-thinking. Thus, as he was so clearly close to Fidel but also trusted by Raúl, it was also logical that his ideas, his youth and his dynamism all marked him out increasingly as representing the future of a steadily redefined 'Revolution', and therefore as the probable medium-term successor to either or both of the Castros. However, this supposition not only made him become identified in everyone's eyes as a future leader, but, in the end, it also seemed to affect the way that he behaved, as he appeared to use his position increasingly to build a base and to act, not least when in the company of foreign politicians and the world media, as though he were indeed such a successor. Hence, in 2009, as Raúl moved into a higher gear (after the hiatus of two years of relative inertia and following the 2008 National Assembly elections) and began to reshape the political structures and personnel to suit his agenda rather than the (by now embarrassingly inefficient and costly) Battle of Ideas, Lage and his fellow 'rising star' Felipe Pérez Roque (see below) were both summarily sacked and removed from positions of power, essentially for having exceeded their brief and having 'played the politician' (and also 'the heirs apparent') too publicly. Such was the antipathy towards the *Grupo* among some in the broader leadership that their dismissal also had an air of 'they had it coming' about it. Interestingly, the sacking (on 2 March) was immediately followed by Fidel's own public criticism of those who had been seduced by what he called 'the honey of power', and then, on 4 March, by Lage's admission of his guilt and his resignation from all of his posts in the Central Committee, Political Bureau, Council of State (to which he had just been re-elected vice president) and National Assembly.

Promoted at the same time as Lage was Roberto Robaina, surprisingly named Foreign Minister in 1993. He was less urbane and more flamboyant than Lage, but came from the same Support Group and UJC stable. In that powerful position, he partly sought to repeat Roa's earlier role, redefining Cuba's external profile in a radically changed world, a role that he largely carried out well (not least by steadily increasing support for Cuba in international forums, and especially in the UN). However, he fell foul of the leadership in 1999, in circumstances which suggested that, rather than exceeding his brief, he had abused his position and authority for personal material benefit. Although not openly accused of corruption, perhaps because his profile had been so high, his fall from grace was so sudden and so spectacular that it was clear that his 'sin' had been great, which, given the sliding scale of 'sackable offences', probably meant at the very least feathering his own nest.

However, he was succeeded as minister by another young Support Group/UJC player, Pérez Roque. Closely associated with Fidel, and especially with the Battle of Ideas (which, in external affairs, meant developing close relationships with Venezuela, Bolivia and the other ALBA countries), he seemed especially blessed by the old leadership and was therefore, like Lage, often spoken of in diplomatic circles (if not as much as Lage was by ordinary Cubans) as a future leader. Hence, it was logical that he fell from grace at the same time as Lage and for the same offences – specifically for excessive 'politicking' and for having engaged (with Lage) in a session of relatively open mockery of Fidel, an incident that was duly filmed by the security services and then presented to the two culprits as evidence of their 'sin' and shown secretly to all party members, as proof of their offence and as a warning to others.

Interestingly, the double sacking confirmed to some extent the importance of not imputing factionalism to the Cuban governing circles, for Lage and Pérez Roque had previously tended to be associated with different, and even opposite, strands of thinking: Lage had been seen externally and internally as a committed 'reformer' (seeking to modernise in whatever way was necessary) whereas Pérez Roque was seen as an integral part of the 'revolutionary' *fidelista* Battle of Ideas.

As part of the post-1993 attempt to rejuvenate the leadership, but, more specifically, as part of the campaign over Elián and then the Battle of Ideas, there were also two, very short-lived, rising stars. Otto Rivero (head of the UJC) spearheaded the Elián campaign, remaining a close confidant of Fidel throughout, and eventually was given specifically vice-presidential authority for the Battle, while Hassan Pérez was the engaging and enthusiastic, if often much criticised, head of the FEU. Their stars fell as quickly as they had risen, as Raúl reshaped the political leadership after 2007.

*The reliable loyalists* However, of all the political personnel changes during this two-decade-long period, three stand out. The first was the case of Ricardo Alarcón de Quesada. Although too young to be a guerrilla before 1959, he had been active in radical student politics before that year. As leader of the law students, he coordinated university activism for the 26 July Movement in 1958, arguing for collaboration with the PSP (thus unusually becoming both a trusted member of the *Llano* and one who agreed with the shift towards the PSP). He then developed a clearly political background: in 1960, he helped to lead the radicals in the hotly contested political battles and changes within Havana University (Thomas 1971: 1286). However, in 1962, he began a career within the Foreign Ministry, taking charge of its Americas section at a time when that meant a close association with the insurrectionary and anti-imperialist policy in the region. In 1966, he began a long and successful period as Cuba's ambassador to the UN, a post he held until 1992. From that position, in fact, he developed a reputation for both efficiency (being praised by Cubans and non-Cubans alike for the skill he showed in negotiations and for his talent for quiet persuasion and tactful diplomacy) and his ability to develop politically useful channels of communication with Washington, where he was usually respected as a sharp, if urbane, operator. It was that experience together with his knowledge of, and contacts in, the United States that, firstly, made him repeatedly useful as a lead negotiator with Washington (this even continuing after he left the ministry, for example in the 1994 post-migration crisis negotiations) and, secondly, brought him further prominence as Foreign Minister in 1992–93.

In 1993, however, he really found his forte and his most important and influential role, as president of the reformed National Assembly; indeed, his promotion to that post (replacing the lesser-known 1990 appointee, Juan Escalona) was seen by many as a key moment in the government's drive to restore some credibility to the National Assembly: bringing an evidently respected, popular and influential politician in to run the Assembly was seen as bestowing it with a prestige that it had not previously enjoyed (Bengelsdorf 1994: 162). After 2008, as elements in the party continued to block Raúl's plans for reform of the economy, Alarcón became a close ally, happily allowing the Assembly and the government to become stronger institutions. So influential and well-liked was Alarcón that, even when Lage was tipped to be 'the successor', many observers continued to identify Alarcón as a possible key player in any such succession and even as a future leader himself. More importantly, despite this, he never allowed such speculation to take over his political good sense (as had happened with Lage and Pérez Roque). When he was surprisingly excluded from the candidates' list for the February 2013 elections, the reason given was ill health; many people subsequently confirmed that this was the truth, although there were also rumours of displeasure among the leadership that he had failed to control his organisation sufficiently.

Overall, in terms of the 1990s promotions, Alarcón was certainly no 'technocrat', since his rise to influence and positions of considerable responsibility clearly reflected his personal talents rather than his specific qualifications, making him closer to the Lazo type of promotion than any other. However, he was equally not guilty of the 'sin' of being a 'politician', so he was able to maintain an enduring existence and influence in ways that others did not.

The rumours surrounding his departure focused on alleged neglect that allowed a fraud to take place. This involved money destined for the high-profile campaign to free the well-known five Cubans imprisoned in the United States in 1998 and sentenced in 2000 for spying on the activities of anti-Revolution groups in the Cuban-American community. Interestingly, Alarcón's apparent demotion was accompanied by the demotion of Naranjo and Barruecos, which pointed in some ways to the final dismantling of all such personalist groupings, not just of the newer Support Group. Equally, in a way, Alarcón's departure from power was the final chapter in the inclusion of ex-*Llano* people in the inner circles; thus, despite his special qualities, relative youth and remarkable longevity in positions of influence, this made him a classic case where a trusted pre-1959 political pedigree and successful post-1959 activism both qualified him for increasing inclusion in the innermost circles, until both age and much-needed reform made his generation, like that of the marginally older ex-guerrillas, dispensable.

The second prominent loyal political actor was Abel Prieto Jiménez. In a way, his trajectory was much more limited and narrowly focused than Alarcón's, since he only ever operated inside the world of culture. A poet and short-story writer, he rose through the ranks of the UNEAC system to become its president in 1991, a post that he retained until 1997. There, however, he showed a well-tuned political awareness, recognising the importance of culture to the whole revolutionary project and many artists' and writers' need to be both consulted and included in the cultural world's new opportunities for hard-currency acquisition. Hence, he made UNEAC both more powerful as a national institution and also more responsive to its members' needs than it had been in the problematic 1970s. As a result, in 1997, he took over from Hart as Minister of Culture, and, from that even more influential position, he proceeded to win a seat at the decision-making table for the cultural world, successfully being noticed (not least by Fidel, who evidently respected Prieto's abilities and willingness to challenge him) and creating the sought-after opportunities for hard-currency earnings, but also enthusiastically enlisting the ministry in the Battle of Ideas, where culture played a fundamental role.

Quite simply, if Hart had rescued the cultural world for the Revolution (after the trauma of 1968–76) and again made culture fundamental to the Revolution's processes of socialisation and nation-building, then Prieto took that process further, not only making culture central to the political process once again, but also giving it a political voice that, to the outsider, defied expectations. When he stepped down in 2012, replaced by a somewhat less charismatic vice president (Rafael Bernal Alemany), it was seen by many in UNEAC as a demotion of culture in the Revolution's priorities; however, there had been ample evidence before that of Prieto's wish to return to writing and to abandon a position in which he was constantly bombarded from below by appeals from the cultural workers and apparatus but increasingly restricted financially from above.

The third such promotion is the one about which we still know the least: that of Miguel Díaz-Canel Bermúdez. As far as the outside world was concerned, he leaped to prominence in February 2013, when, as a fifty-two-year-old, he was elected as Cuba's new senior vice president, replacing Machado Ventura, and was suddenly catapulted into the limelight as the supposedly designated 'successor' to Raúl after 2018. In fact, his rise to influence and authority had preceded that, when, in 2003, he became a member of the Political Bureau, and again, in 2009, when he was named Minister of Higher Education. This was a crucial post at the time, given the newly admitted and publicised problems of poor student quality and the evidence of student discontent. Yet he was no political ingénue, simply someone who had existed 'under the radar' as far as most external commentators were concerned, since his political career until then had largely been in evidence in the provinces. There, in fact, he had quietly risen through the UJC and then the senior party in Villa Clara province, making a name for himself for his efficiency and political skill. As a result, in 2003 he became party leader of the more politically significant Holguín province, from where he continued to attract plaudits for his quiet unsung effectiveness, evidently coming to the attention of a leadership keen to replace overt 'politicking' party activists on the one hand, and ageing and perhaps conservative stalwarts on the other, with a new generation of younger, trusted and efficient 'managers'.

Indeed, Díaz-Canel fitted perfectly the blueprint that Raúl seemed to have created since 2008 in his desire to replace the government that he had inherited in 2006 with people whose political credentials and operational effectiveness could be relied upon.

## Reflections on the changing circles

Where, then, does this convulsive period of leadership change leave us, in the light of the earlier pattern of inner, intermediate and outer circles? Most obviously, a period characterised by crisis, dislocation, urgent reform, reassessment and debate, the weakening and renewed fluidity of the institutional and state structures and the relentless ticking of the biological clock of generational shift had all combined to unsettle, at a time of danger, the carefully preserved but largely organic group cohesion of the overall collective leadership. While the veterans of the old inner circle and intermediate circle may have been reinforced in their influence after 1985–86, and while some of them may have increased their power in pockets and spaces, the reality was that, by the mid-2000s, their hold had been irrevocably weakened, both numerically and in terms of their activism, legitimacy and ability to affect policy-making. The attempt to replace them by introducing a new generation of supposedly equally reliable and ideologically committed activists had resulted in political crisis, the rise of personal ambition and some serious cleavages in the old solidarity. The fact that the influence of the Support Group had been so openly resented, the reduced ability of the old leadership to make sensible and astute political judgements, and the evident and public tension between Raúl (and those supporting his urgent reform agenda) and some recalcitrant elements in the party all indicated the existence of those cleavages. Indeed, so serious were they that, in 2008, Raúl was forced by such resistance to threaten publicly to call an unprecedented Special National Conference in order to make 'generational' (i.e. personnel) changes in the party, and thus outmanoeuvre the 'old guard' – this was a very, and unusually, public washing of dirty linen on issues of policy (rather than corruption), the like of which had not been seen since the 1960s.

At one level, of course, the process had been a result of that biological clock, since death, ageing and ill health had reduced the numerical and even political strength of the old 'core', forcing the leadership to introduce new blood from time to time. For all their evident and genuine commitment (to Fidel or to the old definition of 'Revolution'), the new members simply lacked the veterans' *esprit de corps*, group cohesion and collective legitimacy, and they were also more likely to sympathise with younger Cubans' growing frustration and desire for some sort of generational shift.

Fidel's decision to soldier on into the 2000s therefore played a part in this process of gradual cleavage. While the Elián campaign and the Battle of Ideas might have been both necessary (according to the historical process's logic and even in the light of the short-term impact of the Elián campaign) and effective in briefly rejuvenating an ageing Fidel, by the early 2000s his own physical and even mental frailty soon became an obvious problem. As he fell (twice) and as his legendary ability to lecture Cubans for hours on end, improvising and illustrating arguments with a seemingly endless stream of well-memorised facts and data, began to decline, loyal Cubans started to fear for the stability and flexibility of government. Thus a crucial element of the system's (and the old inner circle's) credibility and legitimacy began to be undermined. While Fidel may never have exercised the supposedly total power that his critics had always alleged and that the 'totalitarian' label assumed, and while even his initial centrality to decision-making may have declined over the decades, the fact was that most Cubans – and certainly those loyal to, or tolerant of, the Revolution (as a system and a unifying myth) – had always believed in his capacity to guide, lead and decide cleverly and with awareness of what they felt. Once that was removed, or at least undermined, the rot had set in, and a new form of governance had to be found. Hence, while his decision to retire might have been stimulated as and when it was by the accident of a serious illness, it was a logical and timely choice, and one might speculate that it perhaps would have come about anyway in the near future. The reasoning was simple: Fidel's awareness may have been impaired in comparison to his earlier ability, but he knew enough (from the Ochoa and Robaina cases and from what the UJC and FEU had learned in 1999–2000 about the thinking of young Cubans) about the risk of remaining in office too long to want to endanger fatally the process for which he had fought since 1953. He too was aware that the system had to adapt.

# 7 | INCLUSION AND EXCLUSION: 'WITHIN' AND 'AGAINST' THE REVOLUTION

Where, then, does all this detail and this trajectory take us in understanding the overall patterns of the Revolution? One obvious conclusion at this stage is that the idea that decision-making was always concentrated only in either Fidel alone (at least until 2008) or possibly, in the early 1960s, in the triumvirate of Fidel, Raúl and Guevara has been at least questioned if not seriously undermined. For we have seen a 'cast of dozens' who at some stage or other have contributed significantly, some in nationally important and even independent ways, but many others in small and narrowly focused ways, to the Revolution's shape, direction and definition. What we have also seen is the remarkable continuity of what we might call the 'core' of those 'dozens': for the Cuban Revolution, as already observed, never suffered from the major leadership rifts or personalist factions of, say, the Russian or Chinese revolutions. Instead, it has been notable for the longevity 'in the saddle' not only of Fidel and Raúl (Guevara, of course, died in battle in 1967) but also of so many of those who were similarly steeled in the fire of battle of the 1953–58 period.

Yet, what we have also seen is a pattern to that unity and that 'togetherness', namely the underlying importance of a collective to which loyalty was expected. That collective was both 'the group' and 'the Revolution', although what the latter actually meant evolved so much over the decades that it lost any clarity that it might have had for some in 1953 or 1959, but, at the same time and for the same reason, it gained in mobilising power and collective identity. As we have seen, that sense and expectation of loyalty affected the leeway given to those who were, in leadership or in responsible positions, part of the three 'circles' of power and influence outlined in Chapter 3, allowing those individuals to stray, question, doubt and err (but never to oppose actively) and still be forgiven and considered part of the 'group'. Indeed, that loyalty almost always overrode other considerations, such as efficiency, ideological conformity or political disagreement, as long as that 'erring' or 'disagreement' was not considered or intended to be against the emerging system and was largely kept 'in house'.

How then can we understand this within any wider patterns, beyond the cases of named individuals and personal relationships? One way is to relate that definable pattern of behaviour and loyalty to two characteristics that have not only been evident from the outset in 1959, but have also helped to shape the direction of things and even the degree of support, loyalty or tolerance of the thousands, if not millions, of Cubans who, since 1959, and with varying degrees of enthusiasm or real commitment, have chosen to remain 'with', and (as we will see) in a real sense 'inside', the Revolution.

## Cuban history and the evolution of a culture of inclusion

The first of these characteristics is the existence of what we might call an ethos or a culture of 'inclusion' (and therefore also of its opposite, 'exclusion'). This developed in the Cuban system especially from 1961, but it had clear roots in the preceding traditions of debates about, and commitments to, the idea of national identity.

There are, in fact, a great many reasons why the emerging Cuban political culture should have produced such an ethos. Firstly, one should probably not overlook the effect of Cuba's geographical identity as an island. As we know from many historical cases, an island identity can easily lead to an island mentality, and both a sense of isolation (and independence of 'destiny') and a collective belief in that island people's 'special' character, uncontaminated by neighbouring territories.

Secondly, one has to take into account the long and contested history of a Cuban national identity. In essence, this refers to a series of historical phenomena. Firstly, while the rest of Latin America's *criollos* (native-born whites) had eventually – by 1828 – welcomed the idea and the reality of independence (despite any earlier reluctance or fear in the first flush of rebellion, broadly in 1808–14), Cuban *criollos*, driven by even deeper reluctance and fears, chose to remain Spanish until that option proved pointless by the 1860s. Secondly, when the idea of separatism finally became an accepted position among enough *criollos*, its first manifestation was not a desire for nationhood but rather for US statehood, advocating annexation by the United States. Thirdly, when a struggle for real independence finally broke out in 1868, the white rebel leadership's surrender, which heralded its formal end (in 1878), was hotly contested by those thousands of (mostly black) Cubans who had seen the long war as a means of achieving their social as well as political liberation. Finally, the whole of the nineteenth century saw a continual influx of Spanish immigrants, increasing even after independence in 1902, which made the island even more *peninsular* (i.e. Spanish) than it had been in 1810 and which in turn created an impossible complexity surrounding the vexed question of who exactly was 'Cuban' and who was 'Spanish'.

On the one hand, from the mid-nineteenth century onwards, more and more children of often loyal Spanish immigrants would become attached to the independence cause, their birth in Cuba and the influence of their peers persuading them to consider themselves Cuban. On the other hand, many recent Spanish immigrants after the 1870s, being generally more politicised than previous immigrants, often sided with the pro-independence dissidents because of their own opposition to Spanish capitalism. Meanwhile, many leading Cuban entrepreneurs and even progressive politicians took US nationality while in exile in the United States, some as a gesture of their opposition to Spain but others because they still harboured annexationist sentiments, even after Cuban independence in 1902. So a consensus about who was 'Cuban' and what that meant remained contested and unclear, and, after 1898, anti-Spanish sentiment remained, to the extent that, from 1902 to 1934, the anger of Cuban nationalists was directed often as much against the power and influence of the still commercially powerful Spanish-born community as against 'US imperialism'.

This complexity, ambiguity and ambivalence were reflected in one underlying principle of the several drafts of the Constitution that rebels and politicians created between 1869 and 1940: the 1897 'rebel' draft, which planned for an eventual republic (Pichardo 1977: 501), and also the final and controversial 1901 document (Pichardo 1986: 76) both contained clauses defining those who could be viewed as Cuban, including ex-slaves born in Africa but also the Spanish who had settled in Cuba.

There were thus deep historical roots to a growing collective sense of a denied nationhood, which, from the 1920s, drove many intellectuals, radicals and nationalists to develop notions of *cubanidad* (Cuban-ness) as part of their search for a clearer and more unified national identity (Suárez 1996). They sought the essence of something called 'Cuba' in any number of characteristics: the countryside and the peasant, the east and especially Oriente province (Kapcia 2000: 159), African-rooted (as opposed to Spanish-influenced) Cuban folk music, a self-deprecating sense of humour (the *choteo*), and a particular racial mixture (ibid.: 86), supposedly creating a 'special' ethnicity that was expressed in Ortiz's *ajíaco* ('stew') as a metaphor for this (Suárez 1996: 12). Therefore, by the 1950s, many Cubans had inherited a sense of their uniqueness, reinforced by their special proximity to the United States and even their quasi-Americanisation in many cultural and social aspects, but without what they perceived as the ignominy of Puerto Rico's quasi-colonial associate statehood. Therefore, a sense of 'us' and 'them' (essential to the emergence of any national identity and any nationalism) already existed, although precisely who constituted 'them' was never entirely clear, being sometimes (for the Left) the United States and its 'imperialism' and at other times (for the Right) the rest of Latin America or the Caribbean, to which many Cubans felt that they did not belong.

Within this deeper and wider historical context, however, three other experiences and perceptions in the 1950s and early 1960s now added to the fusion of influences to exaggerate that sense of 'us' and 'them', at least in the new political leadership and circles of activism. That leadership, indeed, proceeded to project that sense outwards to the wider Cuban population, emphasising a unique national identity (that had produced such a remarkable Revolution) and a shared collectivity.

## The creation of a sense of 'us' and 'them' after 1959

The first was, as we have seen, the shared camaraderie of the Sierra experience, which created that clear and unbreakable 'group identity'; as argued in the preceding chapters, this determined precisely which political actors were 'inside' and which 'outside'. However, from 1960–61, the sense of the 'group' began to extend more generally to include the Cuban population as a whole, with media images, speeches, mass mobilisations, rallies and billboards all helping to create a widespread identification between the *Sierra* (as an idea, as well as an experience, reflecting the essence of 'the Revolution') and the population. While they might not have participated in the fighting itself, the people could be convinced that, by participating in the mass tasks of the new transformation process, serving in the militia from 1959 or educating the illiterate in 1961, they too were reliving the *Sierra*. Thus, when, after the literacy campaign, Cuba was declared the 'First Territory Free of Illiteracy', i.e. the first in Latin America (Montalván Lamas 2011), this was an explicit identification with the guerrillas' establishment of what was called the 'First Free Territory' (in Cuba) in the heart of the Sierra in 1958.

The second collective experience of the 1960s that helped shape that mood of togetherness was the new sense of siege now felt by all Cubans who remained on the island. This really started in 1960, when the first stage of what became total US economic sanctions began, but it was reinforced spectacularly when, in 1961, the long-awaited invasion materialised at Playa Girón (although the fact that all Cubans had expected such an invasion for some time meant that the 'siege' was already real for them), and then, in January 1962, when the United States persuaded all of the region (apart from Canada and Mexico) to break off relations and expel Cuba from the Organisation of American States. Thus, by the time that total sanctions were imposed in 1963, the siege was already in place, this measure simply being the final brick in the wall around Cuba, intended to isolate the island totally. Yet there was one further step in this growing feeling of being under siege: the outcome of the October 1962 Missile Crisis. Many Cubans (and certainly the leadership, publicly) felt a sense of betrayal at the Soviet Union's behaviour in excluding Cuba from the negotiations with Washington – an exclusion that resurrected memories of the 1899 Treaty of Paris between Spain and the United States, which had determined the fate of Cuba without any Cuban participation – and in keeping the Cuban leadership in the dark, and then not taking advantage of the United States' willingness to find a solution in order to achieve a better outcome for Cuba, such as the lifting of sanctions. This therefore led quickly to a growing sense that Cuba could not even count on its new (and geographically distant) allies when it really mattered. After 1963, therefore, although safe from invasion (as a result of Washington's promise in that agreement), many Cubans felt that they were now alone in the world, sometimes defiantly so (after all, they had defeated the 1961 invasion, refused a UN inspection of the missile sites, and showed a willingness to fight, as the real front line in a potential nuclear war) but also at times frighteningly so.

Yet out of this isolation and solitude came a real, and then cultivated, sense of 'us' against 'them', the latter now referring to the whole of that part of the hostile world which sided with either Washington or Moscow. Over the following few years, the Cuban leadership began to encourage guerrilla warfare in Latin America, seeking to overthrow those governments that had 'slavishly' followed the US line and isolated the island, and thereby challenging US power, but also in defiance of Soviet policy and orthodoxy. As a result, relations with Moscow deteriorated steadily, albeit mostly felt indirectly, through Cuban condemnations of the region's Communist Parties, which were, after all, largely following Moscow's dictates. Even as late as 1967, at the nadir of those relations, Fidel declared in Santiago on 26 July (a symbolically memorable date, of course, redolent of notions of struggle and of a very 'Cuban' rebellion) 'Cuba está sola' ('Cuba is alone') (Karol 1970: 340). This was not a plaintive lament but, rather, a defiant declaration of lonely but battling independence. Cuba's self-image of an 'embattled enclave' or David against Goliath (and, in this case, two Goliaths) helped to cement that existing sense of the 'special' character of the island and its people, and now of its Revolution.

The final phenomenon of the 1960s that contributed to this collective sense of unity was the rapid, and then steady, exodus of those who opposed the evolving system and the radicalisation process; this was occurring even before 'Communism' reared its head, but was especially prevalent after 1961. By the early 1970s, over 460,000 Cubans had left, largely the white urban middle class and mostly for Florida (Olson and Olson 1995: 93). Whatever economic damage this exodus may have had (sapping much-needed expertise, with a costly and long-term need to replace a valuable labour force and levels of trained professionalism), the departure of the wealthy (or simply the materially comfortable) was exploited by the Revolution's leaders and propaganda mechanisms. They did this not only by housing thousands of previously homeless or slum-dwelling Cubans in the vacated properties, but also by portraying the supposedly politically motivated emigrants as *gusanos* (worms), traitors not so much to the Revolution (although that question itself struck a popular chord, as most Cubans had benefited from the process and saw the refugees as opposing a valid and much-needed social transformation) as to the *patria*. In this, of course, it helped that their destination was the very country that, since 1959, had opposed a popular process of change and reform, and which, before that, had been seen to keep Cuba neo-colonial and backward.

As a result, the sense of 'us' and 'them' now included a clear message: 'we' were those who had chosen not to abandon Cuba (indeed the phrase *abandonar el país* ('to abandon the country') now became, for decades, the normal way of describing those who had left) but to fight to defend the country, build a new society, with sacrifice and effort, while 'they' included the 'unpatriotic' refugees. Those refugees' decision to leave had therefore taken them beyond the possibility of inclusion in a collective definition of 'Cuba', thereby echoing the sentiments of the earlier Constitution. In fact, it was only in 1980, after the shocking scale of, and response to, the Mariel exodus (when the terms *escoria*, or 'scum', and 'lumpen' were openly used in the media for several days, before a subtle shift was noticed) that a realisation began to dawn that, by then, not all of those leaving were political refugees, turning their back on 'the Revolution', but, rather, many were simply economic migrants (Port 2012). Since then, the Cuban media have been careful to distinguish between what they consistently call *la mafia anticubana* (the 'anti-Cuban mafia') – referring to the implicitly 'treacherous' political elite of the Cuban-American community – and *la emigración* (emigrants). However, the power of the image of 'us' (remaining on the island) and 'them' (who have left) remains strong in certain circumstances; during the long Elián campaign of 1999–2000, one slogan repeated on the specially made T-shirts was *Devuélvanlo a su familia cubana* ('return him to his Cuban family'), the term *familia* being clearly a double reference, to his father and grandparents in Cuba but also to all those fellow Cubans who were marching daily in support of his cause and yearning for him to come back to them. In fact, this whole campaign was also an oblique reference to the traumatic effect of the early emigrations, when families were divided irrevocably by decisions to depart and, even more so, by the infamous 'Peter Pan' operation. In 1960–62, under the control of some Catholic priests but blessed by the church generally, very young Cubans were shipped away from their families in Cuba (in some cases for ever) in order to 'rescue' them from the threat of Communist indoctrination (Triay 1998); that particular campaign, in fact, had reinforced the historic importance of unity among those who remained, in the face of an 'enemy' presented as thinking nothing of dividing the Cuban 'community' on the island.

## Defining 'inside' and 'against' the Revolution

The question of 'inside', however, had already entered the Revolution's lexicon, albeit initially in a very narrowly defined way. June 1961 saw a series of three weekly meetings in the National Library, between worried intellectuals and artists (fearful that the arguments about, and the effective banning of, the controversial *PM* documentary film might presage a policy of restricting artistic expression) and the leadership, which sought to allay those fears. After the meetings, on 30 June, Fidel outlined what was then taken to be the Revolution's first definitive statement of cultural policy, in his speech 'Words to the Intellectuals' (*Palabras a los Intelectuales*); the speech was characteristically long and included all manner of perhaps predictable statements, declarations and assurances, but it especially included one phrase that thereafter reverberated around the world, helping (largely, it has to be said, through its mis-recording in the media and other writings) to confirm the expectations of those outside Cuba who had long feared the stamp of Stalinism. The phrase in question, defining the parameters of cultural freedom in the Revolution, was: 'Inside the Revolution, everything; against the Revolution, nothing' (Castro Ruz 1980: 14); in other words, it was declaring that any cultural manifestation that stayed 'within' the boundaries of what 'the Revolution' represented would be permitted, even if that artistic product did not overtly espouse 'revolutionary' ideas, goals or principles, whereas any manifestation that was explicitly 'against' the Revolution had no place and would not be tolerated.

The important dimension to this statement was not so much the unanswered question (what did 'within' and 'against' actually mean and who would define those terms?), itself enough of an ambiguity to still preoccupy some of those previously fearful, as the precise wording of the binary used. For the choice was not between those 'within' and those 'outside' (which might have been taken as referring to those who were outside the island, but might also have meant those who, rather than writing or painting or composing 'against' the Revolution's tenets, simply did not accept them and ignored them in their works); nor was it between 'for' (the meaning being clear enough) and 'against', but rather 'within' and 'against', an importantly asymmetrical binary. What the phrase was actually saying was that *only* those who acted *against*, openly and unmistakably, could not find a home *inside* the definition of the Revolution and therefore enjoy cultural freedom and possibilities, and that all others would be assumed to be *inside*, since the absence of the term 'for' (instead of 'within') removed the requirement for all artists to be explicitly revolutionary in their work. That wording was crucial to the message, and also to the subsequent misunderstandings. Within no time at all, the version that found its way abroad – and that still, to this day, is repeated ad infinitum – was not the correct one but rather the binary of 'inside' and 'outside', thus distorting the phrase, the underlying message and the policy.

As regards Cuban cultural policy, the interesting thing is that this whole speech did not establish what the Revolution's 'culture' would be henceforth – indeed, one characteristic of Cuban cultural policy pronouncements from that day forward has always been that they do not so much establish something new or set something in stone, but rather they confirm and codify what is already happening (Kumaraswami and Kapcia 2012: 22–3). When Fidel used those terms (and seemed to lay down the law in the rest of the speech), he was not saying anything new, but simply confirming what already existed.

Different groups – most notably those around the *Lunes de Revolución* weekly cultural supplement, which took the lead in seeking to define the new art, the new cinema institute (ICAIC), Casa de las Américas and the artistic contingent within the PSP – had put out early ad hoc and vague ideas on revolutionary culture. However, by 1961, those views had already begun to be replaced by an empirical and evolving set of ideas of cultural democratisation rather than 'elite' art, and an emphasis on Cuban, as opposed to imported, art. Moreover, the speech's tone was no accident for the time: while the literacy campaign was already making inroads into Cuba's illiteracy problem (and creating all manner of implications for literature, let alone for any other cultural form), and while the whole revolutionary experiment had been threatened and then defended in the invasion, the 'luxury' of ideas inherited from North America or Europe was increasingly deemed inappropriate.

However, that speech and that definition were also significant outside the world of culture; for, just as it confirmed rather than determined, so too did it reflect what was increasingly being felt and argued in the wider process of change, rather than what was being determined as 'policy'. In other words, Fidel's cultural definition of either 'within' or 'against' applied to all dimensions of 'the Revolution' in 1961: Cubans were already feeling, or being told, that 'we' (Cuba and Cubans) referred to those who stayed, contributed and defended, even if they did not do so enthusiastically or without doubts, while 'they' were all those who opposed the changes that those same Cubans were risking their lives and sacrificing themselves to achieve.

The point of this is that, by 1961, there were two parallel and mutually influential strands of attitude at play: the broader notion of an 'us' and 'them' inclusion/exclusion, and, within the level of political activists and leaders, the concentric circles of greater and lesser inclusion. As we have seen, in the latter case, 'inclusion' in the inner circles that was based on a person's historic qualifications could last for decades, regardless of performance or of passive, rather than active, involvement, in the same way that 'inside the Revolution' could be presumed to be an innate and indelible condition unless the person concerned chose to *act* 'against'. But what was clear was that either the 'circles' were a microcosm of the wider emerging sense of 'inside', or the latter was the former writ large. Either way, the two were part and parcel of the same unifying ethos of trust, reliability and loyalty, assumed to be inherent until, and unless, there was clear evidence to the contrary. However, this also illustrated an important imperative, as well as an organic assumption, to remain loyal throughout, with no hint of 'against'.

As observed above, this pattern remained largely unchallenged until Mariel, and then again during the *balsero* emigration crisis of 1994 (and the subsequent steady outflow). The year 1994 saw the exodus of some 35,000 Cubans in August and September, responding to growing austerity and unrest. As in 1980, Fidel responded by encouraging would-be emigrants to leave in boats (*balsas*, literally 'rafts'), forcing the US government to enter new migration talks and establish clearer rules on illegal movement. Hence, once the message changed to indicate that most illegal emigrants were now victims, not of the Revolution, but rather, like their Latin American brethren, of imperialism and globalisation, it became possible to present 'forced' emigration as yet another weapon in the 'imperialist' armoury, dividing the 'nation' everywhere and not just in Cuba. The main instrument of this strategy was deemed to be the hated 1966 Cuban Adjustment Act, which had created the unique category of (Cuban) illegal immigrants (to the United States). After arriving, Cubans were allowed to remain for a year and a day, after which they were, unlike all other illegal immigrant groups, allowed US residency status, and therefore eventually were able to apply for citizenship. This now also allowed the Cuban authorities and media to see the Cuban-American community as 'exiled', not politically by Cuba but economically by the United States. Thus, in 1994–95 there were two *Nación y Emigración* conferences organised in Cuba, designed to attract those in that diasporic community who desired cooperation with the island rather than enmity.

What this shift meant, therefore, was that, by the 1980s, there was effectively a third, intermediate, 'layer' of Cubans who were 'inside' and 'outside': namely those who, having left Cuba for economic reasons, were not considered 'against' the Revolution but were officially viewed as being victims of the unequal world order – unofficially, though, they were still rather suspect. Steadily, and certainly by the end of the first decade after 2000, they were usually 'forgiven', however, leading ultimately to the suggestion in 2011–13 of an eventual change in citizenship status.

**The role and nature of debate**

The whole question of migration (and non-migration) was, then, one key factor in creating a powerful and even overwhelming sense of unity in Cuba; the other (mentioned earlier) was the propensity for the evolving system to engage in structured or unstructured 'debates' – or what has, a little more clumsily, been called 'argumentalism' (Kapcia 2000: 254–5) – a pattern and part of a process that was crucial in making this 'inside'/'against' binary a practical principle. The crucial aspect of those 'debates' is that, with some prominent exceptions, they do not fit the model that we expect (from, say, the British or US political practice of parliamentary debates, or, alternatively, from school or university staged debates) nor are they always visible. The logic of the 'inclusion' ethos, and also the 'us' and 'them' binary, means that, firstly, these debates are almost always 'behind closed doors', i.e. for the benefit and eyes of only those involved, and, secondly, they follow defined parameters and even, occasionally, defined forms.

As we have seen in tracing the Revolution's trajectory, these debates have taken very different shapes over the decades. Some have taken place openly – the 1962–65 Great Debate or the 1990s and 2007–11 debates or consultations about reform, not least through the specially created *parlamentos obreros* in factories and workplaces, where one writer described the debates as having 'an unprecedented openness' (LeoGrande 2008: 54); others have been conducted behind the 'closed doors' of the party structures (1970–75); and yet others have fallen somewhere in between ('Rectification' and the contentious Third Party Congress). As we have seen, the two sequential debates of the 1990s were characteristic in that there was a perceived need for them, but also unusual in their length and openness, which combined to make them by far the widest ranging and most public debates thus far, going well beyond the ranks of the party to include mass organisations and especially the trade union confederation, the CTC. The first debate (broadly 1990–93) addressed the most urgent and fundamental question to date, namely how to ensure the Revolution's survival in the face of what was the process's greatest economic (and political) crisis so far. Since the outcome was the crucial set of reforms of 1993–96, it means that, this time, the 1991 Party Congress actually started the debate, rather than (as usual) rounding it off and legitimising the resulting decisions, indicating perhaps the scale of the problem and the genuine need for the leadership to find solutions rather than present people with a fait accompli.

The second debate started almost immediately, but it had more or less finished by the time of the next Congress (1997), although it did in fact continue for some time afterwards, fusing with the post-2000 Battle of Ideas. This time, the issue was not 'how to save the Revolution' (since that had largely been achieved) but, rather, 'what parts of the Revolution should be saved and what parts are dispensable?' This was a response to many Cubans' and many leaders' concerns that the cost of 'saving the Revolution' (the economic reforms) had generated so many social problems and undermined the old collective sense of solidarity so much that it was time to decide on the exact nature of 'the Revolution' that people wanted to save.

This time, the debate went even further than before, enlisting specially created new magazines for the purpose of broaching key questions, broadening the parameters of the debate, and creating a more permissive environment. Among the magazines, especially important were *Temas* (which has since notably set the terms of debate on all manner of hot and contemporary issues, not least with its monthly open forums, *Último Jueves*), *Contracorriente* and *Debates Americanos*. The debate also included organisations hitherto considered outside the political system, such as the Catholic and other churches, which were allowed to set up their own limited-circulation magazines to debate the same issues. Interestingly, as the answer seemed to emerge (that, essentially, what most Cubans wanted, or had always held in their minds as 'the Revolution', were the aims, patterns and ethos of 1959–61, i.e. before the Cold War entered the picture to create opportunities but also distort and constrain Cubans' freedom of action), the successive mobilisations of, first, the Pope's January 1998 visit (which partly resulted from the new dialogue with the church) and then the Elián campaign and the resulting Battle of Ideas also developed.

So what about those debates themselves? How wide or deep have they been, and how effective? Clearly, from what has been said, some of them have been so narrowly focused or so limited (to the ranks of the selective party) that they have not been public in terms of their effect or involvement; others, though, have gone much further, and have involved people more generally, albeit sometimes in rather determined ways.

This is because of the function of the Party Congresses, which is worth clarifying here. Each Congress has usually been preceded by up to a year of discussion of a set of precepts, proposals and suggestions put forward by the party leadership or Central Committee departments; those ideas have then, at the very least, been discussed at the level of the *núcleo*, with amendments and counter-proposals sent back up the system. However, some of the pre-Congress debates (notably in 1986, 1991, 1997 and 2011) were taken outside the party to the mass organisations, and were discussed locally and nationally as a prelude to the party considering the outcomes.

Beyond this, however, regardless of whether the party held a Congress or not, there have been many occasions when significant issues have similarly been taken out to the mass organisations for their members' views, most notably in 1970, 2007 and 2011–12. The latter two were especially revealing. The first followed Raúl Castro's scathing criticisms (on 26 July) of the failings of the system, after which he explicitly asked for that speech to be debated throughout the country, with additional criticisms added as necessary. The result was a vast consultation exercise, with many Cubans having two or more opportunities to 'sound off' in their appropriate mass organisation (most Cubans belonging to two or more of these) and also in the party or UJC, the results being fed up the system to become the basis for Raúl's eventual programme of reform. The second flowed from that: following a similar pattern of step-by-step progression, the debate covered the reform proposals themselves, to which a large number of amendments were made, not least by the CTC, the representative organisation most directly affected by the proposed changes to employment.

What these different examples reflect is the wider reality of the purpose, meaning and patterns of 'debate' in the Cuban system. For it is clear that these debates are not open-ended discussions without an agenda, but rather they are discussions within fixed parameters – to use the *Palabras* terms, 'within the Revolution'. The scope and nature of those parameters are set beforehand (by the party, by speeches, by key magazines, and so on), but there is the possibility of the parameters changing slightly, but not fundamentally, during and in response to the debate in question. Secondly, therefore, it is evident that the debates are more like consultations than open-ended 'free-speech' discussions. Yet the purpose is clear: not only can these exercises be 'sounding boards' and 'safety valves' at times of stress (the 2007 consultation was obviously seen by many Cubans as an opportunity to complain about anything and everything), but they can also serve to legitimise the preferences of those who are setting the parameters. Thus, for example, the outcome of the 2007 consultation was very much as Raúl had expected (partly because he had set the terms of the debate with his preceding speech) and provided him with the ammunition he needed for the higher debates within the party, given the continuing reluctance in those circles to engage in the kind of reform that, by then, he felt was necessary.

There is also, of course, a wider purpose: to cement feelings of identification, belonging and inclusion, namely to provide the mechanisms for a consensus to be seen to emerge among enough Cubans to make it representative of 'the people'. This, therefore, brings it close to the purpose and role of a number of other mechanisms of the Cuban system, namely the functioning of the mass organisations, the use of rallies and parades, and so on (i.e. the various forms of regularly ritualising a collective sense of belonging). Thus, a debate on, say, a leadership speech or a party proposal has the same function as a May Day rally, an anti-US rally on the Malecón seafront esplanade, or a mass organisation meeting, with its known format and its gelling tendencies. There is, however, a key difference: while rallies and more ritual gatherings have a clearly set modus operandi as a mobilisation of 'the masses', a debate has the capacity to generate something of a response *by* 'the masses', which may change the nature of the eventual proposals or decisions.

The 'gelling' element of the debates also has a crucial dimension in leadership-level or activist-level forums: namely that, when the debate is serious, going to the heart of controversial issues (such as the Great Debate or the post-1970 debate), those who 'lose' the debate are rarely marginalised or punished. At worst, they are kept 'in reserve' in some capacity, to be available when next needed, either in a subsequent debate or if and when policy changes. Indeed, this was even the case with Escalante (until his 'serial offending' became obvious and unacceptable in 1968) and Ramiro Valdés, but it may also prove to be the case with more recent individuals, unless their 'sin' is to do with something deemed totally unacceptable, such as conspiracy or corruption.

The overall conclusion from this, therefore, is that the many mechanisms of participation and mass involvement are directly related to the underlying ethos and culture of 'inclusion', which has not only dominated official and unofficial thinking about those Cubans considered 'loyal' or trustworthy and those considered 'beyond the pale', but has also determined the processes of inclusion (but, as we have seen, rarely exclusion) within the leadership and leading activist circles since 1959, or even since 1953. These characteristics, indeed, have been so endemic in the Revolution that they merit a discussion that looks beyond Cuba to see if, and how, they might fit into some broader paradigms.

## 8 | INCLUSION AND COLLECTIVITY: A REVOLUTIONARY CORPORATISM?

### Seeking paradigms

Essentially, what the preceding discussion arrives at now is the need to remind ourselves that the best way of understanding the thinking, particularities and survival of 'the Revolution' is to see them all as components of a delayed process of nation-building, something hinted at in the opening pages and referred to periodically thereafter. This categorisation is important, since one thing that emerges strongly from this discussion, but also from any analysis of the Cuban system, is that, however much the Revolution may have resembled the post-1945 Socialist Bloc polities and however much the leadership's declarations might have resonated for those familiar with that Bloc's ideological manifestations, to simply label the Cuban system as 'Communist' can be as misleading as this study has argued it is to label it 'totalitarian' or 'personalist'. That is not to say, of course, that communism as an idea and Communism as a global system were not influential in the shaping of the Revolution's ideology and political practices, but simply that to equate post-1959 (or, better still, post-1961) Cuba with, say, post-1948 Bulgaria or East Germany is to miss the more important differences and to neglect the particularities of the Cuban system and process.

Instead, it is always advisable to remember some fundamental paradigms that are more essentially helpful for locating Cuba within a broader context: firstly, the process was always seen, and perhaps should always have been seen, as revolutionary; secondly, it was always about realising a long-desired dream of national independence; but also, thirdly, rather than relating it all to our expectations of 'communism', it may in fact be more useful to fit 'the Revolution' into a wider definition of something we currently call corporatism.

The first point is straightforward. The fact that the Cuban polity and political culture, as well as the social and economic structures, went through a process of fundamental and continual change throughout the 1960s means that we have little choice but to read that process as a 'revolution'. This means remembering, as we have seen, that the system – and the state – remained in flux throughout, and that certainties were constantly being challenged. However, the point is that this characteristic also extended beyond the 1960s, as has been argued here: this refers not just to the fluidity of the structures and policies, but also to the process of transformation itself. In other words, the system's revolutionary nature continued to exist, at least in part, well after the 1960s. Certainly, the constant processes of debate, challenge and adaptation (to external pressures and internal crises) meant that stability often evaded the leadership. Hence, to continue calling the system 'the Revolution' was not simply a legitimising rhetoric (as is usually argued about the Mexican Revolution after 1946) but rather a reflection of those constant processes, something that the post-1991 adaptations and reassessments, plus the renewed weakness of the state, made clear.

The second point is also clear enough. A glance at Cuban history (much of which will be addressed below) demonstrates that the whole anti-colonial struggle in Cuba, and certainly from 1868, was driven by an awareness of the systematic denial of nationhood before then (including by many Cubans themselves) and by a growing collective desire to achieve that historic 'destiny'. Even after independence in 1902, that nationhood was in question, given the neo-colonial nature of the new relationship with the United States. This was cemented when the wording of the Platt Amendment was consolidated into both the new republic's Constitution (1901) and the Permanent Treaty with the United States (1903), giving the latter the constitutional right to intervene militarily in Cuba, control Cuba's foreign policy and effectively be Cuba's sole creditor. This status lasted until at least 1934, when it was redefined and when the Permanent Treaty, incorporating the Platt Amendment, was abrogated by the Roosevelt administration. As a result, the power of the underlying nationalism remained and even grew, becoming radicalised. Indeed, one of the fundamental points about the nature of Cuban nationalism from the 1860s is that it was always much more socially aware and more popularly based than many of the comparable manifestations of an emerging nationalism elsewhere in Latin America, where those sentiments often tended to be limited to intellectuals and the emerging bourgeoisie. Hence, in Cuban nationalist discourse, 'nation' always meant more than political independence, which is what made it so powerful, enduring and radical.

It is, however, the third category that is more challenging: the suggestion that we might understand the Revolution within the context of corporatism. Of course, this is because, at first sight, anyone should rightly baulk at the idea of classifying the Cuban Revolution as a form of corporatism, given the common historical association of that term with movements of the right, often close to and either leading to or confused with fascism. What, after all, do Primo de Rivera and Fidel Castro have in common? The answer is very little, if anything at all, although, as we have seen, some critical writers in the 1960s and 1970s did suggest Fidel's affinity with fascism, and Pardo-Llada (critical of the Revolution) claimed that he saw the complete works of Primo de Rivera in the Sierra guerrilla encampment (Thomas 1971: 822), although this seems logistically and politically unlikely.

## Corporatism

However, the term is suggested here not because of that association, but rather because, from the 1960s, political scientists began to develop the range of corporatism into other areas, attracted by the organisational features of the concept and applying it to other, unrelated, movements. As a result, in 1985, Peter Williamson addressed and codified those different meanings of the term.

For him there were already three different forms of the concept. The first was the example we know (above), the several right-wing authoritarian regimes of central and southern Europe, beginning in the early twentieth century and peaking in the 1920s and 1930s. Growing out of a 'social Catholicism' inspired by Pope Leo XIII's *De Rerum Novarum* encyclical (designed to challenge socialism and 'class warfare' by proposing a socially aware politics and class harmony), this strand of political thought, besides providing legitimacy for such regimes (most notably Franco's 'organic democracy'), also gave rise to variants of Catholic Action-related forces, such as the Falange Católica in Chile, eventually creating the Christian Democracy of the 1940s and 1950s.

The second referred to the populist regimes of Latin America in the 1930s and 1940s. While the first variant had a clear-cut ideological impulse, this one (notoriously lacking in any ideological definition) referred more to a form and style of political mobilisation and inclusion than to any set of ideas.

The third variant was the most recent, and, by then, the most widespread: namely the Western European form of post-war consensus politics, the politics of compromise, negotiation and structural involvement (of groups such as trade unions). In this variant, the only parallel with the historically original model was the idea of combining capital and labour in some sort of structure (formally, this was the idea behind Franco's 'vertical trade unions') (Williamson 1985: 7).

For Williamson, despite their obvious differences, these three variants had some things in common: the idea of state regulation of the economic and social order, regulation of production (not distribution), regulation to ensure private ownership of the means of production and labour, and the intermediary function of representative institutions (ibid.: 8–10).

Around the same time, Philippe Schmitter (associated then with studies of the new militarism in Latin America) provided a useful catch-all definition, focusing on the forms and practices rather than on the ideology:

> a system of interest representation in which the constituent units are organized into a limited number of singular, compulsory, noncompetitive, hierarchically ordered and functionally differentiated categories, recognized or licensed (if not created) by the state and granted a deliberate representational monopoly within their respected categories in exchange for observing certain controls on their selection of leaders and articulation of demands and supports (Schmitter 1979: 13).

Indeed, most of the writing at that time on Latin America – notably Howard Wiarda (1973), long interested in 'Hispanic' traditions of corporatism – tended to follow the same line, seeing corporatism as a mechanism of governance rather than a quasi-fascist ideology. However, this attention was drawn as much to the 'bureaucratic–authoritarian' forms of military regimes in Brazil, Argentina, Uruguay and Chile (O'Donnell 1973) as to the well-known 'one-party democracy' system of PRI-dominated Mexico. That said, though, the latter example, with its post-revolutionary imperative towards state-building and integration, and the other Latin American cases of populist state-strengthening integration to cope with the post-1929 crisis and depression, ought to open up possibilities to us here when looking at post-1959 Cuba.

Yet this focus on the functionality of corporatism, while helpful and (*pace* those military regimes of the time) taking us away from the questionable associations with 1920s European authoritarianism, still misses one crucial dimension that sets the Cuban case less within this supposed tradition than in another, more revealing context. That dimension was, paradoxically, hinted at by the original corporatism: namely the combination of an imperative to include rather than to exclude (in the earlier case, arising from Catholic social doctrine), and the association with nationalism and exaltation of the nation. Moreover, in both cases, those impulses were aimed at resisting a perceived threat, although the original variant saw that threat as being posed by an apparently rampant or growing socialism, while this later variant has tended to see it as being posed to the (invariably new) nation by a spectre of civil unrest and economic crisis.

The early corporatism was a response by elites within a fragile capitalist system to a structural crisis at a particular time, as they realised the need for controlled accommodation and enforced unity and stability. In other words, the original version of corporatism was characterised by three features. Firstly, it preached the inclusion of not always willing and otherwise dissonant elements, making the latter into participants whose material satisfaction was attended to, or whose sense of importance was fortified, but whose actual effective involvement was minimal. That is to say, in Gramscian terms, it aimed to persuade enough of the dissident or rebel forces that it was in their interests to acquiesce in their own subjugation at a particular time. Secondly, it emphasised hierarchy, since those systems were always seen as necessarily top-down in power relations and in principle; inclusion may have been stressed but it was never on equal terms. Thirdly, it focused on national unity, ideally based on the notion of 'national identity' (real or imagined) or on consensus of some sort. Essentially, those three features always coalesced more easily in the form of nationalism.

## A post-colonial corporatism?

How far then can or should we apply these tools to a different context and time, namely the Africa and Asia of the post-1945 era of decolonisation? There, the oppositional movements that, in most cases, inherited control of the newly independent nations and became the first governments faced exactly the same range of crises and challenges that the original corporatists had seen forty years earlier, albeit emanating from a different source and with one vital difference. For the decolonising regimes, the crisis was a double challenge of, firstly, a contested and even newly created notion of nationhood, about which there was little consensus (thanks to the legacy and machinations of the colonial regime), and, secondly, a fundamental economic weakness (again resulting from the purpose and patterns of colonial exploitation). Even if those new nations boasted mineral wealth, their economic futures still echoed the weaknesses of post-1820 Latin America: a permanent vicious circle of inadequately income-generating primary dependence and an inability to generate indigenous manufacturing to replace the ever more expensive imports (usually from the former colonial power).

This dangerous mix of problems therefore produced a universal imperative towards solutions that were similar to those advocated by the 1920s' corporatists. Firstly, they needed to find means of inclusion and unification, since colonialism's 'divide-and-rule' strategy had invariably left a legacy of centrifugal interests and forces and a hierarchy of relative privilege and exclusion. In addition, most ex-colonies faced an urgent dilemma over what to do with the remaining colonialist population or with those of the indigenous population who had supported colonialism. Secondly, they also needed to maintain some sort of hierarchy within that unity in order to assert a much-needed stability, only this time it was to be under the tutelage of the former liberation fighters. The crucial difference from the earlier European corporatism was that these new 'nations' were often entities in name only: with a few exceptions (where a definable and recognised nation had preceded colonialism, such as Abyssinia), the new countries had simply inherited the boundaries created by colonialism and, in the case of Africa, the previous century's somewhat haphazard 'scramble for Africa'. Within those boundaries came a not always organic mix of cultures, languages, religions, societies and geographies that had been combined forcibly in the previous colony. Hence, any appeal to nationalism was always somewhat spurious, or at least likely to be marginally effective and contested.

This was indeed demonstrated by the actual practice of much, if not most, of this new post-colonial corporatism. Inclusion might be preached, but in practice it often affected only those groups (tribal, ethnic, cultural, religious or class-based) deemed crucial to gaining independence or to post-independence stability, often reversing the preceding colonial practice of privileging a minority group as the pliant native elite. Therefore, participation was often necessarily controlled, regulated and geared more to creating a sense of belonging (to a new 'nation') than to an effective role in decision-making. Hierarchy, equally, was usually a case of the former rebels becoming the new vanguard, which in turn steadily converted itself into the new elite, usually by forcing a necessary unity through pressure to centralise power within the governing form of the former anti-colonial party or front. Many of the post-colonial systems saw a tendency towards the creation of single-party states, or, as in the Indian case, a political system in which one unifying party (the Congress Party) exercised such effective hegemony that to all intents and purposes (not unlike the situation in Mexico) it was a one-party democracy for many decades.

Yet this brings to the fore a major difference between this variant of corporatism and the original European authoritarianism – and, moreover, between this wave of decolonisation and the previous wave in early nineteenth-century Latin America. This was the reality that most of the rebels tended to be clearly on the left. This was to be expected, given the nature of political evolution in Europe in the early twentieth century (where many of the anti-colonial rebels had studied, worked or campaigned) and given the models that were available and attractive to them at the time (since genuinely new nations by definition lack a prior basis on which to construct the new entity and thus seek models elsewhere) – most notably the Soviet Union (whose economic development under Stalin mesmerised many and cried out to be copied) and the post-1945 Labour government in Britain (whose massive nationalisation drive and creation of a welfare state drew much admiration). If these rebels were not actually Communist (belonging to a pro-Moscow Communist Party), then they almost always defined themselves as being a form of 'socialist'; indeed, the nature of anti-imperialism of the time meant that such a conclusion was almost inevitable. Because the post-independence regimes of early nineteenth-century Latin America had been conservative in their purpose (to prevent racial and social revolt and national disintegration) – however radical the 'first wave' (1810–15) might have been and however 'progressive' their declarations and constitutions – they had all looked either to Britain (as a model of stability) or, more typically, to the United States (as the only example of post-colonial nation-building available to them) for their models of constitutional and political structure (of course, the issue of economic independence never surfaced as a concern at that time). Now, however, the post-colonial leaders had more radical models available to them; these had formed their ideological commitment during the anti-colonial struggles and then often shaped their early attempts at independence and development.

One result of this reliance on new models was, in contrast to the experience of Latin America in the early nineteenth century, a generalised belief in the need for some kind of welfare system. Clearly learning from both the Soviet Union and Britain (but also even from Roosevelt's New Deal), most governing elites of these new nations in this wave of decolonisation saw the desirability (in socialist or progressive principle) and the practicality of seeking to include more effectively, by addressing the inequalities that the old colonial regime had created or perpetuated, and of doing so with some speed.

Finally, most of these new regimes realised the urgency of attacking the underlying problem of colonial economic dependence and thus creating an economic independence to parallel formal political separation. Here again, their models were new, and the inherent leftism of most of the leaders inevitably pushed them in one direction: towards a belief in the state's capacity to develop and industrialise. Again, the models were usually Attlee's Britain (with nationalisation of utilities and basic industries accompanying the new welfare state) and the Soviet Union, where a seemingly backward capitalist country had been dragged in a short space of time, albeit with much human damage, into becoming a nation with an apparently modern agricultural system and a powerful industrial status. Hence, the ideas of rapid industrial development and nationalisation became standards for most of the new governments' programmes.

However, like the earlier European corporatists, they too needed to use, and if necessary create, nationalism. This was entirely logical, since colonialism was always based on a constant and systematic denial of any identity for a colonised territory other than that of a colony (denying either the validity of any preceding independent existence or the possibility of any viable post-colonial independence), until the imperatives of rising anti-colonial feeling in the colony, post-war crisis or political change in the metropolis dictated the need for cautious decolonisation. It was also logical since, to challenge this – and indeed to challenge the colonial power – oppositionists working for independence always needed to create a popular movement against colonialism, building a notion of a national identity (even if one did not exist previously). In this they entered into familiar territory for any student of nineteenth- and twentieth-century European nationalism, namely the need for a cultural decolonisation to be created and disseminated long before the actual political movement for independence. The reason lies in what we might call the essential dichotomy of colonialism.

### The colonial binary of 'problem' and 'solution'

This all raises a critical issue in considering the particularities of the Cuban case of post-colonial nation-building: the long drawn-out and contested processes of decolonisation that, in any example of the passage from colonialism to formal independence (or, in this case, from the sequence of colonialism and neo-colonialism to a drive for greater independence), both necessarily precede the end of colonialism (and neo-colonialism) and also then follow that end, usually for some considerable time. The key points here are the length of time that the processes take, the always contested nature of the processes, and finally their changing character over time.

What we are essentially looking at here is the simple fact that, whatever the metropolis in question, all colonial systems have always depended on the colonised (or at least a significant or leading part of the colonised population) acquiescing in their own subjugation. This might have been for materially practical purposes (because no colonising country was ever able to afford the manpower necessary to police large numbers of the subjugated populations) or because, as Gramsci noted well, any hegemonic system relies on such acqui- escence, but it has been a startling characteristic of all the major 'classic' nineteenth-century colonial experiences, and also of the more subtle domination exercised in the twentieth century by those same powers (and by new expansionist powers such as the United States), which is what became known as neo-colonialism. Indeed, one might argue that the latter needs acquiescence more than colonial- ism does, since it assumes that domination is achieved despite the formal independence of the dominated territory and population, and not because of its dependence.

Essentially, what this has always been is what we might call the binary of coloniality. At this stage, we should probably use the term 'coloniality' (Quijano 2000), referring to a state of mind, rather than 'colonialism', a term now so frequently used as to be perhaps too vague for the complex processes of subjugation and acquiescence that colonialism, as a politico-economic system of domination, always im- plied. It is a binary since it fundamentally proposes, from the outset of the domination, that the colonised people are colonised precisely because they are 'the problem' (with their supposed backwardness, racial inferiority, lack of civilisation, superstitions, inefficiency, un- reliability, inherent divisions, and so on), while the colonial master is by definition 'the solution', correcting or overcoming those innate ills and seeking to bring the benefits of the colonising power's 'superior' civilisation, religion and modernity. Of course, the nature of systems of domination is such that not all of the colonised need to be so persuaded at any one time; indeed, most colonial powers realised early on (perhaps learning from each other and from earlier imperial or colonial experiences) that they really only needed to persuade a section of the native elite to accept the reality and advantages of subjugation. The colonising powers did this either by 'buying them off' (essentially making them a comprador elite) or by persuading them that it was in their interests to accept that, although they were part of the 'problem', the 'solution' nonetheless depended on them attaching themselves to the colonial power as a pliant native elite, essentially governing and controlling the rest of the colonised population on behalf of the colonial master.

That had certainly been the case of the Spanish systems of control in the Americas from the early 1500s, where they soon adopted the idea of the native *cacique* (chieftain) in the Caribbean societies that they found, applying it more widely in the larger and more complex civilisations of Mexico and Peru, and then throughout the colonies beyond those regions, eventually using the native elite (once duly defeated) to run their colonies for them. It was also the system adopted in colonial India from very early on, and then with the Raj, which replicated the pattern with stunning success. Of course, as in many things colonial, Ireland had already represented an outstanding example of this binary.

That system worked, of course, because the same binary was repeated below the level of the wider territory of the colony: the pliant and subaltern elite (intellectual, religious and political) came to believe that, while they were part of the 'problem' in comparison with the colonial master, their closeness to that master (through education, colour or whatever mechanism of distinction was preferred) made them to some extent part of the 'solution' as well, bringing salvation to the benighted masses below them (and, in the process, sustaining their own position of comparative wealth, prestige or power). Hence, it was in their interests to persuade those below them that the same binary was true in their relationship with 'the masses'. In cultural terms, of course, this became solidified in the growth of cultural colonialism, through which the developing native intellectual and artistic elite invariably aspired to find acceptance by the metropolitan cultural elite and on the colonialist culture's terms. In other words, they sought to become part of a 'cultural community' (Kapcia 2005: 13–14 *passim*) that cut them off from their native culture and population but that tied them, for the purposes of prestige, to the high culture of the country or countries that dominated them.

Equally, of course, we should note that the same binary distinction was invariably characteristic of most of the would-be colonising nations before they embarked on their colonial expansion, whether that was fifteenth-century 'Spain' (there being then only the most fragile sense of a 'national' unity of something called 'Spain' behind the Crown's desire to expand) or nineteenth-century Britain or France. Again taking our cue from Gramsci, the whole 'problem–solution' binary was essential to the patterns of domination of both the so-called 'feudal' systems before the mid-1400s and the capitalist systems from the Industrial Revolution onwards, and to all the intermediate patterns whereby the dominated had to be persuaded to acquiesce in their own 'natural' subjugation. Thus, even if we do not accept Lenin's explanation of the origins of nineteenth-century imperialism – i.e. emerging from the limited domestic possibilities of an ever expanding capitalist machine (Christman 1966: 177–270) – it seems incontrovertible that one of the great successes of the whole imperial experience, in Britain or France for example, was the persuasion of an otherwise dissident industrial working class to accept that, while their own subjugation was something to be opposed, the subjugation of others below them might be to their own advantage. This thereby led to them accepting the correctness and desirability of the imperialism in question.

The central issue within this context is that the process of decolonisation that, to some extent, necessarily must precede any movement for independence (real or formal) always has to address this binary, either denying the colonial master any right to be deemed the 'solution' or denying the colonised people's status as the 'problem'. However, so persuasive is the binary in most cases, especially after a sustained and long-lasting colonialism, that neither of those denials is easy or uncontested, even for those most committed to the struggle to find their identity. Whatever the basis of the notion of 'the colonised as the problem' (backwardness, race, inefficiency, untrustworthiness, poverty, or the like), the fact of colonialism contributed in large part to the continuing pervasiveness, as well as persuasiveness, of the binary and the belief in the coloniser's superiority: if 'they' conquered you so easily, controlled you for so long and so effectively, and still held you back, it must be at least partly attributable to 'your' failures in areas such as a lack of unity or determination.

Thus, the decolonisation process has been necessarily long and arduous, usually beginning in hesitant fashion, initially by suggesting that the outsider might not, after all, always or inherently be the 'solution', but also by suggesting, equally hesitantly, that the colonised might have some redeeming features. Indeed, why else is independence a desirable goal? Therefore, the first steps towards an independent identity have tended mainly to involve collective confidence-building, usually heralded and championed by cultural elites. Although (again necessarily) they argue from the cultural viewpoint and use the accepted cultural forms of the coloniser, the cultural elites search for and reproduce forms of the colonised people's 'national' or indigenous culture (music, dance or writing) in terms of 'high' culture – seeking to be accepted by the external 'cultural community' by adopting and adapting aspects of what is seen and presented as an 'authentic' and even 'primitive' and marginal culture. One only has to think of the many examples of musical nationalism in late nineteenth-century Europe (Smetana, Dvořák, Chopin, Grieg, Verdi, and so on) to realise the role and significance of such cultural manifestations: if one's people could be persuaded to be proud of their own culture, then something of a sense of collective belonging and pride could be created. This necessary preliminary stage (what is clearly cultural nationalism) also corresponded to other imperatives: not only did it accord a value to what was seen as authentic, popular or 'national', but it also became a way for the artists and writers expounding it to gain access and recognition inside the European or 'Northern' cultural community, using their own alleged exoticism (from 'the periphery') to become part of the canon established by 'the centre'.

It stands to reason, however, that rarely does the process of political decolonisation take place before the actual effort to achieve independence, unless the colonial apparatus is in crisis, divided or unsure of itself. The essential divisions enforced by any colonial system and process militate against the emergence of a strong and united movement of political self-confidence, especially as colonialism's typical 'divide-and-rule' strategy often relies on elevating a minority group (religion, tribe, region or race) to relative authority in the colony, thereby generating resentment towards that group and preventing any easy unity.

However, if the pre-independence process of cultural, or mental, decolonisation is always difficult and contested, the necessary process that must follow independence is equally challenging and contested. Colonial divisions do not disappear after the colonial master has left and the new elite has emerged, but may well remain and deepen. Moreover, while that decolonisation might have questioned the colonial binary, it has not necessarily reversed it; thus, given the inevitable problems that have almost always followed formal independence, there is often a residual tendency to assume that, although colonialism might have been the 'problem', so too might the ex-colonised have, in part, been problematic, making the post-independence search for solutions to the new problems externally oriented. Colonialism might have gone, but the 'solution' is still likely to be found outside.

## The imperative of nation-building

What then is the point of all this perhaps abstruse discussion in this study? It is essentially to stress the argument that what follows independence is a double process: of continuing cultural decolonisation and of fractured and difficult nation-building. The many examples from post-independence Latin America bear out precisely how fractured and difficult this process can be, for not only were the early years of independence almost invariably characterised by political unrest, fragmentation and economic weakness (with the prominent exceptions of Brazil and Paraguay proving the rule, through their atypical political forms and social constructions), but the process of nation-building in most cases did not really take off seriously for several decades after formal separation. If we consider the many forms and mechanisms of such nation-building (taking the cases of new nations in modern Europe, for example), we can see that many of those mechanisms and forms were missing in Latin America, in some cases until almost the twentieth century. Even then, they remained contested and ineffective until the depression of the 1930s created the space and the need for a more conscious and sustained process to begin.

What might those forms and mechanisms be? The most obvious are the institutions and bodies that make up a strong and cohesive state, because the structure of nation-building is necessarily the process of state-building, to create a viable nation state. These are, for example, a constitution; a civil service; a single, unified and legitimate judiciary and a credible legislative authority (not necessarily an elected parliament, of course); a standing army answerable to the government and not to itself; an education system of some sort (with a degree of central regulation or recognition); national academies of sciences, art, language, and so on. Beyond these institutions, however, there are other visible, but less tangible, processes:

the creation, perpetuation and ritualisation of national 'myths' (of historical events and characters) through a standardised narrative of an accepted national history, historical memorialisation through statues and museums, a currency (with memorialising coinage), a national day and national anthem, but also the processes of national and social integration (of key racial, religious or regional groups) through various means. Of course, all of this assumes a given: that the new nation's economy is sufficiently independently run by the nation's government or has sufficient indigenous resources of sufficient demand abroad to sustain integration.

This is where the experience of most Latin American nations in the period from the 1820s to the 1930s fell down in their nation-building: however successful any given process of visible and memorialising integration and identity creation proved to be (completing some of the above requirements of the process), in most cases neither the necessary social integration nor the economic wherewithal or strength to sustain it were really achieved.

### The Cuban case

Hence, in some respects, the Cuban case was not that different from the situation in, say, Bolivia, Peru or Guatemala, in that, for them, by the 1930s – and perhaps even beyond – real and sustainable economic independence and real and meaningful integration were never achieved, perpetuating the instability, inequality and hierarchy of a century earlier. This was fundamentally because of the two Reciprocity Treaties (1903 and 1934), described below.

But Cuba was quite different in three key respects. Firstly, even if we discount the effectiveness of independence in the rest of Latin America, those countries did at least have some sort of national structures in place by the 1850s (with some of the mechanisms and forms described above) and their governments were able to take some decisions of their own, with political forms that, in most cases, allowed for the rise and incorporation of dissident elements within the elite and the limited 'political' population. Cuba, however, remained formally, overtly and genuinely colonial for eighty years after the rest of the continent had gained formal independence, with all the distortions that that meant: the perpetuation of slavery long beyond it had ceased to make any economic sense (and, with it, the perpetuation of rigid social and racial hierarchies and wide-spread race fears), a systematic discrimination against the majority population within the privileged ethnic group (*peninsulares* always being fiscally, economically and constitutionally preferred over the growing *criollo* population), and the perpetuation of an increasingly corrupt, inefficient and repressive colonial regime beyond the point when the metropolis could afford it in economic or military terms. Therefore all of the divisions that colonialism normally engenders remained fixed and perpetuated even more firmly in Cuba.

Secondly, colonialism in Cuba was, of course, replaced by a more effective neo-colonialism: not, as with the European powers in post-colonial Africa or Asia, under the same former colonial country, but rather under the United States, following its seminal and consciously influential four-year military occupation (1898–1902). Moreover, unlike the later neo-colonial examples, this regime was fixed and legitimised by legal and constitutional means, the contested Platt Amendment-oriented Constitution of 1901 confirming Cuba's protectorate status (and allowing three further military occupations by 1923), reinforced by the 1903 Permanent Treaty with the United States.

Thirdly, as defined by the 1903 Reciprocity Treaty with the United States (and confirmed later by the 1934 version, after the shock of the Crash and the Depression), Cuba's economic relationship with the dominant economic power (investor, market and manu-factured goods provider) was legally established in ways that were only marginally reflected elsewhere in Latin America by Brazil's relationship with Britain and Argentina's Roca–Runciman Pact of 1934, again with Britain. Therefore, Cuba's economic independence was never, formally or informally, a possibility before the 1930s. Even afterwards, with the world sugar economy changing (with a glut of producers and production leading to a market controlled by the consumers), the post-1934 sugar quota agreed annually by the US Department of Agriculture for all those countries seeking access to the US market determined that dependence and monoculture would still be the basic feature of Cuban economic (and therefore social and political) life, with Cuba locked into a relationship as exporter of (low-income) raw sugar and an industry-less importer of (high-priced) manufactured goods.

However, if Cuba differed from the earlier Latin American

processes of decolonisation, it is also important to recognise that the Cuban version bore some significant differences from the other contemporary decolonisation processes with which this study is suggesting that we compare Cuba.

There were, of course, obvious similarities with those processes. Firstly, the same drive for inclusion and unification could be seen from the outset of the insurrection. Although Cuba's colonialism had formally ended sixty years earlier, as we have observed, the strategies of US neo-colonialism in terms of 'divide and rule' were not only no different from those of colonialism but were, if anything, more subtle and, because unseen, they persuaded many Cubans that a close dependence on the United States was either the only option for viable survival or the only desirable one, almost as some kind of superior version of Puerto Rico.

Equally, by 1961, it was clear that, whatever the declared intentions might have been in 1953–58 about calling competitive elections, none of the new leadership (and by no means most Cubans) could countenance a revival of the old party system; hence, post-1959 Cuba showed the same drive towards a single-party system that characterised other contemporary decolonisation processes. In the Cuban case, for over three years that party was a 'classic' united front of the three groups that had either fought the insurrection (the 26 July Movement and the DR) or had sided unconditionally with the Movement late in the insurrection and then in the first months of victory (the PSP) (Sweig 2002: 126). But even before that, as we have seen, the first government of the Revolution was a typical 'front', with only eight of the seventeen posts occupied by 26 July people, the rest being a judicious mixture of ex-Ortodoxos, 'clean' liberals and non-committed social democrats.

An egalitarian welfare drive also figured large among the rebels' early programmes (having been perhaps the defining characteristic of Fidel's 'History will absolve me' speech and document in 1953) and, by 1959, had become more prominent after the Sierra experience. Moreover, the leadership soon discovered that, while the economic revolution could to some extent be either postponed or drawn out, thanks to the new Soviet 'solution' to the old problem of the sugar market, and while the political revolution would take time to work out (given the profound disagreements between all the 'revolutionaries'), the social revolution was urgent, feasible and a practical way of delivering on promises quickly (thus avoiding the familiar post-victory disillusion seen in 1902 and 1934) and also of gaining long-term popular support.

Finally, the new Cuban government, evidently adding Latin America's experience of the 1930s and 1940s (and the templates offered by Raúl Prebisch's UN ECLA example) to the usual British and Soviet models, was soon committed to a programme of rapid development that, as in the other cases, aimed to help Cuba catch up and also to protect the country against the predations of neo-colonialism. Indeed, in many respects, the only differences between the mixed economy model of 1959–60 and the more interventionist model from 1961 was, as the private sector proved inadequate to the task of this strategy (or, in the case of US capital, unwilling to undertake it), that the state had to step into the gap, regardless of any ideological preference for that role.

So the similarities between Cuba and, say, contemporary Tanzania, Ghana, Zambia or Algeria were obvious, confirming the argument that in order to understand post-1959 Cuba better one should ideally compare Cuba not so much with 1945–89 Eastern Europe as with the post-1945 decolonisation experiences. However, whatever those similarities, there were always major differences that led to Cuba's development and political pattern moving in decisively different directions from those of comparator countries.

The first difference was what we might rightly call the 'corporate' character of the rebellion that had brought about the change in 1959, i.e. the growing tendency of the former guerrilla rebels to define 'the group' (as the completely trustworthy, politically reliable and substantially forgivable members of the 'inner circle') by its members' historic 'qualifications' through key moments or episodes of the preceding *lucha*. Having created an apparently unbreakable esprit de corps among those former fighters, and having seen their collective radicalisation take shape, making them the 'true' keepers of the sacred flame, in Cuba the otherwise 'classic' post-colonial nation-building patterns of collective definition and allegiance were overlaid by this tight-knit group loyalty at the top.

The second major difference, obvious though it may be, was the reality of isolation and siege imposed after 1962, as active hostility (and failed invasion in 1961) led to a full economic embargo (still, of course, in place in 2013) and a sustained campaign to isolate Cuba within Latin America and, if possible, further afield. The most evident effect of this was to push Cuba closer to the Soviet Union in many respects, but especially economically, but another was to create something of a defiant 'siege mentality', a constant and even more urgent search for (defensive) unity. Among newly independent societies, this reality is shared only by Israel (which, from 1967, tied itself more closely to both the US side in the Cold War and a strategy of opposition to the other independent states in the region). While the economic effects of that long-term isolation can be exaggerated, the costs were undeniably vast. However, it was the psychological effect that, in this argument, made the real difference, enabling the still popular government to mobilise support for all manner of campaigns in the economy, for social change (e.g. the 1961 literacy campaign) and for political development, always building on a growing identification between the changing meanings of 'Revolution' and *patria* (which itself built on previous traditions in Cuban politics).

The third significant difference was the accelerating departure from the island of over a million Cubans in around fifteen years. Not only did this have clear economic effects and implications for the tasks of nation-building (as we have seen), but it also increased the growing nationalism (as most émigrés sought refuge in a United States increasingly opposed to the reforms that most Cubans desired). It also added a new generation to the long-standing Cuban nationalist demonology of 'betrayal', ensuring that those who chose to be physically 'outside' Cuba would long be assumed to be 'against' the Revolution.

Finally, the fourth (and perhaps most significant) difference was that, while in most post-colonial states the revolutionary nature of the changeover was found in the overthrow of the colonial regime and maybe in the euphoria of the following months, in the Cuban case, the Revolution clearly followed rather than preceded 1959. This was because circumstances combined after January 1959 to create the conditions for a greater radicalisation. Before 1959, while the rebels (especially in the Sierra) were radicalising their ideas as a result of both the struggle itself and contact with a hitherto unknown peasantry – and also due to the impact of those who, like

Guevara and Raúl, already had more militant ideas than most of their cohort – the majority of those who welcomed 'the Revolution' expected something between a substantial overhaul of a discredited system and simply a cleaner version of the pre-Batista regime. Just because they welcomed the idea of 'revolution' did not mean that they were recognisably revolutionary, not least (as several historians have pointed out) because the term 'revolution' was used loosely by even the most un-revolutionary Cuban forces (most notably the PRC-A, the Auténticos, whose claim to be revolutionary harked back to their role in the 1933 events) and often had more to do with the nationalist tradition than with any desire to overthrow it all (Llerena 1978: 38–44).

However, as the previously weak state (no longer as neo-colonial as before 1934, but still fatally weakened by corruption and economic dependence) collapsed between 1952 and 1958, so too did most of the conventional political parties and groups, leaving the new regime with something of a tabula rasa on which to build something genuinely new, as most of the core rebels now intended. Yet the crisis faced by the new regime was one of institutional chaos, especially once the rebels' radical intentions became clear; with every wave of emigration of the increasingly worried middle class, the revolutionary leaders' organisational capacity to create the necessary state for executing all the proposed reforms was weakened further. Moreover, after the political crisis of 1961–62, many of those rebels began to share a jaundiced view of the idea of 'institutionalisation', preferring what one writer called 'revolutionary romanticism' (Dumont 1970: 207) to the creation of structures that could, once again, become a target for takeover by a well-disciplined group (such as the PSP core). Hence, most went along with Fidel's preference for constant mobilisation as the best means of keeping both ideological commitment firm and revolutionary spirits high.

Therefore, it was no accident that, at a time when the proposed single party was going through a slow and painful birth (not emerging clearly until 1965), the many mass organisations that went on to characterise the Cuban system were all created, enlisting most Cubans in the tasks and emerging structures of 'the Revolution' in ways that neither the party (which always intended to be selective anyway, and thus not 'mass' in the same way) nor the emerging state could do. For, as already argued at the start, while the state might remain weak, these bodies substituted for the state, replacing system and structure with a politically crucial mass involvement and organised enthusiasm. That involvement was vital because, as many a labour activist has learned from fellow workers' involvement in sustained strike action, Cuba's leaders realised that the combination of real reform (much of it more revolutionary in implication than intention) and mass campaigning involvement led to a radicalisation of attitudes and demands at the grass roots as well as among the activists. Thus, quite apart from the continuing identification with socialist models (of rapid development and structure) and the pre-1959 basis in patterns and traditions of collectivism, most Cubans' real experience in the heady and 'heroic' (but often austere and 'besieged') years after 1959 was one of a sense of empowerment.

What this suggested, therefore, was that, whatever may have happened to the formerly radical vanguards of most modern anti-colonial struggles once in power, circumstances in and pressures on Cuba meant that the pattern was likely to be different there. Hence, the new nation-building and state-building processes were bound to be more revolutionary than in most other contemporary cases, but they were also always driven by the collective and evident awareness of the 'national' tradition from which the Revolution emerged. In other words, being foot soldiers in the daily building of 'the Revolution' for some time meant much to most Cubans, who remained and (willingly or at least tolerantly) became enrolled in the constant campaigns, organisations, rallies and labour mobilisations, being persuaded to see it all as a continuation of Martí's struggle and therefore (especially after Playa Girón in 1961) as the culmination of that struggle and the end of the history of 'betrayals'.

Finally, perhaps the most significant difference (from contemporary post-colonial experiences) was that nationalism in Cuba was already deeply embedded in the Cuban political culture and did not have to be invented, encouraged or protected. Every historical experience in Cuba from the early nineteenth century had added fuel to the nationalist flames: the persistence of an even more discriminatory and vengeful colonialism, the protection of the slave trade and the late abolition of slavery itself, the length, bitterness and frustrated and frustrating outcome of the 1868–78 Ten Years' War, the following 'Little War' (1879–80) and then the 'successful' 1895–98 War (of Independence), the loss of both Martí and Maceo in that struggle, the four-year US military occupation, the Platt Amendment and the whole legal apparatus of the US neo-colony, the three subsequent military interventions, and so on. By 1959, there was therefore a powerful demonology of the evils and actions of the sequence of colonialism and neo-colonialism. But there was also an equally vibrant and powerful tradition of nationalist struggle to set against that litany: the slave protests and rebellions of the 1820s to the 1850s, the exile of patriotic radicals such as Félix Varela and José Martí, Céspedes's 'Declaration of Yara' of 10 October 1868, the struggle waged by tens of thousands of guerrillas in all three wars, Maceo's defiant 'Protest' in 1878 (to continue the struggle), the commitment and support of the emigrant Florida-based tobacco workers, Martí's self-sacrificing death (and 'martyrdom') in 1895, the dissidence of people such as Mella and Guiteras in the 1920s and 1930s, and so on.

The point here is that, although we can talk of a delayed *nation state*-building process, by 1959 it was clear that *nation* existed, and had long done so, in popular memory (thanks to popular culture, associations, myths and the constant memorialisation of Martí) and in the radical tradition (Kapcia 2000). Even before the flawed nation state emerged in 1902, the idea of a Cuban nation fulfilling its historical destiny to be free and independent had long been entertained in many Cubans' minds, gatherings and cultural manifestations. Indeed, one effect of the social changes and political struggles in Cuba in the second half of the nineteenth century was that conventional radicalism (i.e. socialism and trade unionism) became more inherently nationalist in focus and inspiration, and, conversely, that nationalism was much more radical than it might otherwise have been. Equally, however, the popular memory and radical interpretation of Cuba's past created a widespread tradition of thinking that equated real independence with fierce opposition to imperialism and with a necessary unity (mindful of the fatal divisions that had prevented separatism from gaining ground in the 1820s, and in 1868–78 had conspired to frustrate the long and bloody struggle against the Spanish).

So 'nation' clearly *pre-dated* the 1959 process of nation-building as an idea, but *nation state* did not, or at least not in any full or organic way. For the 1902–34 polity was not, even formally, a nation state but rather an explicitly and legally neo-colonial state, where the dominant economic interests (Cuban and US) accepted the idea of Cuba as a dependent *non-nation*. Equally, while the post-1934 settlement might have been less overtly and less formally neo-colonial, and while some overdue state-building did begin (a national bank, for example, and institutions for 'national' history and language), the ravages of the preceding three decades, not to mention the past 110 years, together with the continuing reality of a dependence cemented by the 1934 Reciprocity Treaty, meant that Cuba was still not an independent nation state, in that the state's inherent weakness and dependence undermined real independence.

## Conclusion

This whole story has essentially been one of four separate narratives, simultaneous and coinciding dramatically and each affected by, and in turn affecting, the others. Partly confirming but also challenging persistent notions of Cuban 'exceptionalism', one of those narratives has been unique to Cuba and to the Revolution, while a second has found a particularly Cuban form. But two belong to a level beyond the particularities of the Cuban 'case', being part of a much wider context in which, it has been argued, we can, and should, understand the Cuban Revolution, past and present.

The first 'typical' narrative has been that of the remarkable cohesion and loyalty within the former guerrilla group of the *Sierra*, a story of named individuals, geographical groupings, personal affinities, shared personal histories and collectively shared political events, where biographical details can acquire later importance. Here, of course, the narrative is 'typical' in that, since the group identity of ex-combatants from a shared state-sanctioned battle is a common enough phenomenon, one can no doubt construct a similar picture of such cohesion and enduring camaraderie among former freedom fighters, especially if anti-colonial (i.e. sharing a 'national' struggle against external oppression). Doubtless, we can find similarities in, for example, the legacy of the Algerian, Vietnamese or Angolan anti-colonial struggles, or the long-fought Chinese revolution. In almost all such struggles, especially where the warfare has been either long or brutal, or where the collective sense of denied nationhood was well established, we can see evidence of a similar group identity among ex-combatants, a willingness to assume that the shared struggle resulted in an inherent affinity that overrode and outlasted political differences and led to a visceral level of mutual trust, especially as the years after the struggle saw a plethora of countervailing pressures, diverging perspectives and even, at times, personal ambitions. In this respect, therefore, the narrative traced here of the 'badge of honour' bestowed by the shared experience of Moncada, *Granma* and Sierra is at one level no different to many another similar guerrilla struggle against notionally superior odds and forces. That said, however, the absence of major splits among the principal leaders and activists in the Cuban case has been truly remarkable – leaving aside the still uncorroborated rumours of the Guevara–Fidel split – and may well indicate something peculiarly Cuban.

The second 'typical' narrative has been on a different level altogether, namely the extent to which the Cuban case shares with any number of post-colonial nation-building experiences certain evident tendencies towards common characteristics. It has been argued that, in that context, we can better understand the overwhelming Cuban imperative of national unity, even leading to the elimination, suppression or neglect of patterns of thought or action seen as being harmful to the unity that colonialism had actively prevented and that, after 'real' independence, was seen to threaten survival. Equally, the importance of a single unified party, encompassing all otherwise centrifugal political parties or tendencies, can be understood as part of the post-colonial drive for unity and unanimity in Cuba. Finally, we can relate the leftism of the Cuban case to the wider pattern of an attraction of 'socialist' models, a defining of the governing philosophy as socialist.

However, what was described earlier was not simply a modification of the Socialist Bloc models but, it was argued, a new variant of what has been generally referred to as corporatism, responding to the external pressures and internal conflicts generated by a previous colonialism and a presently vulnerable independence, while trying to create a nation out of disparate elements or against a previous denial of nationhood and national identity. Essentially, what that corporatism amounted to was not the right-wing variant with which we are historically more familiar but rather a very precise form of the 'incorporating' corporatism of new and struggling nations (rather than the old 'corporate' corporatism), i.e. a very specifically post-colonial nation-building socialist corporatism. Even there, however, it was argued that the Cuban case, while sharing most of those more general patterns, differed slightly through the fundamentally revolutionary nature and impetus of the whole process, which, while still evading notions of 'exceptionalism', made it a sui generis and revolutionary variant of this new corporatism.

In fact, we have seen that the Cuban variant has been character-ised by several things: the ways in which debate has been defined, encouraged and channelled; the approach to dissidence (depending on the extent of the dissenters' 'outside-ness' and 'against-ness'); the tendency to include (but deny) difference (on the basis of race, gender, sexuality or religion); and the greater tendency towards such inclusion after 1990 (including of some emigrant Cubans).

That aspect, indeed, leads on to the third and fourth narratives of this study: the always present and occasionally distorting post-1961 sense of 'siege' in which Cubans have lived on the island, and the effects of the actual process of revolutionary change. The former has, we have seen, created negative patterns – the tendency to exclude, the willingness to coerce, the imperative for conformity – but also positive patterns of inclusion of an often broadly defined 'inside' and a permanent sense of an embattled togetherness, cementing a revolutionary sense of national unity and a powerful awareness of a national heritage and identity. In the meantime, the revolutionary nature of the post-1959 changes has constantly challenged certainties, definitions and stability, but has also created a dynamic sense of the collective. It has been shown here how this all created a powerful awareness of 'us' (Cubans on the island) against 'them' outside (seen as seeking to end 'our' independence or hard-won social benefits), thereby taking the group identity of the *Sierra* and making it into the larger group identity of 'the people' or 'the (always embattled) nation'.

The study began with a questioning of both the reliability of 'Fidel-centrism' in readings of the Revolution and also the overwhelming focus on the 'big' personalities of Fidel, Raúl and Che. The point made from that point onwards, as we have traced the evolution of the narrower group mentality and identity (of the more collective leadership since 1959) and also the nature of the broader national 'group', has been that the key issue in Cuba is not necessarily the much-alleged loyalty to Fidel – although some, such as Borrego, admitted that their respect for Fidel and Guevara led them to accept the correctness of their 'socialism' (Anderson 1997: 410) – but rather loyalty firstly to 'the group' (as broadly defined and as dynamic in formation as this study has made clear) and beyond that to 'the Revolution', not (or not necessarily) as conceived in 1953 or 1958, but rather in 1960–61.

# BIBLIOGRAPHY

Abreu Cardet, J. M. and E. Coredero Michel (2009) *Dictadura y revolución en el Caribe: las expediciones de junio de 1959*. Santiago de Cuba: Editorial Oriente.

Aguiar Rodríguez, R. (2000) *El bonchismo y el gangsterismo en Cuba*. Havana: Ciencias Sociales.

Aladro Cardoso, M., S. Valdés Sánchez and L. Rosendo Eiró (2007) *La Guerra de Liberación Nacional en Cuba, 1956–1959*. Havana: Casa de las Américas.

Almeida Bosque, J. (1987a) *Presidio*. Havana: Editorial del Comité Central.

— (1987b) *Exilio*. Havana: Editorial del Comité Central.

— (1988) *Desembarco*. Havana: Editorial del Comité Central.

— (2008) *La Sierra Maestra y más allá*. Havana: Casa Editorial Verde Olivo.

Alvarez Mola, M. and S. Ravelo López (eds) (2007) *La Expedición del Granma: Selección de documentos*. Havana: Editora Política.

Alvarez Tabío, P. (2004) *Celia: Ensayo para una biografía*. Havana: Oficina de Publicaciones del Consejo del Estado.

Ameijeiras Delgado, E. (1984) *Más allá de nosotros*. Santiago de Cuba: Editorial Oriente.

Ameringer, C. D. (2000) *The Cuban Democratic Experience: The Auténtico years, 1944–1952*. Gainesville FL: University Press of Florida.

Anderson, J. L. (1997) *Che Guevara: A revolutionary life*. London and New York, NY: Bantam Books.

Azicri, M. (1988) *Cuba: Politics,* economics, society. London and New York NY: Pinter Publishers.

— and E. Deal (eds) (2004) *Cuban Socialism in a New Century: Adversity, survival and renewal*. Gainesville FL: University Press of Florida.

Balfour, S. (2009) *Castro*. Harlow: Pearson Longman.

Batista Moreno, R. (2008) *Camilo en el Frente Norte*. Havana: Ediciones Unión.

Batlle Reyes, L. (ed.) (2008) *Blas Roca: Virtud y ejemplo. La imagen de un hombre excepcional*. Havana: Ciencias Sociales.

Bell Lara, J. (2007) *Fase insurreccional de la Revolución Cubana*. Havana: Editorial de Ciencias Sociales.

— D. L. López and T. Caram (eds) (2006) *Documentos de la Revolución Cubana: 1959*. Havana: Ciencias Sociales.

— (eds) (2007) *Documentos de la Revolución Cubana: 1960*. Havana: Editorial de Ciencias Sociales.

Bengelsdorf, C. (1994) *The Problem of Democracy in Cuba: Between vision and reality*. Oxford: Oxford University Press.

'Benigno' (D. A. Ramírez) (1996) *Memorias de un soldado cubano: Vida y muerte de la Revolución*. Barcelona: Tusquets Editores.

Borrego, O. (2001) *Che: El camino del fuego*. Havana: Imagen Contemporánea.

Bourne, P. (1986) *Castro: A biography of Fidel Castro*. London: Macmillan Books.

Brenner, P., M. R. Jiménez, J. M. Kirk and W. M. LeoGrande (eds) (2008) *A Con-*

temporary *Cuba Reader: Reinventing the Revolution*. Lanham MD: Rowman and Littlefield Publishers.

Buch, L. M. and R. Suárez (2009) *Gobierno revolucionario cubano: Primeros pasos*. Havana: Ciencias Sociales.

Castañeda, C. (1998) *Compañero: The life and death of Che Guevara*. New York NY: Alfred A. Knopf.

Castro Ruz, F. (1980) 'Palabras a los intelectuales'. In *Revolución, Letras, Arte*. Havana: Editorial Letras Cubanas, pp. 7–30.

— (2010) *La victoria estratégica: Por todos los caminos de la Sierra*. Havana: Oficina de Publicaciones del Consejo del Estado.

Chomón, F. (1969) *El asalto al Palacio Presidencial*. Havana: Ciencias Sociales.

Christman, H. M. (ed.) (1966) *Essential Works of Lenin*. New York NY and London: Bantam Books.

Clayfield, A. (2013) 'An unfinished struggle? The guerrilla experience and the shaping of political culture in the Cuban Revolution'. PhD thesis, University of Nottingham.

De la Fuente, A. (2001) *A Nation for All: Race, inequality and politics in twentieth-century Cuba*. Chapel Hill NC: University of North Carolina Press.

Díaz Castañón, M. (2001) *Ideología y Revolución: Cuba, 1959–1962*. Havana: Ciencias Sociales.

Domínguez, J. I. (1978) *Cuba: Order and Revolution*. Cambridge MA and London: Belknap Press, Harvard University Press.

— (1990) 'The Cuban Armed Forces, the Party and society in wartime and during Rectification'. In R. Gillespie (ed.) *Cuba after Thirty Years: Rectification and the Revolution*. London: Frank Cass, pp. 45–62.

Draper, T. (1969) *Castroism: Theory and practice*. New York NY: Praeger Publishers.

Dumont, R. (1970) *Cuba: Socialism and development*. New York NY: Grove Press.

Eckstein, S. E. (1994) *Back from the Future: Cuba under Castro*. Princeton NJ: Princeton University Press.

Fagen, R. R. (1969) *The Transformation of Political Culture in Cuba*. Stanford CA: Stanford University Press.

Fernández, D. (2000) *Cuba and the Politics of Passion*. Austin TX: University of Texas.

Fitzgerald, E. T. (1988) 'The "Sovietisation of Cuba thesis" revisited'. In A. Zimbalist (ed.) *Cuban Political Economy: Controversies in Cubanology*. Boulder CO: Westview Press, pp. 137–53.

Franqui, C. (1967) *El libro de los Doce*. Havana: Instituto del Libro.

— (1976) *Diario de la Revolución Cubana*. Paris: R. Torres.

— (1980) *Family Portrait with Fidel*. London: Jonathan Cape.

— (2012) *Camilo Cienfuegos*. n.p.: Christie Books.

García Oliveras, J. (1988) *José Antonio*. Havana: Editora Abril.

Gillespie, R. (ed.) (1990) *Cuba after Thirty Years: Rectification and the Revolution*. London: Frank Cass.

Goldenberg, B. (1966) *The Cuban Revolution and Latin America*. New York NY: Frederick A. Praeger.

González, E. (1979) 'Institutionalization, political elites and foreign policies'. In C. Blasier and C. Mesa-Lago (eds) *Cuba in the World*. Pittsburgh PA: University of Pittsburgh Press, pp. 3–36.

Goodsell, J. N. (1975) *Fidel Castro's Personal Revolution in Cuba: 1959–1973*. New York NY: Alfred A. Knopf.

Graña Eiriz, M. (2008) *Clandestinos en prisión*. Havana: Ciencias Sociales.

Gray, A. I. and A. Kapcia (eds) (2008)

*The Changing Dynamic of Cuban Civil Society*. Gainesville FL: University Press of Florida.

Guanche, J. C. (2013) 'El gesto de Alfredo Guevara'. *La Jiribilla: Revista de Cultura Cubana*, 20–26 April. Available at: www.lajiribilla.cu/articulo/4532/el-gesto-de-alfredo-guevara.

Guerra, L. (2012) *Visions of Power in Cuba: Revolution, redemption and resistance, 1959–1971*. Chapel Hill NC: University of North Carolina.

Habel, J. (1991) *Cuba: The Revolution in peril*. London: Verso.

Harman, C. (1974) *Bureaucracy and Revolution in Eastern Europe*. London: Pluto Press.

Hart Dávalos, A. (2004) *Aldabonazo: Inside the Cuban revolutionary underground, 1952–58*. New York NY and London: Pathfinder.

Hennessy, C. A. M. (1963) 'Roots of Cuban nationalism'. *International Affairs* 39(3): 345–59.

Horowitz, I. L. (2008) *The Long Night of Dark Intent: A half century of Cuban communism*. New Brunswick NJ and London: Transaction Publishers.

Kapcia, A. (1994) 'Political and economic change in Cuba: the significance of Che Guevara'. In M. Rosendahl (ed.) *La situación actual en Cuba: desafíos y alternativas/The Current Situation in Cuba: Challenges and alternatives*. Stockholm: Institute of Latin American Studies, pp. 17–48.

— (1996) 'Politics in Cuba: beyond the stereotypes'. *Bulletin of Latin American Research* 15(2): 247–53.

— (2000) *Cuba: Island of dreams*. Oxford: Berg.

— (2005) *Havana: The making of Cuban culture*. Oxford: Berg.

— (2008) *Cuba in Revolution: A history since the fifties*. London: Reaktion Books.

— (2009) 'Lessons of the Special Period: learning to march again'.

*Latin American Perspectives* 36(1): 30–41.

— (2011) 'Defying expectations: the external profile and activism of the Cuban Revolution'. In G. L.Gardini and P. Lambert (eds) *Latin American Foreign Policies: Between ideology and pragmatism*. New York NY: Palgrave Macmillan, pp. 179–96.

Karol, K. S. (1970) *Guerrillas in Power: The course of the Cuban Revolution*. New York NY: Hill and Wang.

Kirk, E. J. (2011) 'Setting the agenda for Cuban sexuality: the role of Cuba's CENESEX'. *Canadian Journal of Latin American and Caribbean Studies* 36(72): 143–63.

Klepak, H. (2005) *Cuba's Military 1990–2005: Revolutionary soldiers during counter-revolutionary times*. New York NY and London: Palgrave Macmillan.

— (2010) *Raúl Castro, estratega de la defensa revolucionaria de Cuba*. Buenos Aires: Capital Intelectual.

Kumaraswami, P. and A. Kapcia (2012) *Literary Culture in Cuba: Revolution, nation-building and the book*. Manchester: Manchester University Press.

Latell, B. (2005) *After Fidel: The inside story of Castro's regime and Cuba's next leader*. New York NY: Palgrave Macmillan.

Lenin, V. I. (1920) 'The trade unions, the present situation and Trotsky's mistakes'. Available at www.marxists.org/archive/lenin/works/1920/dec/30.htm (accessed 28 September 2013).

LeoGrande, W. M. (2008) 'The Cuban nation's single party: the Communist Party of Cuba faces the future'. In P. Brenner et al. (eds) *A Contemporary Cuba Reader: Reinventing the Revolution*. Lanham MD: Rowman and Littlefield Publishers, pp. 50–62.

Llerena, M. (1978) *The Unsuspected Revolution: The birth and rise of Castroism*.

Ithaca NY and London: Cornell University Press.

López Civeira, F. (1990) *La crisis de los partidos políticos burgueses en Cuba: 1925–1958*. Havana: Ministerio de Educación Superior.

Lowy, M. (1973) *The Marxism of Che Guevara: Philosophy, economics and revolutionary warfare*. New York NY: Monthly Review.

Martínez Heredia, F. (1989) *El Che y el Socialismo*. Mexico: Nuestro Tiempo.

— (2010) *Las ideas y la batalla del Che*. Havana: Ciencias Sociales.

Martínez Victores, R. (1978) *7RR: La historia de Radio Rebelde*. Havana: Ciencias Sociales.

Mencía, M. (1986) *El Grito de Moncada*. Havana: Editora Política.

Mesa-Lago, C. (1974) *Cuba in the 1970s: Pragmatism and institutionalization*. Albuquerque NM: University of New Mexico Press.

Miranda Fernández, L. (1984) *Lázaro Peña: Capitán de la clase obrera cubana*. Havana: Editorial de Ciencias Sociales.

Montalván Lamas, O. (2011) *Cuba: Territorio libre de analfabetismo*. Havana: Ciencias Sociales.

Morales Domínguez, E. (2013) *Race in Cuba: Essays on the Revolution and racial inequality*. New York NY: Monthly Review.

Nuiry, J. (2007) *Tradición y combate: Una década en la memoria*. Havana: Imagen Contemporánea.

Núñez Jiménez, A. (1959) *La Liberación de las Islas*. Havana: Editorial Lex.

— (2005) *En marcha con Fidel: 1962*. Havana: Ciencias Sociales.

O'Donnell, G. A. (1973) *Modernization and Bureaucratic-Authoritarianism: Studies in South American politics*. Berkeley CA: Institute of International Studies.

Olson, J. S. and J. E. Olson (1995) *Cuban Americans: From trauma to triumph*. New York NY: Twayne Publishers.

Oltuski, E. (2000) *Gente del Llano*. Havana: Imagen Contemporánea.

Oltuski Ozacki, E., H. Rodríguez Llompart and E. Torres-Cuevas (eds) (2007) *Memorias de la Revolución*. Havana: Imagen Contemporánea.

Oppenheimer, A. (1992) *La hora final de Castro: La historia secreta detrás de la inminente caída del comunismo en Cuba*. Buenos Aires: Javier Vergara Editor.

Pardo Llada, J. (1988) *Fidel y el 'Che'*. Barcelona: Plaza y Janés Editores.

Paterson, T. G. (1994) *Contesting Castro: The United States and the triumph of the Cuban Revolution*. Oxford and New York NY: Oxford University Press.

Pérez Llody, L. A. (2007) *Rafael García Bárcena: El sueño de la Gran Nación*. Santiago de Cuba: Editorial Oriente.

Pérez Rivero, R. (2006) *La guerra de liberación nacional: Formación y desarrollo del Ejército Rebelde*. Santiago de Cuba: Editorial Oriente.

Pichardo, H. (1977) *Documentos para la historia de Cuba: Tomo I*. Havana: Editorial de Ciencias Sociales.

— (1986) *Documentos para la historia de Cuba: Tomo II*. Havana: Editorial de Ciencias Sociales.

Pogolotti, G. (ed.) (2006) *Polémicas culturales de los 60*. Havana: Letras Cubanas.

Port, L. (2012) 'Hegemonic discourse and sources of legitimacy in Cuba: comparing Mariel (1980) and the Maleconazo (1994)'. PhD thesis, University of Nottingham.

Quijano, A. (2000) 'Coloniality of power and Eurocentrism in Latin America'. *International Sociology* 15(2): 215–32.

Ramos Ruiz, D. (2006) *Roa, Director de Cultura: Una política, una revista*. Havana: Centro Juan Marinello.

*Revolución* (1961) Año IV, No. 726, 17 April: 3.

Roca, B. (1961) *Los fundamentos del*

*Socialismo en Cuba*. Havana: Ediciones Populares.

Rodríguez Rodríguez, I. (ed.) (1989) *AJR: Documentos para una historia de future*. Guantánamo: Editora Abril.

Rojas, M. (1973) *La Generación del Centenario en el Juicio del Moncada*. Havana: Ciencias Sociales.

Rojas Blaquier, A. (2005) *Primer Partido Comunista de Cuba. Tomo 1: Sus tácticas y estrategias,1925–1935*. Santiago de Cuba: Editorial Oriente.

— (2010) *Primer Partido Comunista de Cuba. Tomo 3: El Partido Socialista Popular, su contribución al proceso nacional liberador cubano entre 1952–1961. Estrategia y tácticas*. Santiago de Cuba: Editorial Oriente.

Ruega Jomarrón, H. (2009) *Tradiciones combativas de un pueblo: Las milicias cubanas*. Havana: Editora Política.

Sartre, J.-P. (1961) *Sartre on Cuba*. New York NY: Ballantine Books.

Scheer, R. and M. Zeitlin (1964) *Cuba: An American tragedy*. London: Penguin Books.

Schmitter, P. (1979) 'Still the century of corporatism?' In P. Schmitter and G. Lembruch (eds) *Trends towards Corporatist Intermediation*. London: Sage Publications, pp. 7–52.

Sinclair, A. (1979) *Guevara*. London: Fontana.

— (2002) *Che Guevara*. Stroud: Sutton Publishing.

Suárez, A. (1967) *Cuba: Castroism and Communism, 1959–1966*. Cambridge MA and London: MIT Press.

Suárez, N. (ed.) (1996) *Fernando Ortiz y la Cubanidad*. Havana: Fundación Fernando Ortiz/Ediciones Union.

Suchlicki, J. (1988) *Historical Dictionary of Cuba*. Metuchen NJ and London: The Scarecrow Press.

Sutherland, E. (1969) *The Youngest Revolution: A personal report on Cuba*. New York NY: The Dial Press.

Sweig, J. E. (2002) *Inside the Cuban Revolution: Fidel Castro and the urban underground*. Cambridge MA and London: Harvard University Press.

Szulc, T. (1986) *Fidel: A critical portrait*. London: Hutchinson.

Tablada Pérez, C. (1987) *El pensamiento económico de Ernesto Che Guevara*. Havana: Casa de las Américas.

Thomas, H. (1971) *Cuba, or the Pursuit of Freedom*. London: Eyre and Spottiswoode.

Triay, V. A. (1998) *Fleeing Castro: Operation Peter Pan and the Cuban children's program*. Gainesville FL: University Press of Florida.

Valdés, N. P. (1979) 'Revolutionary solidarity with Angola'. In C. Blasier and C. Mesa-Lago (eds) *Cuba in the World*. Pittsburgh PA: University of Pittsburgh Press, pp. 87–118.

— (2004) 'Presidential succession: legal and political contexts and domestic players'. In M. Azicri and E. Deal (eds) *Cuban Socialism in a New Century: Adversity, survival and renewal*. Gainesville FL: University Press of Florida, pp. 242–58.

— (2008) 'The Revolution and political content of Fidel Castro's charismatic authority'. In P. Brenner et al. (eds) *A Contemporary Cuba Reader: Reinventing the Revolution*. Lanham MD: Rowman and Littlefield Publishers, pp. 27–40.

Vignier, E. and G. Alonso (1973) *La corrupción política y administrativa en Cuba, 1944–1952*. Havana: Editorial de Ciencias Sociales.

Weber, M. (1947) 'The nature of charismatic authority and its routinization'. In M. Weber, *Theory of Social and Economic Organization*, translated by A. R. Anderson and T. Parsons. London: William Hodge & Co. Originally published in 1922 in German as *Wirtschaft und Gesellschaft*.

Whitney, R. (2001) *State and Revolution in Cuba: Mass mobilization and politi-*

*cal change, 1920–1940*. Chapel Hill NC and London: University of North Carolina Press.

Wiarda, H. (1973) 'Toward a framework for the study of political change in the Iberic-Latin tradition: the corporative model'. *World Politics* 25(2): 206–35.

Williamson, P. J. (1985) *Varieties of Corporatism: A conceptual discussion*. Cambridge: Cambridge University Press.

Yaffe, H. (2009) *Che Guevara: The economics of revolution*. Basingstoke: Palgrave Macmillan.

# INDEX

26 July Movement, 10, 11, 23, 26, 32 36, 50, 52–3, 54, 55, 57, 65, 67, 68, 72, 76, 77, 79, 80, 82, 87, 90, 98, 99, 101, 105, 108, 112, 114, 116, 122, 124, 126–8, 127, 128, 130, 136, 138, 150, 151, 176, 214; and PSP, 69–73; naming of, 47

abortion, 90
Abrantes (Abrahantes) Fernández, José, 88, 122, 148, 157
accountability, 20
Acevedo, Rogelio, 83
Acosta, Armando, 29, 70, 103, 121
Agramonte Pichardo, Roberto, 67, 69, 108
agrarian reform, 73, 91, 97
Aguirre, Mirta, 105
Aguirre, Severo, 79, 104, 121
Ala Izquierda Estudiantil, 107
Alarcón de Quesada, Ricardo, 169, 176–8
ALBA countries, 175
*Aldabonazo* newspaper, 42, 110
Aldana, Carlos, 149, 167
Alegría de Pío debacle, 23, 47–9
Almeida Bosque, Juan, 48, 50, 79, 87, 121, 136, 164–5, 171
Ameijeiras, Efigenio, 48, 49, 84, 115, 130, 145
Ameijeiras, Juan Manuel, 84
Amnesty International, 8
Angola, Cuban involvement in, 139, 147, 159, 173
anti-bureaucracy campaign, 10, 20, 119, 124
anti-Communism, 62, 69, 70, 71, 72, 78, 87, 94, 100, 106, 110
anti-loafing law, 124
'Antonio Maceo' Invading Column No. 2, 53
Aragonés, Emilio, 73, 79
Argentina, 213
Artime, Manuel, 111

Association of Rebel Youth (AJR), 13
Association of Veterans of the Cuban Revolution (ACRC), 12, 165
Auténticos *see* Authentic Cuban Revolutionary Party
Authentic Cuban Revolutionary Party (PRC-A) (Auténticos), 41–2, 44, 45, 65, 112, 217

Balaguer Cabrera, José Ramón, 85, 167
*balsero* emigration crisis, 191–4
Barruecos, 'Chomy', 173, 174, 178
Batista, Fulgencio, 23, 35, 43, 59, 70, 75, 77, 78; coup of, 41–2
*batistianos*, 9; execution of, 29; trials of, 75, 125
Battle of Ideas, 20, 26, 38, 61, 153, 161–2, 175, 176, 179, 181, 194
Bay of Pigs episode, 33, 90, 95, 100, 102, 105, 111, 112, 113, 115, 116, 167, 186, 218
Bayamo garrison, attack on, 46
Benítez, Reinaldo, 49
Bernal Alemany, Rafael, 179
Bettelheim, Charles, 118
Bishop, Maurice, 25
black market, 144
black population of Cuba, 171–3
Black Power activists, welcomed in Cuba, 172
Blanco, Eladio, 112
*bonchismo*, 23, 45, 109
Bonsal, Philip, 69
Borge, Tomás, 25
Borrego, O., 223
Boti, Regino, 67, 126
Bravo, Flávio, 25, 35, 79, 102, 121, 130, 147
Brazil, nation-building in, 211
Buch Rodríguez, Luis M., 67, 71, 174
bureaucracy and bureaucratisation, 14–15, 92, 134–5, 145, 152 *see also* anti-bureaucracy campaign

Bush administration, 143

Cabrisas, Ricardo, 127
Calcines, Ramón, 79, 109, 121, 122
Calderío López, Francisco see Roca
    Calderío, Blas
Camacho, Julio, 136–7
Camarioca exodus (1965), 26
Canada, 120, 186
Capdevilla, Jaime, 8
Carpentier, Alejo, 105
Carter administration, 143
Casa de las Américas, 11, 91, 190
Castro, Fidel, 1, 10, 22–8, 31, 35, 36, 40,
    48, 49, 58, 61, 68, 69, 70, 71, 72, 73,
    74, 75, 78, 79, 80, 81, 83, 86, 90–1,
    94, 95, 97, 100, 101, 102, 107, 108–9,
    120, 121, 122, 123, 126, 136, 141, 150,
    152, 155, 158, 164, 173–4, 178, 182; as
    Commander in Chief of Rebel Army,
    67; as orator, 181; as student activist,
    45–6; assassination plot against, 111;
    charismatic authority of, 3; criticism
    of, 78; 'Cuba está sola' declaration,
    187; decision to continue serving,
    181; decision to retire, 181; defence
    speech of, 46; 'History will absolve
    me' speech, 25, 214; ill-health of, 22;
    meets intellectuals, 96; mockery of,
    176; preference for mobilisation, 217;
    relations with Celia Sánchez, 55–6;
    relations with Che, 30, 34; relations
    with Support Group, 175; supposed
    differences with Raúl, 139; 'Victory
    Caravan', 36; view of Soviet invasion
    of Czechoslovakia, 132–3; visit to
    United Nations, 91; 'Words to the
    Intellectuals', 189–92 see also Fidel-
    centrism
Castro, Raúl, 22, 26, 28, 30, 31, 35–9, 40,
    48, 49, 52, 53, 54, 55, 59, 68, 69, 71, 72,
    74, 79, 86, 87, 88, 95, 105, 107, 116, 121,
    123, 124, 136, 138, 155, 156, 163, 165, 166,
    169, 174, 180, 182, 217, 222; criticism
    of failings of system, 195–6; named
    as second-in-command, 36; reform
    programme of, 177, 195; supposed
    differences with Fidel, 139

Castroism, use of term, 4
Catholic Action, 45
Catholic Church, 20, 189, 194, 202
Catholicism, social, 200
caudillismo, 3–4
Cayo Confites expedition, 110
Ceballos, Fernández, 112
Ceballos Parejas, Segundo, 74
Central Committee of PCC see Cuban
    Communist Party, Central Committee
Centre for Martí Studies, 134
Cepero Bonilla, Raúl, 67
Céspedes, Carlos Manuel de, 6, 49;
    'Declaration of Yara', 219
Chávez, Hugo, 25
Chibás, Eduardo ('Eddy'), 42, 47, 55
chibasismo, 42
China, 37
Chinese model, 39
Chomón Mediavilla, Faure, 48, 51, 60, 79,
    106–7, 122, 130
choteo sense of humour, 185
Cienfuegos, Osmani (Osmany), 79, 105,
    136–7, 150–1
Cienfuegos Gorriarán, Camilo, 6, 31, 48,
    49–50, 52, 53, 71, 72, 73, 82, 86, 114,
    116, 165
Cienfuegos military mutiny, 93
Cintra Frías, Leopoldo ('Polo'), 82
Civic Resistance Movement (MRC), 50,
    57, 82, 93, 108, 112
civil service, purging of, 9
coercion, 8; accusation of, 6
Cojímar discussions, 87, 88, 98, 103
Cold War, 14, 62, 77, 194
collective leadership, 3, 4, 131, 182, 222
collective sense of unity, 185–9
collectivity, 198–223
Colomé Ibarra, Abelardo, 83–4, 139, 158
coloniality, use of term, 207
Column No. 6, 36
COMECON, 61; collapse of, 5; Cuban
    membership of, 132, 134, 140
    (refused, 118)
Comintern, 43, 44
Committees for the Defence of the
    Revolution (CDRs), 12, 16, 102, 116,
    134, 160

Communism, 4, 42, 43, 52, 53, 69, 77, 95, 97, 99, 102, 106, 110, 112, 117, 187, 189, 204; Cuban version of, 114, 119, 198; orthodox, 97–105, 118 see also anti-Communism

communism, as ideal, 76, 93, 198

Communist Party of Italy (PCI), 69

Communist Revolutionary Union Party, 43

comunitario movement, 161

Confederation of Cuban Workers (CTC), 12, 38, 78, 101, 131, 170, 193; battles in, 77–9

Conjunto Folklórico Nacional, 172

Constitution of Cuba, 30, 140, 160, 199

contraception, 90

Contracorriente magazine, 194

Copextel enterprise, 168

core leadership, 22–40

corporatism, 200–2; Hispanic traditions of, 201; of new nations, 221–2; post-colonial, 203–6; revolutionary, 198–223; use of term, 198

corruption, 12, 38, 39, 42, 65, 71, 145, 151, 155–7, 175, 213

crèches, 90

criminality, petty, 13, 161

criollos, 183–4, 213

crisis of 1989–94, 159–62

Crombet, Jaime, 149–50

Cruz, Agustín, 73

Cuban Adjustment Act (1966) (USA), 192

Cuban Communist Party (PCC), 13, 14, 29, 31, 32, 43, 59, 89, 98, 101, 102, 108, 110, 111, 119–20, 140; Central Committee, 83, 85, 89, 90, 92, 103, 109, 125, 128, 130, 141, 149, 157, 165–6, 167, 195; Congresses of, 15, 16, 19, 194–5 (first, 132, 136; second, 136; third, 1986, 146, 151, 152, 153,157–9, 193; fourth, 37, 163, 193; fifth, 1997, 163, 193; sixth, 38–9, 163, 166); creation of, 4, 11; membership of, 134; Political Bureau, 15

Cuban Five, 17

Cuban People's Party (Ortodoxos), 26, 42, 65, 112

cubanidad, 185

Cubela, Rolando (also Cubelas), 51, 106–7, 111, 113

cultural colonialism, 208

cultural community, 210

cultural policy, 189–92; disputes over, 96

culture, and institutionalisation, 141–3

Curbelo, Raúl, 79

Czechoslovakia, Soviet invasion of, 132–3

debate, role and nature of, 192–7; system of, 18–21 see also Great Debate

Debates Americanos magazine, 194

decentralisation, 144

decision-making, system of, 16, 18

Declaration of Havana (1960), 31, 109, 120

decolonisation, 203, 204–6, 209, 211; cultural, 206; in Cuba, 214–15; political, 210

de la Torriente Brau, Pablo, 108

del Pino, Rafal, 155

Del Valle Jiménez, Sergio, 79, 82, 121, 136

democracy, direct, 3

Democratic Socialist Tradition, 43

Department of State Security (DSE), 17–18

dependency theory, school of, 118

Díaz, Angel, 46

Díaz, Marcos see Roca Calderío, Blas

Díaz-Canel Bermúdez, Miguel, 179–80

Díaz Lanz, Pedro Luis, 71

Directorio Revolucionario see Revolutionary Directorate

'divide and rule' strategy of colonialism, 203, 210, 214

dollar, US: influx of, 162; legalisation of, 13

Domenech, Joel, 121

Dominican Republic, 88; planned liberation of, 23, 31

Dorticós Torrado, Osvaldo, 79, 89, 90, 92–4, 109, 121, 126, 130, 136

Draper, Theodore, 3

Dubček, Alexander, 133

Echeverría, José Antonio, 25, 45, 51, 80, 106

education, 5; spending on, 20

embargo *see* United States of America (USA), embargo against Cuba

emigration, of middle class *see* middle class, emigration of

Escalante Dellundé, Aníbal, 10, 73, 76, 79, 94, 98–9, 113, 122, 123, 130, 131, 196; affair of, 79–81, 100, 115, 116–17, 128

Escalante, César, 79, 103

Escalona, Dulce María, 103

Escalona, Juan, 177

Espín, Vilma, 45, 48, 54–5, 74, 89–90

exclusion, 182–97

executions, 6; of *batistianos*, 29

ex-guerrillas, 7, 81, 85, 89, 97, 103, 114, 115, 120, 136, 138, 142, 143, 158, 164, 165, 166, 168, 215, 220; and the military, 82–6 *see also* guerrillas

exodus, 187–8, 216; *balsero* crisis, 191–2 *see also* Camarioca exodus, Mariel exodus, middle class, emigration of *and* migration and non-migration

factions, question of, 64, 137–9 *see also* micro-faction affair

Fajardo, Manuel, 48, 50

Falange Católica (Chile), 200

Federation of Cuban Women (FMC), 12, 89, 90

Federation of Secondary Education Students (FEEM), 12

Fernández, José Ramón, 167–8

Fernández, Omar, 111

Fernández Font, Marcelo, 51, 57, 94, 110, 115, 118, 127, 128, 130, 137

Fernández García, Manuel, 67

Fernández Rodríguez, Angel, 67

Fidel-centrism, 1–5, 22, 222–3

Figuereido, Carlos, 88

First Free Territory, 186

Florida, Cubans in, 187

folk music, Cuban, interest in, 185

*Forbes* magazine, 25

Frank País Second Front, 36

Franqui, Carlos, 66, 93, 110–11, 130, 164; *El Libro de los Doce*, 48–9

Frías, Ciro, 50

*funcionario*, use of term, 15

Fundamental Law (1959), 30

G2 security apparatus, 17, 88, 125

Gandhi, Indira, 25

García, Calixto, 49

García, Guillermo, 48, 50, 54, 79, 88, 121, 130, 136, 147, 157

García, Raúl, 136

García Bárcena, Rafael, 45, 57

García Buchaca, Edith, 104, 131

García Martínez, Calixto, 85

García Oliveras, Julio, 88, 122

García Vals, Francisco ('Pancho'), 70, 73, 103

General Intelligence Office (DGI), 17, 125

general strikes, 44, 50, 66, 112

Gil, Elena, 89

Gómez, Máximo, 6

Gonzales, Edward, 137

González, Elián, 161; campaign, 176, 181, 188, 194

González Carbajal, Ladislao, 102–3

Gorbachev, Mikhail, 143–4, 149, 151, 154, 164

Gramsci, Antonio, 207, 208

*Granma* expedition, 23, 29, 36, 47–8, 50, 52, 53, 54, 55, 58, 60, 81, 83, 84, 86, 115, 122, 129, 164, 168, 221

*Granma* newspaper, 92, 111, 121, 126

Grau San Martín, Ramón, 42

Great Debate (1962–65), 33, 63, 116, 117, 119–20, 127, 128, 132, 138, 149, 193, 196

Grobart, Fabio, 121

Guatemala, 62

Guerra, Secundino, 121

guerrilla strategy, failure of, 125

guerrilla warfare, 9, 33; in Latin America, 187; theory and practice of, 31; urban, 121

guerrillas, 29, 41, 81, 107, 113, 186 *see also* ex-guerrillas

Guevara, Ernesto 'Che', 6, 22, 26, 28–35, 40, 48, 49, 52, 53, 60, 66, 69, 73, 74, 75, 76, 79, 86–7, 93, 94–5, 97, 103, 106, 118, 119, 120, 122, 123, 127, 138, 158, 165, 182, 217, 222, 223; death of, 121, 133; departure from power, 33–4; ideas of, 154 (inapplicability of, 121); *La guerra de guerrillas*, 31; mythification of, 28; *Pasajes de la guerra revolucionaria cubana*, 31; president of National Bank, 28, 32; relations with Fidel, 34; *Reminiscences*, 49; travels from Cuba, 30; UN speeches of, 28

Guevara Valdés, Alfredo, 11, 74, 95–6, 98, 131

Guillén, Nicolás, 105

Guiteras, Antonio, 6, 65, 219

*gusanos*, use of term, 7, 188

Gutiérrez Menoyo, Carlos, 106

Gutiérrez Menoyo, Eloy, 51

Haig, Alexander, 6

Hart Dávalos, Armando, 45, 47, 56–7, 67, 79, 91, 92, 94, 121, 128, 130, 136, 142–3, 178, 179

Havana Cultural Congress, 128, 141

Havana Party, 166

health, spending on, 20

hegemony, 207

Helms-Burton Act (1996) (USA), 2

Hernández Rodríguez del Rey, Melba, 47, 56, 81–2, 130

hierarchy: of corporatism, 202; of post-colonial systems, 204

homosexuals, harassment of, 62

housing, for homeless and slum-dwelling people, 187

*Hoy* newspaper, 43, 59, 78, 98, 111, 128

Human Rights Watch, 8

ICAIC cinema institute, 11, 96, 104, 190

Iglesias, Joel, 83, 131

illiteracy *see* literacy and literacy campaign

imperialism, origins of, 209

inclusion, 182–97, 202, 203, 214, 222; and collectivity, 198–223; culture of, 183–5

independence, desirability of, 209

individualism, 13, 14

inner circle, 41, 46, 47, 56, 57, 59, 60, 85, 87, 96, 114, 129, 136, 137, 150, 152; ageing of members of, 163; changing nature of, 162–80; early, 81–2; introduction of younger politicians into, 173; new, 122–9; PSP

membership in, 95; women in, 89–92 *see also* 'within' and 'against' the Revolution

Institutional Revolutionary Party (PRI) (Mexico), 145

institutionalisation, 9–10, 19, 135, 140, 146, 217; contested, 132–9; culture and, 141–3; resistance to, 119

Integrated Revolutionary Organisations (ORI), 10, 13, 76–7, 79–80, 94, 98, 116–17, 140

intermediate circles, 129–31

International Monetary Fund (IMF), 20

Israel, 216

JUCEPLAN agency, 126

Lage, Marcos, 137

Lage Dávila, Carlos, 38, 150, 174–5, 177

Lazo Hernández, Esteban, 169

Lenin, V. I., 12, 209

Leo XIII, *De Rerum Novarum*, 200

Lezama Lima, *Paradiso*, 142

*libreta* ration book, 14, 20

literacy and literacy campaign, 29, 33, 92, 119, 186, 191, 216

literary production, 11

*Llano* group, 50–1, 56–8, 60, 66, 77, 78, 92–5, 113, 114, 115, 130, 131, 142, 151, 176, 178

Llanusa Gobel, José, 56, 127

Llerena, Mario, 50

localism, rise of, 160

López, Antonio ('Ñico'), 46, 88

López Fresquet, Rufo, 67

*Lunes de Revolución*, 96, 104, 190

Luzardo, Manuel, 79, 121

Maceo, Antonio, 6; 'Protest', 219

Machado, Gerardo, 42, 43, 44

Machado Ventura, José Ramón, 136, 165–7, 168, 169, 179

*mafia anticubana*, use of term, 188

Malmierca, Isidoro, 121, 136

Manley, Michael, 25

Mao Zedong, 6, 122

March, Aleida, 70, 89

'Mariana Grajales' platoon, 55, 89

Mariel exodus (1980), 7, 26, 188

Marinello Vidaurreta, Juan, 43–4, 76, 93, 104, 121

Martí, José, 6, 41–2, 218; 50th anniversary of, 45; centenary of, 35; death of, 219; ideas of, 172

Martín, Miguel, 101, 121

Martinez, Julio *see* Roca Calderío, Blas

Martínez Páez, Julio, 67

Martínez Sánchez, Augusto, 36, 67, 78, 79

Martínez Villena, Rubén, 108

Marxism, 33, 74, 76, 85, 94, 101, 108, 172; of Che, 28, 29, 30–1, 32–3; of Fidel, 26; orthodox, 118

Masó Revolutionary Movement (MRM), 55

mass mobilisations, 20

Matanzas Party, 166, 169

Matar Franye, José, 102, 121, 122

Matos, Huber (Hubert), 37, 71–2, 126, 164; arrest of, 72, 87, 95, 112

Matthews, Herbert, 1, 58

Mederos, Elena, 67

Mella, Julio Antonio, 6, 44, 108, 219

Mendoza, Jorge Enrique, 125

Menéndez, Alfredo, 103

Mesa-Lago, C., 138

Mexico, 36, 42, 47, 53, 54, 120, 186, 204

micro-faction affair, 102, 109, 122, 123

middle class, emigration of, 10, 63, 171

migration and non-migration, issues of, 192

Mikoyan, Anastas, 88

Milián Castro, Arnaldo, 121, 136, 140–1

military, ex-guerrillas and, 82–6

Military Unit for Assisting Production (UMAP) work camps, 6; closure of, 105, 142; creation of, 123

Militia of Territorial Troops, 17

Ministry for Tourism (INTUR), 150, 158

Ministry of the Interior (MININT), 31, 148, 155, 157; Liberation Department, 125

Miret Prieto, Pedro, 47, 54, 69, 74, 88, 126, 136

Miró Cardona, José, 67

missile crisis, 24, 95, 115, 116, 120, 186

Miyar Barruecos, José Miguel ('Chomy'), 91

Moncada barracks, attack on, 23, 35, 36, 46, 52, 54, 56, 60, 81, 82, 83, 86, 89, 115, 122, 129, 164, 168, 221

Montané Oropesa, Jesús, 46, 47, 48, 82, 83, 130, 174

*Monthly Review*, 118

Mora, Alberto, 118, 127

moral economy, 19, 24, 33, 118, 132

Morales, Calixto, 49, 71

Morales, Evo, 25

Morán, Chao, 49

Morgan, William, 51

Movimiento de Liberación Dominicana (MLD), 88

Movimiento Revolucionario del Pueblo (MRP), 112

Mujal, Eusebio, 77

*mulato* population of Cuba, 100, 171

*Nación y Emigración* conference, 192

Naranjo Morales, José A. ('Pepin'), 85, 122, 173, 174

narratives of the Revolution, 220–3

nation: exaltation of, 202; predates nation-building, 219–20

nation-building, 198–200, 206, 218, 221; imperative of, 211–12; in Cuba, 212–20

National Assembly, 18, 27, 130, 132, 140, 151; presidency of, 109, 169; reform of, 160

National Association of Small Farmers (ANAP), 12

National Culture Council (CNC), 11, 96, 104, 135, 142

National Federation of Sugar Workers (FNTA), 78

National Institute for Agrarian Reform (INRA), 32, 75, 97, 99–100, 125

National Liberation Front (FLN) (Algeria), 97

national myths, creation of, 212

National Revolutionary Militias, 12

National Revolutionary Movement (MNR), 45–6, 57–8, 70, 142

National Student Front (FEN), 50

national unity, promotion of, 202

National Workers' Front (FON), 50

National Workers' Unity Front (FONU), 77

nationalisation: in Britain, 204–5; of non-agricultural enterprises, 118–19
nationalism, 21; creation and use of, 206; in Cuba, 218; musical, 210
nationhood, 203–4
neo-colonialism, in Cuba, 213
Neto, Agostinho, 147
New Left, 118
'new man', 32–3
Nicaragua, 143
Nicolau, Ramón, 70
Non-Aligned Movement (NAM), 30, 120
Noriega, Manuel, 156
*Noticias de Hoy*, 11
*Nuestro Tiempo* group, 74
Ñúnez Jiménes, Antonio, 29, 74, 75, 96–7, 99, 131, 174

Ochoa, Arnaldo, scandal of, 145, 155, 181
Office of Revolutionary Plans, 75
Oltuski (*sometimes* Oltusky) Ozacki, Enrique, 45, 57, 66, 67, 71, 94, 130
Operation Just Cause, 156
Operation Mongoose, 16
Ordoqui, Joaquín, 79, 104
Organisation of American States (OAS), Cuba expelled from, 125, 186
Ortega, Daniel, 25
orthodoxy, in relation to USSR, 137
Ortodoxos *see* Cuban People's Party
OSPAAL network, 150
outer circles, 114, 129–31
over-staffing of jobs, 14

Pacto de Pedrero, 51
Padilla, Heberto, 61, 141, 142
Padrón González, José Luis, 158
País, Frank, 45, 47, 48, 54, 56, 59, 93
Panama, 143; US intervention in, 156, 159
Paraguay, nation-building in, 211
participation, system of, 20
patronage, networks of, 145
Pavón Tamayo, Luis, 104, 142
Pazos, Felipe, 32, 67, 106
Peña, Lázaro, 79, 101, 121, 131
peasantry, 216
People's Councils, 160

People's Power system, 14, 15, 20, 126, 132, 134, 136, 151, 160, 169
People's Socialist Party (PSP), 9, 10, 11, 24, 25, 29, 33, 35, 36, 37, 42, 51–2, 57, 58, 65, 66, 67, 68, 69, 70, 71, 72, 74, 76, 77–81, 87, 92, 93, 97–105, 110–11, 112, 113, 115, 116, 117, 121–2, 123, 124, 127, 130, 131, 132, 133, 135, 138, 140, 176, 214, 217; after 1959, 95–105; and 26 July Movement, 69–73; criticism of, 111; in inner circle membership, 95; naming of, 44; return of, 139–43; third congress, 43; sixth congress, 99, 101; survivors, 128–9
Pérez, Antonio, 136
Pérez, Faustino, 48, 49, 51, 57, 66, 67, 95, 112, 115, 130, 150–1
Pérez González, Humberto, 132, 146, 148
Pérez Hernández, Faustino, 45
Pérez Roque, Felipe, 38, 175–6, 177
periodisation of the Revolution, 61–4
Permanent Treaty with the United States (1903), 199, 213
personality cult, 5–6
Peter Pan operation, 189
Pina, Victor, 87
Piñeiro, Manuel ('Barbarroja'), 124–5, 130
'pink tide', 121
Pino Machado, Quintín, 71
Pino Santos, Oscar, 74, 75
Pioneers, 12
Platt Amendment, 66, 213, 219
Playa Girón episode *see* Bay of Pigs episode
*PM* documentary film, 96; banning of, 189
political prisoners, 8–9
politics of passion, 20–1
Ponce, Juan, 48
Popular Movement for the Liberation of Angola (MPLA), 137
Portuondo, José Antonio, 105
Prebisch, Raúl, 215
Prieto Jiménez, Abel, 27, 178
Prío, Carlos, 25, 45, 52, 101
'problem' and 'resolution', colonial binary, 206–11
property owning by foreign capital, 173
prostitution, 13; growth of, 161

public sector jobs, cutting of, 38
Puente Blanco, José, 111

Quevedo, Angel, 111
*quinquenio gris*, 7, 11, 62, 104, 135, 142

race, Cuban attitudes to, 171–3
racial mixture of Cuba, 185
racism, 100
radicalisation, 216
Radio Rebelde, 110, 125
Ramírez, José, 102, 121
Ramos Latour, René, 51
Rapid Response Brigades, 18
Ray Rivero, Manuel, 57, 58, 67, 95, 105, 112
Reagan, Ronald, 6, 17
Reagan administration, 143
rebel alliance of 1959, 68–9
Rebel Army (Ejército Rebelde), 50, 66, 67, 68, 69, 72–3, 76, 82, 87, 102
Reciprocity Treaties (1903 and 1934), 212–13, 220
Rectification, 19, 61, 148, 150, 168, 173, 193; explanation of, 153–7
Redondo, Ciro, 48, 49, 53
religion, as opium of the people, 172
religious believers, 6; tolerance of, 160
remittances, 161, 171
rendering of accounts, 134
*Revolución* newspaper, 11, 59, 74, 78, 110, 111
Revolution: changing meaning of, 216; daily building of, 218; extension of, to Latin America, 34; loyalty to, 223; paradigms of, 198–200; popular participation in, 217–18; seen as personified in Fidel, 27; use of term, 199 *see also* narratives of the Revolution
Revolutionary Armed Forces (FAR), 7–8, 17, 36–7, 38, 40, 82–6, 87, 88, 89, 105, 107, 111, 124, 135, 139, 156, 159, 165
Revolutionary Confederation of Cuban Workers (CTC-R), 12, 77, 101
Revolutionary Directorate – 13 March (DR), 10, 51, 67, 69, 79, 80, 104, 106–7, 111, 117, 122, 124, 130, 214; naming of, 51

Revolutionary Insurrectionary Union (UIR), 23, 45
Revolutionary Offensive, 20, 118, 144
Revolutionary Police Force (PNR), 84
Revolutionary Socialist Movement (MSR), 45
Revolutionary Student Directorate (DRE), 45; change of name, 51
Risquet, Jorge, 76, 124, 136–7
Rivero, Otto, 176
Roa García, Raúl, 69, 107–10, 175
Robaina, Roberto, 175, 181
Roca Calderío, Blas, 43, 59, 73, 76, 79, 80, 100, 111, 114, 121, 122, 130, 136, 140, 158
Roca-Runciman Pact (1934) (Argentina), 213
Rodríguez, Armando, 49
Rodríguez, Carlos Rafael, 36, 44, 58–9, 66, 73, 76, 99–100, 103, 104, 114, 115, 118, 121, 128, 132, 136, 137, 140, 158
Rodríguez, Fructuoso, 51
Rodríguez, Héctor, 138
Rodríguez, José Luis, 174, 178
Rodríguez, Lester, 35
Rodríguez, Luis Orlando, 85
Rodríguez, Marcos Armando, 104, 107
Rodríguez, Reinaldo, 49
Rodríguez García, José Luis, 169
Rodríguez Rodríguez, Luis Orlando, 67
Rojas, Ursinio, 121
Ross Leal, Pedro, 170
*rumba*, rehabilitation of, 172
Russian Revolution, anniversary of, 166

Salon de Mai exhibition, 142
Salvador, David, 51, 58, 77–8, 111–12
Sánchez, Celia, 48, 54–6, 74, 89, 174; as Fidel's confidante, 90–1; relations with Fidel, 55–6, 55
Sánchez, Universo, 48, 49, 85
Sánchez Arango, Aureliano, 77, 112
Sánchez Pérez, Manuel, 155
Santamaría, Abel, 47, 79, 81–2
Santamaría Cuadrado, Haydée, 11, 47, 48, 54, 56, 59, 81–2, 89, 91–2, 127, 130
Sardiñas, Lalo, 53
Schmitter, Philippe, 201

schools: experimental, creation of, 92; nationalisation of, 92
Schools of Revolutionary Education (EIR), 76, 102
Second Front *see* Sierra del Cristal Second Front
security services, 16–17
self-employed sector, 13, 38
Serguera, Jorge, 125, 131
Serra, Clementina, 121–2
sexual education programmes, 90
sexuality, 6
siege mentality, 216, 222
Sierra del Cristal Second Front, 83–5, 102; veterans of, 122–6
Sierra experience, 23, 26, 28, 81, 82–6, 111, 115, 119, 168, 185–6, 221
Sierra group, 49, 50–1, 53, 54, 56–8, 60, 76, 95, 113, 123, 124, 157, 164, 220, 222
Sierra Maestra, 48, 59
single-party system, 214
Sixth Column, naming of, 84
slavery, 184, 212–13; late abolition of, 218
slaves, protests of, 219
socialism, 68, 202, 205, 218; of the Revolution, 65, 70
Socialist Youth (JS), 13, 25, 35, 37, 52, 93, 95, 102, 105, 170
Sorí Marín, Humberto, 67, 73, 111, 112–13
Sotús, Jorge, 50
Soto Prieto, Lionel, 76, 95, 98, 101–2, 131, 149
South Africa, negotiations over Angola, 137
Spain, attitudes to, 184
Spanish system of colonial control, 207–8
Special National Conference, 180
Special Period in Peacetime, 13, 61, 153, 160, 162
Stalin, Joseph, 5, 204
Stalinism, 76, 104, 189
state: changing nature of, 116–17, 162–80; monolithic concept of, 9–18; regulation by, 201; strong, needed for nation-building, 211; weak, 11, 16, 217
strikes *see* general strikes
sugar: Cuba as exporter of, 62, 214;

Cuban dependency on, 19; estates, 55; harvest targets for, 26, 119, 132; sales to USSR, 103; US quotas for, 213 (cuts in, 30)
supercow, plan to produce, 25
Support Group, 173–6, 178, 180
Syria, Cuban brigade in, 139

Tarará group, 73–5, 89, 96
*Temas* magazine, 194
Territorial Militia Troops, 143
Thatcher, Margaret, 2
Third Worldisation, 142
Tiempo Nuevo group, 96
Torres, Félix, 71
Torrijos, Omar, 25
trade unions, 43, 44, 77
Treaty of Paris (1899), 186
Tricontinental Conference, 120
Triple-A organisation, 77, 112
triumvirate, 22–40
Trudeau, Pierre, 25

*Último Jueves*, 194
UMAP camps *see* Military Unit for Assisting Production (UMAP) work camps
unemployment, 20, 165
Union of Communist Youth (UJC), 13, 149, 162, 174, 175, 179, 181
Union of Cuban Writers and Artists (UNEAC), 7, 105, 178–9; prize for poetry, 141
Union of Soviet Socialist Republics (USSR) 7, 24, 30–1, 34, 37, 40, 61, 62, 63, 64, 80, 100, 104, 106–7, 113, 117, 119, 120–1, 122, 123, 132, 133, 135, 137, 154, 166, 204, 205; as model, 138, 140; collapse of, 5, 13; Cuban delegation to Moscow, 115; Cuban personnel trained in, 151; foreign policy of, 143; Hungary issue, 108; international strategy of, 43; invasion of Czechoslovakia, 111; relations with Cuba, 186, 187, 216; sale of sugar to, 103, 214; Sino-Soviet split, 122
United National Workers' Front, 50
United Party of the Cuban Socialist

Revolution (PURSC), 10, 13, 103, 117, 119, 140, 158

United States of America (USA), 16, 18, 20, 42, 43, 75, 78, 100–1, 121, 151, 156, 159, 186, 199, 207, 214, 216; annexation by, advocated, 184; change of Cuba policy, 143–4; embargo against Cuba, 5, 8, 63, 118, 120, 143, 186, 216 (intensification of, 21); Fidel's attitude to, 25; foreign policy of, 62; migration talks with, 192; neo-colonialism of, 219; policy assumptions of, 27; relations with Cuba, 2; support for Batista, 66

Universidad Popular, 102

universities, reform of, 92

University Students' Directorate (DEU), 42, 45

University Students' Federation (FEU), 12, 162, 181

Urrutia Lleó, Manuel, 67, 68, 71, 72, 92–3

'us' and 'them', creation of sense of, 185–9

Valdés, Ramón, 123–4

Valdés, Raúl, 73

Valdés Menéndez, Ramiro, 48, 49, 53, 71, 79, 87, 88, 91, 106, 116, 121, 136, 147–8, 164, 165, 168, 196

Valdés Mesa, Salvador, 170

Valdés Vivó, Raúl, 25

vanguard: concept of, 33; formation of, 41–60

Varela, Félix, 219

Vatican, 69

Vecino Alegret, Fernando C., 82, 139

*Verde Olivo*, 142

Vietnam, 94

Vivó, Jorge Antonio, 98

voluntarism, 33

voluntary labour, 134

Weber, Max, 3

welfare systems, 20, 204, 205, 214

Wiarda, Howard, 201

Williamson, Peter, 200–1

'within' and 'against' the Revolution, 182–97, 222

women: brought into labour force, 124; in the inner circle, 89–92

Youth Labour Army (EJT), 123

*zafra*, 135